The Sourcebook Of Magic

A Comprehensive Guide To The Technology Of *NLP*

L. Michael Hall, Ph.D.
&
Barbara P. Belnap, M.S.W.

Crown House Publishing Limited
www.crownhouse.co.uk

First published by

Crown House Publishing Ltd
Crown Buildings, Bancyfelin, Carmarthen, Wales, SA33 5ND, UK
www.crownhouse.co.uk

and

Crown House Publishing Ltd
P.O. Box 2223, Williston, VT 05495-2223, USA
www.CHPUS.com

First published 1999
Reprinted 2000 (twice), 2001, 2002, 2003.

British Library of Cataloguing-in-Publication Data
A catalogue entry for this book is available
from the British Library.

ISBN 1899836225

LCCN 2002109966

Printed and bound in the UK by
Bell & Bain
Glasgow

Table Of Contents

List Of Figures

The Basic Patterns

Foundational Patterns

Primary NLP Patterns For Transformation And Excellence

Patterns For Incongruity Of "Parts"

Patterns For Identity And "Self"

Patterns For Neuro-Linguistic States

Patterns For Languaging And Re-Languaging

Patterns For Thinking Patterns, Meta-Programs, And Cognitive Distortions

Patterns For Meanings/Semantics

Acknowledgments

First, we want to acknowledge those directly responsible for the birth of NLP as we have it today:
John Grinder and Richard Bandler,
Robert Dilts and Judith DeLozier,
and Leslie Cameron-Bandler.

Second, we would like to dedicate this work to two Magicians who further pioneered the NLP Model:
Tim Hallbom and Suzi Smith

And third, we would like also to acknowledge the numerous other unnamed NLP trainers who have likewise extended this field, and those who will continue to do so.

Preface

Welcome to "Solution Land!" Swing the doors open wide and step right up to the next level of helping both yourself and those you choose to assist to a double portion of the most powerful and dynamic changework and action strategies known to mankind. Herein lies a wealth of resources, strategies, and skills that will assist you, the agent of change, in making your life more powerful, pleasurable, and productive than you thought possible. What you will find within these pages will enable you, the NLPer, to effect deep and pervasive change and transformation in yourself and others from the inside out.

How many times have you asked yourself, "Just how can I help myself or another to really attain a *better* or *higher quality of life,* to achieve the wants and needs, desires and dreams that are possible in life?" How often have you searched and sought after techniques, skills and strategies to do just this?—those tried and proven to work.

My search for answers has led me to study many different technologies and the developers who created them. Originally, I began seeking an understanding of **problems** and what caused *the problems.* Later, it became clear to me that what I had true interest in concerned *solutions,* not problems. I wanted to know what *actions* a person could take to make improvements, "additions and editions," in their lives. What I found along this path to what I call "Solution Land" was the field of Neuro-Linguistic Programming—NLP—and its trail of resources, strategies, and skills.

Yet, I had difficulty in finding a clear and precise handbook, a guide, that would provide me with the essence of what we now recognize as NLP. I was seeking a work that made the key distinctions empowering me, the helper or the "helpee," to have ready access to sequential solutions when I needed them most. In this work you will access strategies and skills with which to launch and accelerate your results and accomplish what you may not have even thought possible—real and long-lasting, pervasive improvement in quality of life, change, not as a result of talking about what you want or don't want, but *"Taking Action"* to make it happen!

I have personally used this guide for nearly a year and many of the techniques for over ten years consistently. The explanations of the changework and personal transformation patterns have proved to be extremely helpful in developing a mind frame of under-standing, a positive expectancy for change to get out of 'problem land' enabling you to propel yourself forward, towards what you want.

If you buy any book on NLP changework or technology this year, or are looking for a comprehensive and complete work to capture the power and energy of NLP, take this one home with you...take it truly home, to the level of MIND.

I am grateful to Michael Hall and Barbara Belnap for allowing access to the technology of NLP with such clarity and heart. I might well end by asking, "Just how much can you help yourself and others to transform and to come alive!?"

E. Keith Lester, M.A.
Lakeland, FL, September 1997

Foreword

"**Why** did you write this book?" she asked.
"And **for whom?**" he chimed in.
"**For what purpose?**" yet another asked.

It began one day when Barbara and I caught a vision of collecting *all* *of the central NLP patterns* by which we can create resourceful-ness and excellence in everyday life. We dreamed about collecting and putting them into *"one wonderful volume."* Working in the context of managed care herself, Barbara conceived the idea of using *the NLP patterns* as a book of "brief psychotherapy" for therapists. This seemed to make sense. After all, managed care in the USA focuses on both *brief* and *high quality* therapy. So we thought we would identify the cognitive-behavioral processes within NLP and specify *how to* use this powerful change model in a step-by-step fashion.

So we created that ordering format in our minds, and then chaos (as it so often does) crashed our party. This transpired because, as we began gathering NLP patterns and organizing them into this work, Barbara kept experiencing *"thought balls"* about who else we could include in our focus. She had ideas about others who would also want to have this *one volume of NLP patterns*—NLP trainers, beginning and advanced students in the domain of neuro-linguistics, teachers, and Human Resource people in corporations who provide training in communication, team building, and personal effectiveness, therapists, parents, etc.

But this idea for an expanded audience messed up our original plans. It also messed up Keith Lester's original *Preface* to this work. Nor did I find that it settled well for myself. After all, my style in research, writing, and in planning and organizing materials operates from establishing a concentrated focus and staying with it until I complete a project.

Nevertheless, I did make the change in focus. After all, what *magician* worth his or her salt defaults to inflexibility? As we made the change in the text's focus, it meant shifting from directing this work to words therapists to presenting all of the **basic and central patterns** of *NLP* so that readers could easily translate and apply them into multiple domains:

- Business
- Education
- Psychotherapy
- Personal effectiveness
- Sports and athletic coaching
- Interpersonal relations
- Communication enrichment
- Negotiation, mediation, conflict resolution
- Etc.

Thus it came to pass.

We collected all of the core patterns that have come to distinguish NLP as a "magical" realm of change, transformation, personal development, and "the technology of excellence." Then another *thought ball* came crashing into the realm of our consciousness. "What about all the people who may read this work who don't any have expertise with NLP, but just know the basics?" For those, I therefore put together a very brief and succinct introduction to NLP's magic.

In this way, this volume took its present form. Here we offer primarily a concise presentation of NLP with a fairly exhaustive display of *the patterns of "magic"* or, as the title suggests, **The Sourcebook Of Magic**.

"Magic" Huh?

In NLP, we typically use the term *"magic,"* **not** to designate external magic whereby we change the laws of physics. It refers rather to the seemingly wild, wonderful and "magical" effects that occur when we know *the structure of subjectivity.*

When we do not know *how* human subjectivity (mind, emotions, motivation, health, language, etc.) works, it leaves us *clueless* about experiences (i.e., their *whys* and *wherefores*) and about change (i.e., *how* to transform things, the leverage point of change). When we *do not* understand human functioning (cognitive-behavioral or neuro-linguistic functioning), it leaves us "in the dark" about how to improve human efficiency, happiness, and effectiveness. We therefore live in a world of darkness and confusion about the role of "language" in human consciousness, neurology, and health.

Conversely, when we do understand *the structure of subjectivity* (i.e., the central focus of NLP), it gives us a working knowledge of the "magical wands" at our command for change, continuous improvement, health, happiness, success, and excellence. In other words, knowing *the leverage point* in the human system of mind-emotion, memories, hopes, desires, and fears, etc., provides us with a place from which we can do some magic for fun and profit, for development of excellence and for making a significant contribution to human welfare.

Hence, the neuro-linguistic model itself, and the techniques for "running your own brain" (the patterns themselves), essentially provide us with a *sourcebook of magic*. This reflects the theme from the first books in this field, *The Structure Of Magic* (*Volumes I & II*, 1975 and 1976). It reflects the works of *Magic Demystified* (1982), *Magic In Action* (1985), and *The Secrets Of Magic* (1998).

Now as it happens, the founders of this domain—a linguist (Dr John Grinder) and a student studying computer programming who then became an unofficial Gestalt therapist (Richard Bandler)—specified *the very structure of magic* as lying within the human *representational systems*. These "language" systems of mind-body include not only words and sentences, but other "languages" as well, "languages" that operate at various logical levels.

At the primary level we have *sensory-based* sights, sounds, sensations, smells, and tastes (i.e., the VAK) that make up the "language" of the sensory modalities of awareness. Within this level, we have *the qualities* (properties, distinctions, features) of the modalities. Recently Hall and Bodenhamer (1998) have noted that these have been inaccurately labeled *sub*modalities. These distinctions do not actually exist at a lower level (especially *not* at a lower logical level). These *qualities* and *characteristics* of the visual, auditory, and kinesthetic modalities comprise the features that stand out as salient inside (or within) each of these awareness modes.

When we move up from the non-linguistic level of sight, sound, and sensation (the sensory modalities), we come to the first level of propositional language—*sensory-based words.* Here we have the empirical language of science, testable by the senses.

Next we move up to another level and to another kind of "language"—*evaluative language.* Here we interpret and evaluate from the previous language and create a higher level abstraction. And this process of abstracting can, and does, continue up to more and higher levels. Eventually, we get to the meta-level of metaphor and story.

What significance do all of these levels of consciousness have in actual experience? Considerable. Because when we change any of these various *languages of the mind*—our internal sense of reality itself changes. And when that happens, *magic occurs.*

Learning The Incantations Of "Magic"

In detailing here the NLP Model with its basic patterns, we offer two kinds of "understandings." The first has to do with *a theoretical kind of understanding*, the second with *a practical kind of knowledge*. Together, these understandings empower us to "run our own brain."

In the first part of this book, you will learn how your brain operates and how to run it. Doing this then empowers you to take charge of your life, build enhancing maps, move into social and relational contexts with more grace and joy, and achieve the outcomes you want in order to increase your overall effectiveness.

These *kinds of knowledges* also separate how we experience "problems" and solutions. **Knowing** *that* we have a problem, and even knowing *why* we have that problem in terms of its causes and origins, differs radically from knowing *what to do about* the problem.

The first knowledge gives us theory, explanation, and causation. Here we can specialize in formal and technical knowledge. Here we become an expert in explanations. Here we know **about.** The second knowledge endows us with wisdom, practicality, and transformation. Here we know **how**. It gives us *how-to* knowledge to make us experts in changing.

In this book, we have provided only a little bit of the first knowledge and a whole lot of the second knowledge. In the first chapters you will find an overview from the cognitive psychology field of the new domain—**Neuro-Linguistic Programming (NLP).** In the chapters that follow, you will discover multiple patterns of transformation that give you *know how* for taking effective action with regard to various problems and challenges that can sabotage effectiveness.

Caveat Emptor

We have designed this book as *a concise NLP reference manual* (i.e., a sourcebook of magic) with nearly a hundred specific patterns. We have designed it in such a way that, ideally, it will facilitate your practice and use of neuro-linguistics as you work with yourself or others. And yet, as we do this, we do **not** want to leave the impression that *merely reading* this book will make you a master in this field. It will not.

As with any experiential set of learnings, to **master a field** you have to *practice the skills and patterns* with others in the context of high quality training and under the tutelage of qualified people. The "magic" occurs in the overall effect and sometimes speed of a process. But **mastery** involves so much more.

Therefore, in using these NLP patterns and becoming highly skilled with them, we highly recommend that you avail yourself of the required training in both the verbal and non-verbal aspects of this model. This will enable you to practice the patterns in a safe and wise context. When you do so under the supervision of qualified and expert trainers, you will get the specific coaching and insights that will enable you to hone these skills and effectively integrate them into your person. To further encourage you to do this, we have included an Appendix of NLP Training Centers in the USA and the UK.

Of course, when you contact any of these Training Centers, do inquire about whether that particular Center operates from a set of criteria and conducts its training as *a competency based* training. Personally we do not believe in the "correspondence course" approach to NLP or in the short training programs that promise mastery in five days. Instead, look for those programs that provide the necessary depth and quality essential for becoming an effective practitioner.

A Touch Of General Semantics

Now the phrase *"neuro-linguistic training"* actually began way back in the 1930s and 1940s under the tutelage of Count Alfred Korzybski. In fact, he used "neuro-linguistic trainings" as a part of his *modus operandi* for founding the field of General Semantics (GS).

In his landmark work, *Science And Sanity: An Introduction To Non-Aristotelian Systems And General Semantics* (1933/1994), Korzybski established the distinction between map and territory. His constructivist epistemology set the basic framework for NLP, influencing Richard Bandler and John Grinder in their first work, *The Structure Of Magic*, as well as anthropologist Gregory Bateson (*Steps Toward An Ecology Of Mind*, 1972) who contributed to the presuppositions and theoretical underpinnings of NLP.

In this work, I (MH) have used my background as a General Semanticist to utilize some of the linguistic formulations that Richard and John did **not** bring over into the Meta-model. Korzybski argued that these *extensional devices* provide the human race with *tools* (or technologies) for both science and sanity. As you read this work, you will note these formulations in the writing itself. For those unfamiliar with GS, this work may present itself to you as of a unique and strange format. For a fuller work on the linguistic contributions of GS to NLP, see my work, *The Secrets Of Magic* (1998), that extends the Meta-model using some of the Korzybskian "magic."

> ***Quotation Marks (" ").*** As an extensional device these mark off terms and phrases, which, to varying degrees, present questionable neuro-linguistic mapping. *"Quotes"* indicate that the reader should handle with special care some word, term, or phrase. For example, words like "time" and "mind" (that we typically take for granted and assume that we know the meaning of) involve several kinds of distortion that make them problematic. These represent not only nominalizations, but also terms that one can use in multiordinal ways.

Hyphens (-). This device enables us to deal with dichotomized and fragmented maps. As used in the phrase, *"neuro-linguistic programming,"* hyphens reunite the world torn apart into *elements* (hence "elementalism") that do not, and cannot, stand alone. GS uses hyphens to heal the elementalism and dualism that has so thoroughly affected the West. Hence, "mind" *and* "body" references nothing tangibly real—only a linguistic fiction. So with "time" *and* "space." Yet mind-body and the time-space continuum do reference real phenomena and give us a more true-to-fact map.

Et cetera or *etc.* Used here, not as a trite, over-used term due to bad habit, but intentionally to convey a non-Aristotelian attitude. Why? Because in the infinite world of the territory, *no map can say it all.* To remind us of this *non-allness* in the world, we use "etc." **Etc.** alerts us to avoid thinking that we have "said it all," or that what we have thought or understood brings an end to the subject. As you read, let "etc." cue you to think about the many other things that we could add. If in deletion we leave character-istics out, in "etc." we remind ourselves of this mapping phenomenon.

E-Prime/E-Choice. Simply, English without (or primed of) the verb "to be." When we *prime* English of this false-to-fact verb (is, am, be, being, been, was, were, etc.) we eliminate two entirely erroneous problems: *the "is of identity"* ("He is an American") and *the "is of predication"* ("That chair is red"). These "ises" map out false-to-fact representations to thereby misrepresent the structural relationship of the terri-tory. That creates problems for sanity—for adjusting to the territory. (See Appendix C also.)

Process language. Since reality at the quantum level (as we now know it via modern physics) exists as much as "a dance of electrons" and sub-atomic parts, *"thing" language* creates all kinds of problems in representation. We need a language that describes a dynamic world. We need more of a *process language*, consisting of verbs, actions, functions, and processes. This corresponds to the emphasis on **de-nominalizing** nounified terms in NLP (see chapter 7).

... . When you find a series of dots (...) within a quotation, we have simply deleted part of the quotation. When you find such *in a set of instructions*, we use that to signify, "Stop, go inside your mind...and experience these words and instructions fully."

If you get lost, there is a glossary and index at the back of this book.

Pattern Sources

Where did these patterns come from? Who created them? What other individuals played a key role in evolving them to the form that you find here?

NLP primarily arose from Richard Bandler's discovery of Fritz Perls' work. In fact, Richard, hired by Dr Robert S. Spitzer, edited his first book, *Eye Witness To Therapy* (1973), while an undergraduate. (This book has been coupled with *The Gestalt Approach*, written by Perls, and is now published as *The Gestalt Approach And Eye Witness To Therapy*.) As a senior Richard received permission to teach a seminar class on Gestalt therapy. Spitzer then introduced him to Virginia Satir and later hired John Grinder and Richard Bandler to edit some tapes of Virginia's work which became the book *Changing With Families*.

Thus most of the original patterns, representational systems, reframing, parts parties, Meta-modeling, integration of parts, etc., came from Perls and Satir. We can hardly say that any of these patterns "belong" to anyone or that anyone exclusively developed them. Actually each reflects the growing, evolving knowledge of the field—the "time-binding" process of Korzybski. And, of course, knowledge and use of these patterns will stimulate a person's creativity to find new and productive uses. If you, or someone you know, did play a key role in the development of a given pattern, send us your information and we will most gladly put it in the next edition.

Because you can run some of the patterns on yourself, and others necessitate having someone run the patterns on you, you will find varying formats. For the most part, when you find an expression such as, "Now have the person imagine floating above his/her Time-line..." you generally have a pattern that requires someone to coach and facilitate the process. Yet we have discovered that, with almost all the patterns, most people can run them on themselves after they have been led through them repeatedly, especially in a supervised coaching context. Everything habituates. And so, running your brain using these wonderfully magic patterns will also habituate.

Michael Hall, Ph.D.
Colorado, Spring 1999

Part One

The NLP Model

*The Source Of The Magic
For Transformation And Excellence*

Chapter 1

Introduction To NLP Magic

Magic Has Structure

When we don't know *how* something works or how it operates and the principles that drive it, we live "outside the secret" of what seems like magic. Do you recall any moment wherein you suddenly experienced the shock of finding "magic" in your world?

How does flipping this switch turn on the lights?

You've got to be kidding! You mean by typing on this keyboard and pushing these sequences I can send e-mails around the globe?

You mean you put this food in the microwave and push these buttons and it will cook the food in seconds?

To an outsider to the *secret* of the magic, things often seem preposterous, incredible, unbelievable, non-sensical, etc.

How can the world be a globe that turns around the sun? That's crazy! So how come we don't just all fall off?

What wild flights of imagination! To think that we can build flying machines. Next thing you'll know—he'll think we can fly to the moon!

As an uninitiate to the secrets, such wild and wonderful ideas and experiences can only seem like "magic." And yet knowing what we know today about gravity, aero-dynamics, the electromagnetic spectrum, artificial intelligence, information processing via parallel processing units, etc., we no longer think of such things as *"magic."* We view them as just *"knowledge."*

Now *suppose* similarly we learn some of the "secrets" of the magic that occurs in the human brain-and-neurology system? Suppose we know the factors, components, and principles that govern human neurological *information processing* so that we gain insight into how the bio-computer of our brain and nervous system works? Suppose we become initiates to how the human *internal world* that we refer to as "mind," "emotions," "personality," "genius," etc., works? Further, suppose we discover its structure of "magic" and, as with processes in other sciences, we can identify, specify, and effectively work with those *"patterns"* of magic? Now just suppose that... .

When you fully imagine this dream of pushing the limits of scientific discovery into the internal, subjective and phenomenological world of human beings, you have stepped into the world that we call **NLP—Neuro-Linguistic Programming.**

The "Magical" World Of Human Subjectivity

Actually, the breakthroughs in this domain of human *Neuro-Linguistics* have surpassed the limits of what many people can even *imagine as possible.* Similar to the way scientific discoveries in physics, electronics, quantum mechanics, etc., far exceed even our science fiction imaginations—so NLP has also surpassed what many in the field of human functioning, psychology, and communication ever thought possible in their wildest dreams.

"What incredible discoveries?" you ask.

- Altering a phobic response that has lasted for decades in as little as ten minutes

- Modeling the internal processes (strategies) of "genius" and teaching others to replicate them consciously

- Discovering the components of "consciousness" that make up the "building blocks" of "mind," "emotion," "personality," etc., in order to engage in some human "design engineering"

- Finding and reprogramming the structure of "meaning" in human neurology and processing to eliminate negative and dysfunctional meanings and replacing them with enhancing meaning

- Using hypnotic states to program one's autonomic nervous system processes for health and effectiveness

- Changing limiting and sabotaging beliefs

- Intentionally and consciously evolving human consciousness and skills

- Completely transforming toxic states of self-contempt, loneliness, boredom, despair, seriousness, etc.

Wild dreams? Not any longer. NLP has actually developed *models that make such human technologies possible*. In the twenty-four years since the first Neuro-Linguistic Programming book appeared (*The Structure Of Magic*, 1975), incredible discoveries have come to light that encourage us to think of the human neurological system of mind-and-body as a "computing" or information processing system that we can program. Having specified a paradigm about *how human subjectivity works*, NLP has made available a set of distinctions that initiates us into the very secrets of what otherwise seem pure "magic." And with these secrets about the structure of magic, we can now direct the processes involved.

In 1977 Richard Bandler and John Grinder revealed what they designated as "The NLP Ten Minute Phobia Cure." They revealed it *by doing such*. They would work with a person with a phobia and make it such that they didn't have it anymore. The person would walk in and couldn't even talk about the phobic item (whether an elevator, a snake, public speaking, conflict, etc.) without feeling the panic, distress, and fear. Then after a few minutes of running them through a specific pattern—they would feel surprised to find that they couldn't get the panic back. Magic.

Further, what made this "magic" seem even more spectacular was that they only *talked* to the person. Word magic! Or at least—so it seemed. Yet in spite of the seemingly "magical" nature of this process, the two co-founders of this new domain knew and simply worked with the very structure of the magic.

If in 1977 they had performed such wonders and with no explanatory model, they would have had a single piece of "magic" and no understanding of how it worked, how to teach it, how to replicate it, or how to discover more of the same. But they did have *an explanatory model.* They also spent several years developing supporting tools, patterns, and processes for their work. They further had legitimizing ideas which they had gathered from such domains as behaviorism, neurology, linguistics, cognitive psychology, general semantics, etc.

This explains why they did not dismiss their "magic" as mere flukes. John and Richard had discovered the structure of the magic. So the transformational technology that began to emerge from cutting-edge models of information processing, cognitive psychology, and linguistics in the early 1970s led them to more discoveries. And since that time, the technology of magic has continued to develop.

The Story

Neuro-Linguistic Programming came together when two men, both outside the field of psychology (therefore without its inherent biases), initiated a tremendous *paradigm shift* using their model of human functioning. Thomas Kuhn (1962) describes *outsiders* to a paradigm as those who typically bring about *revolutions in science.*

One man (Dr John Grinder) came from the field of linguistics and, specifically, transformational grammar. The other man (Richard Bandler), could claim no expertise whatsoever, except he had a natural and wonderful genius. As a young college student he could only lay claim to an innate genius in replicating (or modeling) patterns. In school at Santa Cruz in southern California, Richard studied mathematics and computer programming.

Together they stumbled upon some *pieces of genius and excellence in human functioning.* It just so happened that Richard met Virginia Satir and then Fritz Perls through working at Science and Behavior Books. The publisher first asked Richard to listen to audio and video tapes of Satir and transcribe them. Later he sent Richard to one of her trainings to run the sound equipment and to record the family system processes.

As he ran the sound system for Virginia, Richard says he would play rock music in the sound booth *and* listen to Virginia through his earphones. And as he did so, he picked up on seven of Satir's patterns that she used in her work that seemed so magical.

Later he said, "You simply use seven patterns and continually re-cycle through those seven." She inquired as to what this young twenty-one-year-old kid thought were her seven patterns. He enumerated them—to her surprise. Richard later told me (MH) that she said she knew four of the patterns, but had never articu-lated the other three, but that he had correctly identified them.

The next genius that Richard met was Fritz Perls. He became acquainted with him via audio- and videotapes. Dr Spitzer (1982) later noted that Richard would sometimes mimic Fritz so well that he caught himself calling Richard "Fritz." About that time, Fritz died. Dr Spitzer, who had an unfinished manuscript of Perls's, asked Richard to work on editing it. Richard selected various teaching films of Fritz and transcribed them, which then became the book *Eye Witness to Therapy* (1973).

From these experiences, Richard got permission as a senior in college to begin conducting a Gestalt Awareness class at the college. Terrence McClendon (1989) described this in *The Wild Days: NLP 1972-1981.* In those class sessions Richard "became" a Fritz Perls from having learned Gestalt therapy only by modeling Perls' patterns as gleaned from tapes and books. Dr Grinder entered the scene at this point having become Richard's supervisor for the course. McClendon writes,

> *John with his brilliant modeling skills from linguistics in conjunction with Richard who had the experience in behavioural modeling skills and his knowledge in the new contemporary systems of psychotherapy, formed a relationship which later on proved to be exceptional and beneficial to both.* (p. 10)

Richard wanted to understand more about his own skill in repli-cating patterns. And inasmuch as the patterns that he replicated with Virginia and Fritz primarily involved language, John provided the linguistic analysis. Reportedly, John promised to enter the adventure if Richard would teach him how he did it.

Richard, having worked as a computer programmer in modeling human tasks, breaking them down, and compiling programming formats, and John, a linguistic expert who modeled the structuring of language, then became engaged in a new form of modeling— **modeling human excellence.** Consequently, Richard and John set out to *pull apart the component pieces* that enable the human brain (actually the entire mind-body nervous system) to become *patterned.* This lead to their asking all kinds of questions:

- What comprises the components of a sequence?
- What initiates the sequence?
- How does the sequence work?
- What else happens?
- What distinctions does the brain make?
- How does it sort and code these awarenesses?
- How does language facilitate this process?

Bandler and Grinder began this exploration viewing the human brain as a "computing" information processing unit that can become "programmed" with "programs" for thinking, emoting, behaving, etc. As **structure** drives and informs language, mathematics, music, etc., so structure also determines and runs human processes. As we can program a computer to do human tasks (e.g., working with numbers, adding, multiplying, word processing, etc.), so similar processes must occur in us at neurological levels.

After all, some people have the ability to perform high level math. Others, (e.g., Perls, Satir) have a "program" to use language eloquently and "magically" to bring about significant personality changes.

How do these "programs" work? What comprises their component parts? What creates the programming? How does one change such programming? How can one train one's conscious and unconscious mind to develop the necessary intuitions to run such programs?

The paradigm shift that Bandler and Grinder initiated grew out of their collaboration. Eventually the results of this became the field of **Neuro-Linguistic Programming (NLP).** Immediately upon studying Perls and Satir, they published two volumes of *The*

Structure Of Magic—books about therapy and language. Virginia Satir and anthropologist Gregory Bateson wrote the introductions. These revolutionary books established the foundation of the technologies that formed the field of NLP—the field of modeling human excellence.

As they brought those books to press, Bateson introduced them to another magician, hypnotist Milton Erickson, M.D. Bandler and Grinder immediately modeled Erickson's marvelous language and non-language patterns that formed his skills in hypnosis. The next year (1976), they produced two volumes of the hypnotic techniques of Erickson (*Patterns, Vol. I & II,* 1975, 1976) which led to finer distinctions in the NLP model.

There you have it. Using the formulations of linguistics, General Semantics, and cognitive psychology (especially George Miller, Karl Pribram, Eugene Galanter, etc.), Bandler and Grinder modeled the models that they found in such diverse fields as Gestalt, Family Systems, and Ericksonian hypnosis. They didn't create a new field of psychology. Instead, they created a *meta-field.* Through modeling, they sought to discover and understand the patterns and structures that *work.*

Each of these highly skilled wizards of communication facilitate wonderful life-changes when they talk with clients. What did they have in common? They adopted an entirely new focus—one never before used in psychology. Namely, outside of the "theories" that explain *why* it works, **what processes describe how it works?**

This summarizes the heart and passion of NLP: modeling, searching for processes and the "how," and disdaining the "why," and focusing on experiences of excellence rather than on cases of pathology.

Psychology for a hundred years had operated from a completely different orientation. Based on the medical model and physical "hard" science model, it looked at pathology (at distortions, perversions, pain, distress, etc.), seeking to understand the source ("where did this come from?", "why is this so?"), and wanting empirical, external proof.

The paradigm shift completely uprooted the old formulations in psychology. The "why" question which had focused clinicians entirely on knowing the source of a difficulty, in one fell swoop became irrelevant. Suddenly a new focus emerged: *"How" does it work*? Empiricism, modernism, and positivism gave way to post-modernism, phenomenology, and constructionism. The basic question changed from "What 'is' the real nature of this problem?" to "How has this person constructed his or her felt and experienced reality?"

The Patterns Of NLP

Since those early days, the field of NLP has generated trainings, workshops, conferences, journals and publications, thereby giving birth to **change patterns.** These gave people a way to "run their own brains" in new, creative, and productive ways. Some of these patterns radically transform a person from feeling caught up in immense pain and distress to feeling free to live a more sane and empowering life. Some patterns delineate *the secrets of genius* so that "ordinary" people can learn to do new and marvelous things. Some patterns simply identify the component pieces and sequences of basic living strategies—how to speak up assertively, how to eat sensibly, how to negotiate in business contexts, how to parent with loving firmness, how to read more intelligently, how to spell, etc.

From the mundane to the sublime then, NLP patterns give *step-by-step instructions for "how to run our own brains."* They provide us with knowledge about *how to* "program" our organic and neural bio-computers to create highly efficient experiences.

This means that while NLP has lots of psychotherapeutic applications, NLP does not merely describe another psychology. It began there. Having modeled two psychotherapists and two schools of psychology—it started in the field of therapy. Yet the co-founders, and those who followed, did not keep it there. NLP describes a much larger field, namely, *the field of human subjectivity,* and even more pointedly—**the field of human excellence.**

Part of the radical paradigm shift that NLP brought to psychology has to do with its focus. Prior to the cognitive psychology revolution in the 1960s, psychology had primarily focused on understanding the "why" questions:

- Why are people the way they are?
- What causes people to get so messed up?
- Where does human psychopathology come from?

In response different psychologies invented different reasons and explanations: Freud used various Greek mythologies to explain the sexual drives which he held responsible for most problems; Adler explained the "why" in terms of inferiority; Jung explained the "why" in terms of the collective unconscious, and so it went. Almost everywhere therapists focused on the source, *assuming* that people had to understand the "why" to get better.

Bandler and Grinder challenged that assumption calling it "psycho-archeology" and "psycho-theology." Coming from the Cognitive-Behavioral models of Korzybski (1941/1994), Chomsky (1956), Miller (1956, 1960), the semi-cognitive, existential, and humanistic model of Perls, the systems model of Satir, the cybernetic model of Bateson (1972), etc., they introduced a new focus. As inheritors of the Information Processing models of the cognitive revolution and computer science era, they focused on the "how" questions:

- How does this or that brain work?
- How do "minds" get programmed in the first place?
- What comprise the components of information processing in the mind?
- What representational components comprise "the difference that make a difference?"
- How does the programming work?
- How can we interrupt, alter, and/or transform the programming?

The Structure Of "Subjectivity"

NLP, as a modeling field of human subjectivity and excellence, focuses primarily on *how things work:*

- How does language work?
- How do human "minds" function?
- How many styles of "thinking," processing, representing, sorting, etc., can we find?
- What difference do different processing styles make?
- What sequence of thoughts, representations, etc., create a human program?
- How can we run or program a brain to run more efficiently?

With this emphasis on *structure*—the early developers of NLP began inventing and constructing all sorts of "patterns" for changing behaviors. These structured processes operate in human experience (consciousness, representation, feeling, etc.) as **human technologies for change and excellence**.

In that sense, these transformational patterns offer to the social sciences (communication, relationship, thought-emotion, states of consciousness, etc.) technological advances that we have seen for several hundred years in the hard sciences.

Transformational Patterns—
"Magical Incantations For Growth And Excellence"

We offer this brief synopsis of NLP in order to hook your interest and capture your fascination in this model and its patterns (which we refer to as "techniques" or "technologies"). Since so many patterns have emerged, and so many more will emerge, we have focused on *the original patterns* that empower people to "run their own brains" as they construct subjective "realities" that will enhance their actual functioning. We have here written out and condensed those patterns to give you *the know-how knowledge,* hence the step-by-step format.

No single volume to date has collected all of these NLP patterns in this kind of format. We have written this book to fill that void. Previously, one would have had to purchase dozens upon dozens of books to locate these patterns. Typically a person can find three or four patterns in a given book, although some may have ten or fifteen patterns. Books have even been written that only have one pattern in them! We have usually referenced works that continue more in-depth presentation of a given pattern. We have also sought to provide, for those new to NLP, a picture of the extensiveness of this empowering and paradigm-shifting model.

You will find in the next chapter a very brief overview of *the essentials of the NLP Model*. We have presented this so that even a neophyte to this field can immediately begin using these *know how* patterns. We trust also that this collecting and organizing of patterns will assist the NLP veteran by providing an easy access to the patterns. Perhaps this will, in turn, stimulate additional creativity as practitioners use patterns, or component pieces of patterns, to create new arrangements.

From the beginning, the NLP founders recognized that this model functions not only remedially, but also *generatively*. Using both the model and its technologies, NLP offers processes for creating new and unthought-of *patterns of excellence*. This enables us to develop and evolve more and more as we actualize more of the human potentials available. May that be forever true of your adventure into this domain!

Conclusion

As a model for "running your own brain," Neuro-Linguistic Programming offers not only a theoretical model, but also actual *patterns* for doing so. These *human technologies* for change, transformation, and renewal enable us to examine the maps that we have built as we have moved through life, and to update those that don't serve us well. In the pages to come, we will introduce this positive, solution-oriented model and then articulate cutting-edge *technologies of the mind-body* for becoming increasingly resourceful in the way we live our lives.

Chapter 2

The NLP Model

Design, Language, And Components

What do you need to know to work with your own *Neuro-Linguistics* or the *Neuro-Linguistics* of another person?

Briefly, NLP refers to **modeling human excellence** in order to create cutting edge human "technology" (or "magic") that allows us to improve our quality of life. We model human excellence by finding, identifying, eliciting, and designing various patterns or "programs" that work within the mind-body (neuro-linguistic) nature of our experience.

We have the following three components that make up our *Neuro-Linguistics:*

Neuro: the voluntary and autonomic nervous systems through which we process experiences via our five senses (visual, auditory, kinesthetic, olfactory and gustatory) and our "made-up" sense, *language,* (which we call "auditory-digital"). This highlights the importance of human neurology and physiology as part of the human information system.

Linguistic: language and non-verbal symbol systems by which we code, organize, and attribute meaning to neural representations (re-presentations). "Linguistic" does *not* refer only to words and propositional language, but to all symbol systems: the sensory systems of visual, auditory, kinesthetic, etc. and the non-propositional symbol systems of mathematics, music, art, etc.

Programming (also, processing, psychology): the process of getting ourselves into regular and systematic patterns of responses (habits). Unfortunately, when people don't know to relate this term to *the computer metaphor* out of which it arose, they tend to contaminate it with ideas of "manipulation," "control," etc. Yet, in context, "programming" operates as just another word for patterns and refers to the organized "plans" and processes that can become installed in human functioning.

The Components Of "Mind" Or Consciousness

One of the early NLP books carries a title that highlights the focus of this model. *Using Your Brain—For A Change* (1985) describes the centrality of *"thought"* and locates NLP as a cognitive-behavioral model. Rational-Emotive Behavior Therapy (REBT, formerly RET) similarly focuses on "thoughts" as primary in driving human experience. In REBT, however, "thoughts" show up primarily as words, self-talk statements, and beliefs, and more recently as internal imagery.

NLP accepts this analysis of the cognitive nature of human mental processing, *and* it doesn't stop here. It enhances the cognitive model significantly by extending its analysis of "thought" to include the five sensory *modalities* (modes) of awareness. These include:

- Visual (pictures, sights, images)
- Auditory (sounds, noise, music, etc.)
- Kinesthetics (sensations, feelings)
- Olfactory (smells)
- Gustatory (tastes)

We summarize these sensory modalities as **the VAK** (visual, auditory, kinesthetic). The VAK comprises the basic components of "thought" or our **representation systems** (RS) by which we *represent* (literally, re-present) information. These representations comprise the language of our bio-computer and so by using these *representational systems* we not only *re-present* information to ourselves but program ourselves.

Figure 2.1

The Representational Systems Of Modalities And Submodalities

Modalities:		Submodalities:
V — visual		
A — auditory		Within each modality
A$_t$ — auditory tonal (sounds, music)		we have the *qualities*
A$_d$ — auditory digital (words)		or finer distinction
K — kinesthetic or bodily sensations		that cue the body,
K$_v$ — visceral (gut sensations)		informing it *how* to feel
K$_t$ — tactile (touch)		or respond.
K$_m$ — meta (= emotions)		
O — olfactory		
G — gustatory		

Since we experience "awareness" via these sensory components, treating the VAK or RS as our programming language gives us a way to understand, model, and transform experience. Bateson noted (in his introduction to *The Structure Of Magic*), with both surprise and regret, the genius of Bandler and Grinder to pick something as simple as the senses to use as the core components of human representation.

Bandler and Grinder constructed the NLP model of "mind," "personality," "experience", etc., using the VAK as *a notational system*. In doing this they provided a simple, yet profound, way for describing with precision our subjective internal experience. Prior to this, "introspection" had always failed to produce any accurate, useful, or legitimate approach. Even though modern psychology, beginning in the 1880s with Wundt's introspective method, sought to identify the "table of elements" in thought, with a precise language, such introspection proved unwieldy and ultimately untrustworthy.

With the introduction of the notion that sensory systems comprise the elemental components of thought, NLP provides a precise language for describing and manipulating the introspective world inside consciousness. This new precise "language of the mind" also provides a way to describe the processes (or *strategies*: "sequences of representations") that we use in our minds-and-bodies to create our programs that make up our unique models of the world.

Thus, "in the eye of the mind" we make "sense" by using our see, hear, smell, and taste senses to code information, whether past experiences (memory) or imagined experiences. Each sensory modality provides us with an additional *language of the mind*. Beyond them, at a meta-level, lie the symbolic systems for representation and coding. This obviously includes language, along with math, music, poetry, proverbs, stories, etc. Each modality provides additional avenues for coding and representing structural information or programs.

The domain of **submodalities** refers to the *qualities* of our RS which allow us to speak with *even more precision and specificity* about the contents of our thoughts. What significance does this have? It essentially provides *the finer coding* (or encoding) for the "mind." Through these finer distinctions we get to the very structure or process of the thinking that "programs" human neurology for feelings, reflexes, behaviors, speech, skills, etc. So, in addition to the *forms* of cognition (VAK and A_d), NLP relies upon submodalities to specify *differences*.

Paradoxically, however, to recognize, detect, and observe *submodalities*, you have to "go meta." You have to *step back* from your sights, sounds, sensations, etc. (the VAK) and *notice* them. Do I have this coded in color or as a black-and-white picture? How high or low do I have the sound volume? What tone and tempo encode this awareness of the sound?

This means that, while the finer *distinctions* of the VAK occurs *within* the mode of awareness, to observe such, we have to "go meta" (above or beyond) the representation. Then, from there, we can make alterations and transformations in the coding. This differs from the traditional NLP explanation. For a fuller description and understanding, see Hall and Bodenhamer (1999, *The Structure Of Excellence*).

Some of these *qualities* and *characteristics* of the RS function in a way similar to the off/on switches of 0 and 1 in a computer (thus offering digital distinctions). Through awareness and recognition of submodalities we can make distinctions between closely related, but different, experiences. What codes the difference, for example, between *thinking about* a fearful event and *experiencing it as such*? Traditional psychology has spent decades coming up with "explanations." Unfinished traumatic memories, weak ego strength, too many dysfunctional defense mechanisms, an undeveloped psycho-sexual or psycho-social stage, etc.

The developers of NLP asked a different question, *"How* do each of these experiences work?" From that they came up with a very different conclusion. To merely *think about* experience, one simply needs to code it from a second perceptual position, from a spectator's point of view, as if watching a movie. To *freak out and go into hysterical emotional reactions* one simply needs to step into the movie and "be there." Step out and it changes. Step in and it changes. Off. On. The secret lies in the coding. We don't need more explanations.

Figure 2.2

Specific Qualities And Distinctions In Each Representational System

Visual:

- location of images
- distance
- snapshot or movie (still or moving)
- number of images
- bordered or panoramic
- color or black-and-white
- shape
- form
- size
- horizontal and vertical perspective
- associated or dissociated
- 3D or flat (2D)
- brightness (from dull to bright)
- foreground and background contrast

Auditory:

- location of sounds
- distance
- number of sound sources
- kind of sound (music, noise, voice)
- whose voice
- tone
- volume (from low to high)
- quality (clarity, intelligibility or lack thereof)
- pitch (from low to high)
- melody.

Kinesthetic:

- location of sensations
- what sensations
- still or moving
- pressure
- area and extent
- intensity
- temperature
- moisture
- texture
- rhythm

And in the **auditory digital system of language**:

- location of words
- sensory based or evaluative
- simple or complex
- of self and/or of others
- current or dated.

Processing Levels

NLP operates not only as a model, but also as *a model-about-models*, as illustrated in *Figure 2.3.*

Neurologically, we first *map* the territory of the world as we generate non-language representations using our sensory channels (the VAK). These *neurological representations* exist at a level below, or prior to, words. Then, to think *about* those RS, we *map* at a higher level. We make *a linguistic map* by using words, symbols, metaphors, etc. Language functions as signals about signals—a meta-level.

Within the level of modalities, we have the domain that we have come to know as *submodalities*. This term, *"sub*modalities," however offers a mislabeling. These discrete facets of the VAK do *not* actually exist at a lower logical level ("sub") to the modalities. They actually comprise the features and characteristics *within* the representation. And yet this set of distinctions (submodalities) does explain and govern much of "the magic" that occurs in many of the NLP patterns. In applying submodalities, we make finer distinctions about the coding of an experience, and that, in turn, leads to greater precision in designing strategies and working with subjective experiences.

Finally, at the top level of the figure, note the meta-modality of language. This describes our sixth sense inasmuch as by language we talk *about* our senses; the meanings we attribute to what we see, hear, and feel.

Figure 2.3

The NLP "Information Processing" Model

More Abstractive Language (the Milton Model)
↓ ↑
Linguistics (a meta-level signal)
Evaluative Language
↓ ↑

Sensory Language
MODALITIES
↓ ↑
Sensory Based Representations (Neurology)
Visual / Auditory / Kinesthetic / Olfactory / Gustatory Representations
Submodalities
(Specific Qualities within Each Representational System)

Higher Information Processing Levels

Above the neurological and language RS, we have an area noted in *Figure 2.3* as the meta-level.

"Meta" (a key word) refers to something "above" or "beyond" something else. When something stands in a meta relationship to something else, it exists at a higher logical level and refers to, or stands as "about", a lower level.

When we move up the continuum on the figure, we find the *meta-level phenomena*: beliefs, values, criteria, frames, presuppositions, metaphors, narrative, etc. Here we have also developed **meta-level technologies**: Time-line patterns, the V-K dissociation, ecology checks, Milton-model (hypnosis), Core Transformation, Meta-belief change work, Reframing, etc.

At the primary level, thoughts induce states. The coding (and sub-qualities of the RS code) of sights, sounds, and sensations moves us into a mind-body state of consciousness. This continues as we move up the scale. When we turn our states **reflexively upon** other states, we create and experience states-about-states (fear of fear, calmness about anger, joy about learning, love about loving, etc.). Hall (1995) designated these states-about-states as *Meta-states*.

The Meta-states model (1995) makes *even more explicit* these internal processes that occur at these higher levels. We have long known that phenomena at these **higher logical levels** *drive* and control the lower levels (i.e., "primary states"). The Meta-states model makes this explicit and shows how it works. So we have put it at the higher levels, **above** the level of the RS.

Logical Levels Of States

A primary state refers to a state such as those that involve *primary emotions* (fear, anger, joy, lust, relaxation, pleasure, disgust, etc.). A Meta-state, by contrast, refers to those states that contain thoughts-and-emotions **about** a primary state: anger at one's fear, guilt about one's anger, feeling upset about one's disgust, fear of one's fear, depression about one's fear, etc.

States-about-states (*Meta-states*) explains the critical importance of the unconscious frames that govern our presuppositional lives. It also explicitly details Bateson's insights about meta-levels. Bateson argued that we can discern **meaning** not only via the words or syntax of a structure, but by considering the larger *contexts* within which the words and syntax occur. This explains how Meta-state technology can have such pervasive and generative effects in change work.

The Meta-states model explains many of the so-called "failures" which some people have experienced with NLP. Essentially, they have worked with a meta-level experience or phenomena using primary state technology. For instance, to test kinesthetic anchoring (see the Anchoring Pattern), one might have a person access a state involving meta-levels rather than primary levels and set a sensory-based (VAK) anchor for resilience, proactivity, self-esteem. One might then fire off the anchor at a later time and, finding it would not re-access that state, one might then conclude that "NLP does not work."

Meta-level theory explains that, while we can anchor primary states with sights, sounds, and sensations (VAK), Meta-states need *a meta-mechanism* (like language, higher level linguistics, symbols, etc.) in order to anchor such experiences. After all, self-reflexive consciousness operates at a meta-level to the basic modalities level.

The Meta-states model distinguishes between **primary and meta-states**. Primary states (e.g., fear, anger, etc.) generally refer to the territory *beyond* our skin. We use such states to cope and master things. Meta-states deal with high level abstractions: self, time-space, morality (good/bad; right/wrong), relationships, values, beliefs, emotions, etc. Meta-states inherently involve recursive, self-reflexive consciousness which enables us to reflect on our thinking (i.e., meta-think), feel about our feelings (meta-emote), talk about our talk (meta-communicate), etc.

Primary level anchors set up a neurological "learning" whereby outside stimuli condition our response. Anchors, as *conditional stimuli*, function as NLP's user-friendly version of classical conditioning. We anchor *content*.

When we set an **anchor at a meta-level** (the Learning II level), we anchor *the method* of how we process the learning context, rather than the learning itself. Bateson designated these anchors as "context markers" (trigger, suggestion, word, etc.). They identify the frame of reference under which we operate. These access the context, which triggers a different kind of processing. Here we have *meta-anchors*.

Words generally comprise these context markers or meta-level anchors. We can include (as meta-level anchors) most evaluative terms, terms about classes and categories, complex equivalences, meta-frames about meanings, cause-effect terms, meta-programs that refer to one's meta-processing level, etc. Anchors that contain a meta-level within them involve the auditory-digital representation system. (Do you find many of these terms new and strange? They make up other facets of the NLP model that we will gradually define as we progress!)

Figure 2.4

Logical Levels Within The Representations

		Presuppositions
		Meta-Frames
Technologies:	*Meta-States* (States-about-states)	Core Transformation

The Meta-model, ↓ ↑ Reframing
Time-Lines, Beliefs/Values
Ecology Checks, _____ V-K Dissociation
Milton-Model (Hypnosis) **Linguistics** (a meta-level signal)

Evaluative Language

Sensory Language
Technologies; **MODALITIES**
Eye Accessing Cues **Sensory Based Representations** (Neurology; VAK RS)
Pacing
Anchoring
Collapsing Anchors

Submodalities Specific Qualities in Each
Technologies: Representational System
SBMD Shifting
Contrastive Analysis, Swishing

The Mechanisms Of Change
Understanding How The "Magic" Works

Given this model of human functioning and patterning, how do we explain "change," transformation, pathology, renewal, etc.? How do the *human technologies* incorporated in the *transformation patterns* work? How does this technology function to effect change and transformation in human affairs?

First, the *transformation technology* functions as all *Cognitive-Behavioral psychology models function—by the cognitive-emotive mechanism of representation.* We don't operate on the world directly, but indirectly, through our maps of the world. NLP combines the best of the cognitive movement and the best of the behavioral movement. Written with a hyphen, *cognitive-behavioral* recognizes that both factors operate in our mind-bodies as an interactive system. This model incorporates the best also from the neuro-linguistics of General Semantics and from the family system model of the MRI (Mental Research Institute) that generated the Solution-Oriented Brief Therapy model. All of the explanatory mechanisms that one finds in those domains, apply here.

As a cognitive-behavioral model, we begin with the post-modern recognition of *constructivism*. This means that the internal representations we have of the world—we have **constructed** and store in our nervous system. The human experience involves creating internal *representational maps* **of** the territory.

Thus, as we process, code, and construct our internal model(s) of the world (our cognitive-emotional schemas or paradigms) we experience, feel, communicate, and behave. Our sense and experience of reality come from our maps *of* reality. Therefore, when we change our maps—we change our reality. This summarizes the basis of human transformation.

As a meta-psychology model, NLP began by exploring how human programming (learning, conditioning, experiencing) gets coded at the neuro-mental (or neuro-linguistic) level. As a result, NLP generated a working pattern of *the structure of human subjectivity.*

Korzybski (1941/1994) noted that in the process of "abstracting" information from the world—we make **a map of reality**. He formulated the now-classic map-territory distinction, "The map is not the territory." He also noted that, if our map has a similar correspondence (the correspondence theory of truth) or a usefulness so that it leads us to the places we want to go (the pragmatic theory of truth), then, *as a map*, we can work effectively from it. If it meets neither of these criteria, then it functions as a "problem" to us and needs changing, updating, or deleting!

NLP, incorporating Chomsky's transformational or generative grammar, formulates a map-making model using three "modeling processes." These include **deletion, generalization, and distortion**, which refer to the fact that, as we handle the billions of bytes of information per second striking our nervous system, we delete most of this information, generalize a good bit of it, and distort the rest of it. As a result of our abstracting via these processes, we create a paradigm. We model the world and then use our nervous system and "mental" constructs to navigate our way through life.

As such, we then recognize that cognitive-behavioral mechanisms ultimately mediate our experiences. We create our reality through our perceptions. This map of the territory differs radically from the territory itself. If our experience of reality seems most limited, problematic—then the problem lies in our paradigm, not in the world. Thus it becomes a case, not of the world's existing as too limited and impoverished, but that **our map of the world** suffers from impoverishment.

Our *neuro-linguistics* thus describe the central mechanism that mediates our experiences. When we change our neuro-linguistic structure (how we use our languages of the mind and our physiology), we change our reality and our experience.

On To The Patterns Of Human Technology Or Magic

Understanding how we use the representational systems and their submodalities and how they put us into mind-body states (neuro-linguistic states), and how we all model the world using the processes of deletion, generalization, and distortion, **we can now track down the patterns** that create our subjective experiences. Such "strategy" analysis allows us to effectively work with subjective experiences.

Using cues to neuro-processing such as eye accessing cues (Appendix A), linguistic markers, non-verbal calibration, physiology, etc., we can obtain the person's internal formula, program, or strategy that runs their experiences. This formula gives us an inside track to the structure of their subjective pain and distress.

*The NLP model does not consider people broken, **only their maps!*** People work perfectly well. NLP operates from the same premise that has become a password in Narrative Therapy:

> *"The person is not the problem;*
> *the problem is the problem!"*

Pathology occurs in our neuro-linguistic **maps** *of* the territory. Operating from poor and impoverished maps results in impoverished and limited ways of living, thinking, feeling, relating, behaving, etc.

The change process then requires another set of patterns by which we can disrupt old patterns and co-create new, more effective patterns. Patterns, as step-by-step processes, can help people bring about their transformation.

Enough explanation and theory—*on to the patterns!* In the pages that follow, you will find pattern after pattern for effectively working with human maps. Each pattern has a brief description of the concept, and sometimes an explanation, and sometimes additional information about the source of the pattern.

We have written each pattern as a step-by-step process. From time to time we have even written some of the language in script form. We did it this way intentionally. We wanted to provide enough content so that even those unfamiliar with a pattern could immediately use it knowledgeably. We also wanted to avoid reducing the patterns to mere outline form, assuming your acquaintance and memory, choosing instead to present them as well-constructed, complete and effective change pieces.

Structural Outline Format

In this book we have sorted *"problems"* (i.e., challenges, difficulties) into the following **categories**. We have provided this *classification of types or kinds of "issues"* so that the reader can use them to more effectively choose, work with, and apply the various NLP patterns. This categorization thus provides a way to sort and separate "problems." In choosing to organize the NLP patterns in this way, we have used this category list as **the organizational structure** for the following chapters. Thus, we can think about human difficulties falling into the following areas:

- **Parts**—suffering from two or more "integral parts" in conflict
- **Identity**—suffering from having one's sense of self in distress
- **States**—experiencing problematic, unresourceful and/or emotional states of consciousness
- **Language**—experiencing cognitive errors in self-talk and languaging oneself in negative and distressful ways
- **Thinking Styles**—suffering from cognitive and perceptual distortions or simply inappropriate meta-programs
- **Meanings**—suffering from limiting beliefs and diminished meanings
- **Strategies**—suffering from not knowing how to engender a piece of desired behavior (micro- and macro-behavior)

We offer this purely arbitrary system simply as a way to manage and chunk the following material. Obviously, a person may suffer from incongruity when one part of the self wants to play during work time and work when it is time to play. We could also frame this as a person struggling with beliefs about such conflicts and what this implies about their identity, the states they get into, etc. Each represents a *constructed frame of reference* and therefore neither exists as more "real" or "true" than the other. Each has different degrees of usefulness.

Further, we do not think of these categories as exclusive ones. They merely offer us one way to sort out human difficulties and the factors that prevent us from experiencing our full potential. We have sorted them in this way simply so that we may address them with various patterns in the NLP arsenal of techniques. Thus, if a particular pattern does not shift a "problem," simply go to another category that may allow you to construct the "problem" in a different way, and see if the technologies there will allow you to transform it.

Figure 2.5

The NLP Algorithm

Present State **Desired Solution State**

Description: specifically   Specific description in
how does it create a problem?   terms of well-formedness

Bridging to—
Kinds of resources needed to move

- Parts—suffering from having two or more "parts" in conflict
- Identity—suffering from having one's sense of self in distress
- States—experiencing problematic unresourceful states of consciousness
- Language—experiencing cognitive errors in self-talk and languaging oneself in negative and distressful ways
- Thinking styles—suffering from cognitive and perceptual distortions or simply inappropriate meta-programs
- Meanings—suffering from limiting beliefs and unenhancing meanings
- Strategies—suffering from not knowing how to achieve a piece of desired behavior (micro- and macro-behavior)

This diagram enables us to think about a "problem" in terms of *moving from* present state *to* desired state. This accordingly allows us to analyze the "problem", first in terms of how we currently experience it, think about it, feel it, the strategies and internal representations that comprise it, etc. (present state analysis). We can then move our consciousness to consider the desired state that we want to achieve and similarly analyze it.

Doing this analysis then raises resource questions—questions about how we *move from* one state to another and how we create *bridges* between them.

- What resources do we need to move from present state to desired state?

- What human technologies within the NLP model will assist us in moving from present state to desired state?

- What internal representations, submodalities, meta-programs, strategies, etc. will assist with this?

And now, the patterns.

Part Two

NLP Patterns

The Incantations For Transformation And Growth

(The Sourcebook)

Chapter 3

The Basic Patterns

Patterns For Running Other Patterns
(Meta-Patterns)

Having examined the NLP Model in chapter 2, you have just about everything you need to use the NLP transformation patterns that you will find in this book. *"Just about,"* however, implies that you will need to add a couple more pieces before getting out your magic wand and using this book as a sourcebook of incantations for growth and change.

On previous pages, we introduced the concept of logical levels. This leads to a crucial distinction in human experience between **content** and **process.** Further, because this distinction plays such a crucial role in what follows, we thought it best to offer some additional explanations regarding it before turning you loose.

Content describes the what and the details. It refers to both the juicy details about what someone did, when, where, and with whom, and also includes the boring details. It generally describes the primary (and sometimes the sole) place upon which most helping models focus.

Process, by way of contrast, refers to *how* something operates, to its *structure*. And, as a model about models, NLP adds a whole new and higher dimension—it focuses primarily on **process**.

In the area of content, people want to know detail upon detail of all the facets that make up an experience:

- When did that terrible thing happen to you?
- By whom?
- And how did you feel about that?
- And what else?

In some therapies, practitioners even believe that if you go over and over and over the details enough—eventually people will get over the hurt. (Yes, they may eventually become desensitized to it, or just plain bored!) Of course, sometimes going over it again and again only reinforces the generalizations made in and from the traumatic event, thus reinforcing the problem. Every visit to the therapist only deepens the pit!

In NLP, we don't do that.

In NLP, we want to know about **the process of an experience in terms of its structure,** not specific details. Bandler has said, "Therapists are far too nosey—far too nosey." To discover the structure, we have to *go meta*, to a higher level, and, from that meta-position, look at the structure of the representations, the submodality qualities and distinctions, the conclusions and abstractions that the person made *about* the experience, etc. And this explains the power of this model to change things so quickly and thoroughly.

We can think of word processing on a computer as fairly comparable to human processing *structure*. Suppose you wanted to change a letter or document that you typed using a particular software for word processing. Now suppose you decided you didn't want the text to start on the first line of every page, but several lines down. How could you change that? You could go in and then, page after page, you could make that *content change* at each specific location in the document. **Or,** you could forget about the text itself, and instead go to a "Format Menu." Then from there you could type in a command that would, in effect, change the entire document for you. At this higher level, in one fell swoop, you would change everything. Working on the change in this way makes a transformation at a *structural level*.

Further, when we transform a program at a meta-level, we create pervasive, system-wide changes. NLP seeks to do precisely this regarding *human texts* that tell our stories and plot our futures.

Programs To Run Programs

In a later chapter we will introduce the NLP Meta-programs. These higher level *programs* function in human consciousness much like *an operating system* functions in a computer. They run our style of perceiving, sorting for information, and processing data. When we change one of them, we often create pervasive change over our entire mind-body system.

The same tends to happen with **these first NLP meta-patterns**. We introduce them here because they exist as more than just specific *transformation patterns*. They essentially give us the ability to use this model and to apply the technology to a wide range of things. A therapist would need them in working with a client. So would a manager in working with and through the people in his or her organization. And so would a parent, a salesperson, or anyone working in the context of self or other people.

The First Meta-Pattern

Where do we begin? Where should a therapist begin with a client? Or a manager with the people he/she oversees and manages? In NLP, we begin "with the end in mind"—with the outcome that we desire to attain. So we typically ask ourselves or another:

- "What do you want?"
- "If you didn't have your difficulty, what would you like to have instead?"
- "Where do you want to go upon getting to your destination?"

Before introducing specific *transformation patterns*, we need to know what we, or other persons, want, what desired outcome we should go for. We begin then with the concept and the meta-pattern of *well-formed objectives* or outcomes. After that we will present other meta-patterns needed to engage someone in the transformational process itself.

#1 Well-Formed Outcomes

Concept. A primary characteristic of the cognitive-behavioral psychology model lies in its hands-on, experiential approach as well as its directness. This contrasts with the indirect and non-directive style of Rogerian and Psychoanalytic schools. From Erickson's direct hypnotic approach, to the co-created directedness of Solution-focused Brief therapy, to the coaching style in NLP for "running your own brain," and the confrontational approach in REBT of arguing against and training a person to stand up to irrational cognitive distortions, all of these models operate with *an eye on the desired outcome.*

In other words, these models of human functioning operate from a highly *intentional* state with a constant view of the objective or outcome. They focus on questioning such as:

- "What would you like to accomplish today?"
- "How can I assist you in dealing with this difficulty?"
- "If a miracle happened tonight, and tomorrow you didn't have the problem, how would you know?"
- "What would let you know?"

NLP offers a model for developing **Well-Formed Outcomes**. Inasmuch as this process functions as a pattern itself—we introduce it as **the first pattern**, actually a *meta-pattern*. This pattern uses the criteria of well-formedness to create effective goals that motivate and empower because we have formed them *well*. We have structured them so that, by their very design and make-up, they pull us into our future, fit our criteria and the form for effective goal fulfilment.

Well-formedness In Desired Outcomes

On the surface, "setting goals" sounds like an easy and simple thing to do. Yet the fact that most people have great difficulty with goal-setting and goal fulfillment suggest otherwise. It suggests that the process of moving from one's present state to some desired state involves more complexity than appears on the surface.

In this pattern for Well-Formed Outcomes, we have identified the key factors that enable us to identify what we want and to organize our responses so that we can take definite and positive steps to make our desires and hopes real. This pattern also provides an informed way to work with someone in assisting and facilitating their process of attaining desired objectives. This pattern engages others (clients, customers, friends, children, etc.) in a response-able way by taking their words and concerns at face value and helping them to map their goals more intelligently.

Using this model as a map for *designing goals with others* enables us to bypass many of the problems that traditionally arise in helping situations. Namely, that some people:

- Don't really want to change
- Don't feel ready to change
- Fear change, etc.

Further, using these criteria, we can engage in goal-focused conversations in business, personal relationships, and therapy. This creates a new orientation for all involved—a solution-oriented focus.

Key Criteria That Make An Outcome Well-Formed

1. **State it in the positive.** Specifically describe what you *want*. Avoid writing goals that describe what you do **not** want. "I do *not* want to be judgmental." Negation ("not") in the mind *evokes* what it seeks to negate. "Don't think about Elvis Presley." "Don't think about using your wisdom to live life more graciously." Rather, describe what you do want. "If you don't have this problem occurring, what will you have occurring?" "If we had a video-recording of your goal, what would we see and hear?"

2. **State what you can do—what lies within your area of control or response.** If you write something like, "I want others to like me," you have not written anything that you can *do*. Consequently, *that* goal will **disempower you**! State things that you can **initiate** and **maintain**, things within your response-ableness. What specific actions could you take this week to

either reduce your difficulty or to eliminate it altogether? What one thing could you do today that would move you in that direction?

3. *Contextualize.* Define and emphasize the specific environment, context, and situation needed to reach your goal. Don't write, "I want to lose weight." State specifically how much weight you wish to lose, e.g., ten pounds within two months. This gives your brain information about what to do! Identify the place, environment, relationship, time, space, etc., for this new way of thinking-feeling, behaving, talking, and so on. Finally, "Where don't you want this behavior?"

4. *State in sensory based words.* Describe specifically and precisely what someone would see, hear, and feel. Whenever you use an abstract or vague word, specify the behaviors that someone could video-tape. Not, "I want to become charismatic in relating to people" but, "I want to smile, warmly greet people with a handshake and use their name..." Asking for see-hear-feel language, over and over, eventually re-trains us to think in terms of behavioral evidences. This makes our goals more real and less abstract or vague.

5. *State in bite-size steps and stages.* Chunk the outcomes down to a size that becomes do-able. Otherwise the goal could become overwhelming. Not, "I will write a book" but, "I will write two pages every day." Not, "I will lose fifty pounds," but, "I will eat ten fewer bites per meal!"

6. *Load up your description with resources.* What resources will you need in order to make your dream a reality? More confidence in your ability to speak in public? Then write that as a sub-goal. As you think about living out this new objective in the next few weeks, what other resources do you need? What about assertiveness, resilience, confidence, the ability to look up information and check out things for yourself, reality testing, etc.?

7. *Check for ecology.* Does this goal fit in with all of your other goals, values, and overall functioning? Do any "parts" of self object to this desired outcome? Go inside and check to see if this goal is acceptable to all the parts of self.

8. *Specify evidence for fulfillment.* How will you know, in addition to the previous criteria, when you have reached your goal? Make sure you have specific evidence for this.

Using these criteria, either with self or with others, provides a way to quality-check our objectives. This enables us to form our desired outcomes so that we code and map them in a well-formed way about the future we want to create. Smart goal-setting will take us where we desire to go.

Well-Formedness In Desired Outcomes	• State it in the positive • State what you can do • Contextualize • State in sensory-based words • State in bite-size steps and stages • Load up your description with resources • Check for ecology • Specify evidence for fulfillment

#2 Pacing Or Matching Another's Model Of The World

Concept. Pacing or matching another's model of the world describes the second meta-pattern technique. "Pacing" refers to the process of *matching* another person's words, values, beliefs, posture, breathing, and other facets of ongoing experience.

Pacing or matching a person's behaviors describes *the structure of* what we call *"empathy"* or *"rapport."* In other words, as we enter into the other's conceptual mental-emotional world, and use their language, value words, frames of reference, etc., we take on their way of thinking and feeling about the world—their model of the world. We thereby take "second perceptual position," and this **matches** their "reality."

Reflecting back to another person his or her own map of reality communicates our understanding, confirmation, and empathy. Bandler and Grinder (1975, 1976) noted that most people use a favored representational system (VAK). As we listen for the predicates people use in these categories, and use them in our communications, we *linguistically pace (or match)* others' reality. This creates "a yellow brick road" right to their heart.

If someone says, "The way I see things right now, I can only see things getting worse and that makes me feel really bad...," we would use similar *visual* and *emotional terms*. To say, "I hear what you're saying" shifts to the auditory channel and fails to pace the person. To say, "It looks like things have turned dark in your world..." would fit.

Because pacing represents such powerful technology, you can find books devoted to creating rapport—learning how to improve your awareness of, calibration to, and reflection back of, the responses of another person.

#3 Calibration To Someone's State

Concept. Calibration refers to using our sensory awareness to develop an intense focus that allows us to detect another's mental-emotional state, mood, experience, etc. Calibrating a machine refers to learning its unique responses and gauging it. Calibrating to another human being entails learning to use sensory awareness (eyes, ears, skin, and other sensory receptors open and inputting!), to recognize the unique facets of another's experiences as he or she processes information, goes in and out of states, etc.

Bandler and Grinder (1976) identified *eye accessing cue patterns* as one key set of responses to pay attention to. Eye accessing cues refer to a person's eye movements as he or she "thinks," processes information, "goes inside" to make meaning of words or referents, etc.

As a general pattern, the majority of people move their eyes up to visualize. They move their eyes laterally (side to side) when internally hearing and talking in self-dialogue. And they move their eyes downward when accessing feelings. Further, given the existence of the right and left hemispheres, a normally right-handed person will look up and to their left when remembering visually, laterally to their left when remembering auditorially or in words, and down and over to their left when remembering highly valued feelings. (For a diagram of this, see Appendix A).

Similarly, a right-handed person will normally look up and to their right to create imagined pictures, laterally over to their right to construct sounds, music, and words, and down and right to access normal feelings and constructed feelings. Treat these accessing patterns as generalizations and always calibrate to the unique person with whom you communicate. Cerebrally reversed people will remember and construct experiences in an opposite way.

Eye accessing cues then provide us with some indication as to which *representation system* (RS) a person may access while thinking. We can also calibrate to other neurological signs such as breathing, muscle tone, physiology, skin color, etc. All of the early (1970 and 1980) NLP books provide a great deal of detailed information on calibration and pacing.

Calibration plays a crucial role in communication, teaching, and psychotherapy, because every person has his or her own unique way of experiencing and responding. One important area for calibration involves detecting when a person agrees or disagrees with us. Can you tell? Some people respond in obvious ways that leaves no doubt, others in less obvious ways. Some people show only the most minute changes to indicate "Yes, I am with you," or "No, I do not follow or agree." (For an exercise on calibration to "agree"/"disagree" see Appendix B).

#4 Checking The Ecology Of A Pattern

Concept. The human technology of running a "reality check" and an "ecology check" on our thoughts-emotions, experiences, states, beliefs and value hierarchy offers a pattern that operates at a higher logical level than content. This phrase "checking ecology" refers to "going above or beyond" (meta) our current experience (or someone else's) and asking *about* it.

- Does this state, belief, idea, feeling, etc., serve you well?
- Does it enhance your life or limit you in some way?
- Would you like to change this programmed way of thinking, feeling, behaving?
- Does this way of functioning empower you over the long run?
- Will this make you more, or less, effective?

Moving to a meta-position, or a meta-level of observation, and evaluating the overall effect of a belief, behavior, or response enables us to "evaluate our evaluations." This gives us the technology to do a *reality check* on every pattern. And in so doing we have a way to keep our lives balanced within all of the contexts and systems in which we live.

Human consciousness operates as a mind-body *system* of interactive parts. All of the component pieces interact. So when we influence one component in the system, this usually has repercussions on the other components. Consequently, this pattern for checking ecology focuses on making sure that a proposed change or new behavior will operate productively and take into consideration all of our outcomes and values.

After all, un-ecological change will either not last or it might even create conflicts or more problems. So if we do not take into consideration the overall impact of changes, we can create change that may look really good on one level, but on another, invite disastrous effects.

Various Ecology Frames Exist In NLP

- *Conflicting outcomes* suggest that, when a person doesn't obtain a desired change, this occurs because he or she has good reasons for not achieving those changes. To achieve a goal without first taking care of conflicting outcomes may create harm. With this pattern we can check for ecology.

- *Present state outcomes* assume that every behavior/response has some useful function. Since this function will work in a unique way for each person, it becomes important to identify and preserve this function when making a change. So we ask, "What will I (or you) lose with this change, belief, or behavior?"

- *Questionable presuppositions* imply that sometimes change does not occur because it does not fit with either the person's external or internal reality. When we want to change something, we should also examine the presuppositions behind that desire. Frequently people ask for motivation to get more done, when what they really need may involve a better way to decide whether they should do the thing in the first place.

Ecology Checks to Make

- *Incongruence.* Do we (or others) respond congruently when thinking about making a change? Watch and listen for incongruent responses as the person describes or experiences the desired outcome. If he or she responds incongruently, then explore one of the following three questions:

  a) Do we (or they) have one or more parts expressing conflicting outcomes?

  b) Do we (or they) have a conflicting part that continues to play an active role when we inquire about the desired outcome?

  c) Do we have sufficient sensory acuity to detect the incongruence?

- *Forecast possible problems.* "What problems could arise by the proposed change? Will it get the wanted outcome? What will the person lose by getting the behavior?" (Any gain always involves some loss, even though minor.)

- *Deletions.* As we gather information, check for anything not mentioned. Have we considered the internal responses, processing, and external behaviors of all other relevant people with respect to the proposed change?

The Pattern

1. *Invite the person to step back or up.* Upon identifying any thought, representation, belief, value, pattern, experience, state, etc., step back and think *about* (meta) that experience. "And as you think about..."

43

2. *Invite an evaluation.* "...and you can notice if it serves you well or not, whether it limits or enhances your life, if every part of yourself finds it useful or unuseful..." "Does this empower or limit me?" "Does it expand and open up more choices, or create new and different limitations?"

#5 *Flexibility Of Responses*

Concept. This meta-level skill, or pattern, involves cultivating within ourselves (or others) more flexibility in responding. Contrast with the opposite—rigidity of response. This means that we constantly check the ongoing and current outcomes. When we discover a set of responses that we do not want, *we "do something different."* In so doing, we operate from the basic NLP Communication Guideline Principle:

> *The meaning of our communication*
> *lies in the response we get —*
> *regardless of our intention.*

So when we discover that the response we receive differs from the response we want, we shift the triggers and stimuli that we offer. If we keep offering the same stimulus, time after time, we will get the same responses —and more of them!

The NLP model encourages our development of flexibility by presenting the realization that each person operates out of his or her own model of the world. And, however it works, *it works*. It may not work well. It may not work to achieve what the person wants, but it works.

NLP does not operate from a closed-system and rigid model that "human nature" is "the same" in all humans. Rather, NLP views each person as operating with and from a unique and idiosyncratic set of patterns. Depending upon how a person has *constructed* his or her reality, his or her responses *make sense* in that construction.

We thus begin by discovering and calibrating to that "reality" so that we can figure out **how that particular system of meaning works**. Once we have done the work of calibrating and pacing, we ask the person to run an ecology check on their system. This allows *them* to discover and determine if their system of thoughts, beliefs, values, and programs works to enhance their life, or not. Obviously, this helps us to engage another person *without imposing* our beliefs, values, perceptions, etc. And in this process, it encourages active involvement, motivation, ownership, responsibility, etc. Overall, it makes for a respectful way to interact with others.

Our own flexibility develops as we recognize that everybody operates from a map of reality, that we all navigate and make decisions based on our maps, that most of our maps come from early childhood, and became installed through cultural, family, educational, religious osmosis—*and that we humans typically do not know that our maps "are" not real* in an external way. We typically grow up **not** questioning our thinking. Rather, we just **assume** that if we "think" something —it must "be" real! ("I think—therefore I am.")

To the extent then that we *believe in our beliefs*, we have little flexibility. To the extent that we *question our beliefs* and recognize them as mental constructs (and inherently fallible), we develop greater flexibility and tentativeness. (By the way, both *believing and questioning* our beliefs describes a meta-state construction which we will present more fully later.)

The Focus Of The Meta-Patterns

In one sentence, the primary goal-directed **focus** of the NLP model involves *moving a person from a present state to some solution state by clarifying the difficulty and bringing various resources to bear that will move him/her from the present state to the outcome state.*

This focus makes the entire process of *applied human technology* solution-oriented and resource-oriented. While problem origin, facets, and nature play an initial role in the process, we do not believe that we have to know the source of a problem to solve it. In fact, to develop too much of a *problem consciousness* tends to reinforce the problem causing us to focus on it. Rather than psycho-archaeology as we mentioned earlier (Bandler, 1975), we shift to a more positive solution outcome focus.

This **outcome focus** underscores the importance of becoming clear about our objectives and goals and the criteria that enable us to design well-formed solutions. It underscores the importance of *thinking in terms of resources* for bridging the gap:

- What resources do you need to reach your goal?
- What resources have you lacked that prevented you from moving there?

Overall, this approach creates a here-and-now focus so that *what* we do today, and *how* in this moment we use our "past" or our "future", how we map out reality, how much responsibility we assume, etc., become the primary concern.

#6 State Elicitation

Concept. One of the most crucial NLP skills involves the ability to effectively evoke responses, experiences, memories, etc., from ourselves or another. By eliciting states, beliefs, RS, submodalities, resources, etc., from self or other, we can discover the form of an experience. This, in turn, allows us to replicate it (e.g., in terms of motivation, creativity, resilience, etc.). We do not have to observe blankly such resources, merely wishing that we could access them too. Via eliciting, we can discover and model internal programs. Elicitation can also transform experiences by replacing old difficulties with new resources. This transformation plays a crucial role in effective communicating, persuading, and motivating.

During elicitation, people will essentially *"go inside"* their "memory" to the internalized *referents* that they have stored. Eye accessing cues will provide some indication of their VAK processing. When a person takes an internal trip, give them time to process. If we talk during their TDS (transderivational search), it may interrupt the process.

The Pattern

1. *Move to an uptime state.* Open up all of your sense receptors so that you can input all of the sights, sounds, sensations, etc., presented. ("Uptime" refers to adopting an "up", or alert, orientation to the external world).

2. *Assist the person in accessing the state.* "Think about a time when you felt..." (then name the state, e.g., confident, creative, honest, forthright, in love, etc.). Eliciting the structure without the person's having entered into that state reduces our exploration so that the person just talks *about* it rather than re-experiences it. Lack of accessing the state removes the person one level from the experience itself and will result in more of the person's *theory* about it rather than the experience.

3. *Elicit as pure a state as possible.* If you ask for a "strong belief," pick something that the person doesn't have laden with emotionally significant issues. (e.g., "I'm a worthwhile person".) Pick something simple and small (e.g., "I believe the sun will rise tomorrow." "I believe in the importance of breathing."). The mental processes of the experience will involve the same structure and, with less emotion, we can get "cleaner," and more direct information about the structure.

4. *Express yourself congruently and evocatively.* In eliciting, remember that your elicitation tools consist of the words you say and how you say them in terms of your tones, tempo, body posture, etc. So speak and sound in a way that accords with the subject. Speaking congruently will evoke the state more effectively. If the person gets stuck recreating the state, ask, "Do you know anyone who can?" "What would it feel like if you became them for a few minutes and did it?"

5. *Allow the person time to process.* If the person doesn't seem to access the state, have them pretend. We refer to this as the "as if" frame in NLP (see the pattern for "as if"). "What would it be like if you could?" "Just pretend that you can for a moment, even though we know you really can't... ."

6. *Begin with non-specific words and non-specified predicates* (e.g., "think, know, understand, remember, experience," etc.). This allows the person to search for the experience in his or her RS.

7. *Follow up with specific predicates.* As you notice the accessing of certain RS, help the person by using sensory-specific words. If they use a visual predicate, then you can follow up with a visual, "And what do you see...?"

8. *Use good downtime questions.* Use questions that presuppose the person has to "go inside" to get the information or experience. "Downtime" refers to an internal state in contrast to the sensory awareness state of "uptime." When we do not have access to the information or experience, we have to use our strategy to go inside and get it.

9. *Identify the submodalities.* Once the person begins accessing, focus on the form and structure of the experience by getting the person's submodality coding.

In eliciting, we help the person to become conscious of factors that normally operate outside the range of conscious awareness. Here, our own patience, positive expectation, and acceptance make it easier for the other to access the information.

#7 State Induction

Concept. Sometimes we (or another) seem **unable** to access a particular resourceful state, way of thinking, feeling, acting, relating, etc. If we cannot reach a desired resourceful state when we need, then we will feel "stuck," i.e., at an impasse, without coping skills. To assist with this, we have three foci for accessing and inducing a resourceful state. We use these processes to move ourselves down *"the royal roads" to state* (Hall, 1995) of "mind" and "body." These include:

- *Remembering a state.* We can use our memories to "recall a time when" we thought, felt or experienced the particular resource. "Have you ever X?"

- *Creating a state.* We can use our imagination to wonder about "what would it look, sound, and feel like if..." In this way we can construct the components that make up the state. Using the "as if" frame will enable us to find information coded in various modalities and submodalities and to construct the resource state we desire.

- *Modeling a state in someone else.* "Who do you know who thinks, feels, acts, relates, etc., in this resourceful way?" "Have you seen or heard them do this?" "Imagine yourself taking their place for a day, as you step into their body, looking out of their eyes, and you can be them for a while as you learn their strategy..."

The Pattern

1. *Catch a state in process and anchor it.* If we stay in uptime with our sensory awareness alert to the experiences of others, we will develop the skill of catching "states" as they occur. By accessing and anchoring these states, we can assist that person to learn how to control his or her own subjectivity.

2. *Ask someone to specifically remember the state.* "What did that state of...feel, look, sound like when you experienced it?" "Recall a time when you felt safe and secure..." (or any other resourceful state from memory). Have the person use his or her creative imagination about the components that make up the state. "Begin to allow yourself to simply imagine walking in with calmness and presence of mind..."

3. *Intensify· the state.* Turn up the representations. After accessing the representations that induce a state, amplify them to strengthen the intensity of that state.

   - Identify the *driver submodalities* that make the representations sensory rich and full. What submodality really drives or kicks in this state for you?

   - Use various linguistic intensifiers. What would you need to say to yourself that would crank up this state so that you sizzle?

4. *Access the physiology of the state.* To use physiology to access states, we put our body into the kind of posturing, movements, breathing, etc., that corresponds to the state. "Show me with your body, your posture, etc., what it would feel like if you fully and completely experienced X." "How would you breathe?"

5. *Gauge the state.* "How much do you now experience that confidence? If you gauged it between zero for not-at-all, and ten for totally, what would be your score?

#8 State Interrupt

Concept. Sometimes we get into mental states and emotional states that do not serve us well at all. When that happens we need to **break state** or to **interrupt** the pattern and stop the functioning of the ongoing strategy.

The process of breaking or interrupting states occurs every day because our states of mind-and-body do not stay the same. We experience multiple states and shift our patterns naturally. By developing awareness, this enables us to take charge of altering our states and those of others. A "state" of consciousness (a mind-body or neuro-semantic state) involves internal RS (VAK, submodality qualities, beliefs, values, decisions, etc., and physiology), and whenever we alter these components we can alter or interrupt the state.

The Pattern

1. *Identify the current state.* What state has this person accessed? What state of mind have they entered into? Their state of body? Their state of emotion?

2. *Alter some significant factor of the state.* Change any "driving" submodality in VAK modalities. Listen to that voice as Donald Duck speaking. Hear it as if it came from a distance. See it in black-and-white, etc.

3. *Interrupt.* Doing almost anything new, different, weird, or unexpected will interrupt a state. Stand on your head up against a wall. Use the "T" hand signal for "time-out." Shift to a sexy tonality. Look up in the sky, and ask, "Is that Halley's comet?" State your telephone number backwards.

A good pattern interrupt will *jar consciousness so that it cannot continue* with its current internal representations and physiology. If you journal your states (we have a process for this in the chapter on states), you have an excellent opportunity for noticing the natural pattern interrupts that occur in your life. Because our states constantly get interrupted and altered, knowing, and having access to, several good "pattern interrupts" enables us to stop some states from becoming too powerful or overwhelming.

#9 Anchoring

Concept. Anchoring, as a pattern, provides a user-friendly version of Pavlovian conditioning that allows us to handle "experiences" (internal, subjective experiences—memories, emotional states, awarenesses, skills, etc.).

Behind anchoring we recognize the principle that, neuro-linguistically, **things become linked together in our very neurology**. When we do, we can then *trigger* this or that experience (state, thought, emotion, response) by experiencing one piece of its make-up.

Pavlov discovered this principle in working with experimental laboratory dogs. He observed their unconditioned response to meat powder which activated their saliva glands. To this response he then attached another trigger (a bell) and found that exposure to the meat powder with the bell soon conditioned the dogs to salivate to the ringing of the bell. They learned this response by linking up neurologically "the sound of a bell" to "meat powder" and, since their autonomic nervous system would salivate to "meat," it taught that part of their neurology to salivate to the sound of a bell.

In humans, VAK stimuli constantly get associated with various states of mind-emotion-physiology inside us. These stimuli (or anchors) create our *responses* for thinking, emoting, etc. We begin life with a neuro-physiology loaded with unconditioned responses. Then, when in a responsive state (e.g., pain, pleasure, fear, anger, etc.), **another stimulus** becomes attached to the stimuli. These responses can become so associated (in our associative cortex) with the original stimulus that they can *set off the response*. We call this a "conditioned response" because we have conditioned the person to learn it.

This explains the origin of our "buttons." Such "buttons" essentially operate as the "bells" that get us to salivate! In general semantics we refer to this process as a *"semantic reaction."* This means that the "meaning" or "significance" of the stimuli exists in terms of the response it elicits *in us*. This explains the meaning of *meaning*. A "meaning" consists of a neurological linkage between a stimulus and a state, hence "neuro-semantic." This generates, in NLP, the formula that sets up several linguistic patterns that create the foundation for **reframing meaning**.

Figure 3.1

The Structure Of Meaning

External Stimulus *equals or leads to Internal Significance/State*

$$(ES = / \rightarrow IS)$$

Such an association (a neuro-semantic association) can even become linked and conditioned in us apart from our conscious awareness, since this process involves the functioning of our entire neuro-physio-psychological state. This description also accounts for *the state-boundness of information*. When we have accessed a state, all of our learning, memory, communication, perceptions and behavior operate as state-dependent.

So what? We all have anchors set in our neurology! As a semantic class of life, living in the world where billions of stimuli occur, we inevitably get things linked together. And many of these connections do not serve us well. They just wire us up with lots of "buttons" so that we experience emotional states (semantic reactions) to certain stimuli.

Now we can explore these neurological linkages. "What kind of anchoring situations have you had?" or "Which ones would you like to change?" On the downside, we find that many people do not associate *resourceful states,* but *unresourceful states,* to challenging situations. In other words, they have linked up meanings that put them into a negative neuro-semantic state in response to some trigger.

An anchor then operates as *a sensory stimulus* that has become so *linked to a specific state* that it can instantly put one into that state in a way that "feels" automatic, immediate, and beyond one's control. Recognizing that **this neurological mechanism** empowers us to set up useful anchors, we can change "internal experiences" (states) so they can serve as resources.

This also indicates the extent to which we live in *a symbolic world.* We take in various stimuli as "symbols" and then react/respond to those symbols which create our semantic world or reality. When we create our symbolic/semantic model of the world, we respond to the world via our symbols (meanings: memories, imaginations, beliefs) rather than to the stimuli *as stimuli.*

The result? Our *meanings* begin to carry far more importance than mere stimuli and eventually become stabilized into beliefs, values, attitudes, etc. Anchors function as *triggers* for *state access.* Anchoring uses an element of an experience to bring back the full experience. Anchoring can occur in any sensory system and also in the language system. Finally, anchoring re-induces states without the need to "think" about things.

The *key anchoring factors* involve:

- State intensity: at the peak of an experience.
- State purity: distinct, discrete, specific.
- Anchor uniqueness: unusual, precise, distinct, replicable.

The anchoring pattern gives us the ability to work with association and dissociation as states (as in the phobia cure). We can also anchor an unresourceful cue picture to a resourceful desired outcome picture and *Swish* our brains (the Swish pattern). We can anchor resourceful states so that we can later "fire them off" and re-experience them. Thus, the general purpose in anchoring involves managing an experience so that we can access it at will.

The Anchoring Pattern

1. *Decide on a behavior, state, or response you would like to recreate.* Also identify what kind of an anchor (cue system or trigger) you want to set (e.g., a silent hand movement, a smile, an unobtrusive touch, a word).

2. *Elicit a response.* Ask a person to remember, imagine, or think about a state and go back and remember it fully... . In eliciting the response, make sure that the person has an **intense** response (something worth anchoring).

3. *Calibrate to and detect the response.* Because anchoring links a new stimulus to a response, notice when a person has a response, and calibrate by noticing eye accessing cues, body gestures, posture, breathing, movement, etc.

4. *Add a stimulus.* Now, to the person's response add a sight (make a face or gesture), sound (make a noise), sensation (touch) or word. Always anchor with *unique* triggers, and do so in all of the sensory systems (this creates redundancy which makes it stronger).

5. *Test.* Break state and then re-trigger the stimulus and notice if the response occurs again. If it does, then you have anchored the response.

#10 Accessing Positive Intention

Concept. When "negative" behaviors occur, we typically think of them as driven by a "bad" intention. Most psychotherapy operates from that assumption as well. In NLP, we start from an entirely different basis. We deal with problematic emotions and behaviors by *assuming* that they serve (or served) some useful purpose of value and importance. This attitude lies at the heart of reframing: "Every behavior has a positive value—in some way, for some purpose, at some time."

To find, access, and/or create a *Positive Intention* in a behavior enables us to adopt a more effective reaction to the behavior and the part that produces it. We then have more control over it. This cuts out the negative looping that results when we turn our psychic energy against ourselves in hating or resenting some emotion or behavior. Behavior that puzzles and/or confuses us actually only demonstrates that most of its context lies outside our awareness. This process involves asking a person or some part of a person what it hopes to accomplish of value.

The Pattern

1. *Identify a problem or difficulty.* This works especially well for problems which seem to serve no useful purpose.

2. *Find the part responsible.*

> "Some part of you produced this response or behavior. As you allow yourself to become aware of that part of you, some thought, emotion, or belief, you can begin to ask that part what it sought to do of positive value for you. What did you seek to accomplish of importance through it?"

3. *Continue asking the positive intention question.* Sometimes we have to get the outcome of that outcome, and the meta-outcome of that outcome, and do this several times before we find an objective that seems "positive." So keep recycling through the question until you find the positive intention.

Conclusion

While textbooks now classify NLP as falling within the Cognitive-Behavioral school, it is also now seen as encompassing several other fields:

- family systems (Virginia Satir)
- existential humanistic psychology (Perls, Rogers)
- transpersonal psychology (Assagioli, Maslow)
- the neuro-sciences
- linguistics (Chomsky)
- General Semantics (Korzybski)
- hypnosis (Erickson)
- logical levels (Bateson), etc.

NLP itself began, not as a school or even within a school, but as a meta-school as it created models of various therapies and processes. From the beginning, it sought to apply modeling principles to how things work.

We have identified **ten Meta-patterns** that enable us to run *the Patterns of Transformation* that follow.

Meta-patterns:

1. Well-Formed Outcomes
2. Pacing or Matching
3. Calibration
4. Ecology Checking
5. Response Flexibility
6. State Elicitation
7. State Induction
8. State Interruption
9. Anchoring
10. Accessing Positive Intention

Chapter 4

Parts

Apart Of The Whole
—Warring Parts

Patterns For Incongruity

Sometimes one facet of ourselves will conflict with another facet. The classical work/play conflict serves as a good example. We want to get some work done. So we start to do it. Then a little voice, or thought, in our head pipes up and says, "Wouldn't you rather do something *fun*?" Later, we go outside to play or to take a walk, and a little nagging voice in our head pipes up again, "You ought to be inside taking care of business." On such occasions we feel conflicted. This may take many forms. We may feel: indecisive, anxious, inwardly torn, stuck, procrastinating, etc. "I want to develop the skills of strength, firmness and assertiveness *and* I want to be loving and understanding so that I don't hurt people's feelings." "I want to passionately go after my dream, but I want to feel safe and secure financially and not risk anything."

In this chapter we offer numerous *patterns for the resolution of such conflicts*—strategies that enable us to become more integrated, whole, and at peace with ourselves.

(As an aside about the term "part(s)," we use it here simply to designate *a facet* within the whole system, and do not use the word in an elementalistic way. Nor do we actually or literally think of these "parts" as separate entities. This language simply maps out that different facets within the system can create problems and distress for the system.)

#11 The Collapsing Anchors Pattern

Concept. A "state of consciousness" always involves both mind-and-body. When we experience two states, which radically differ (relaxing and tensing, feeling afraid and joyful), operating at the same time within us, they tend to interfere or interrupt each other. So what can we do about this? We can access and anchor each (with different anchors) and then fire them off simultaneously. Doing this forces our *one neurology* to deal with the messages and experiences of the two states so that they collapse into one response. We cannot think-and-feel calm *and* tense simultaneously. So, when we communicate to our nervous system to do both, this usually results in a "collapsing" of the anchors and states. Sometimes this results in confusion, disorientation, interruption, and even some slight amnesia.

This technology enables us to change a response that does not work very well. By using this **Collapsing Anchors pattern**, we pair a powerful negative anchor with a powerful positive one. When the collapse occurs, we will experience a loss of both responses. This technique works especially well for changing feelings and behaviors (programs) resulting from prior experiences (in other words, old, unuseful anchors). It also utilizes "unconscious" processes and therefore does not necessitate that we consciously need to understand the process. We use this pattern when we have two states conflicting and sabotaging each other. Or, if we have an unresourceful state (an old anchored experience) that interferes with life, we can now let that response collapse into a more resourceful state.

The Pattern

1. *Access an unresourceful state.* Invite, elicit, or just catch a person in, a negative state and set an anchor for it. To do this with their conscious awareness, invite them to talk about it while including the qualities of their sights, sounds, sensations.

2. *Break state.* Stop, interrupt and have them set that state aside.

3. *Access a resourceful state.* Ask the person to think about the state that they would prefer to operate from. "What would you like to experience when in that situation?" Describe it fully: "What would you see, hear, feel, smell, taste? What words would you say to yourself?"

4. *Amplify and anchor.* As the person accesses the resourceful state, have him or her double the size of their pictures, to make the voice stronger and more intense, or to make whatever submodality shift they need to do to amplify the state. When they eventually reach a peak in this resourceful state, anchor it.

5. *Again break state.*

6. *Fire off the unresourceful anchor and then immediately fire off the resourceful anchor.* Hold each anchor and let the neurological processing continue—asking the person to "just experience this state fully." Hold the positive anchor longer than the negative anchor.

7. *Test your work.* After you have broken state again, fire the anchor for the unresourceful state or ask the person to try and recall their previous negative state to see if it returns. If it does not, you have succeeded in collapsing that anchor.

8. *Refresh the resourceful anchor.* As a good ecology process, go back and re-access the resourceful state, making it stronger, brighter, bigger, or whatever submodality amplification intensifies it, and re-anchor it.

#12 The Parts Negotiation Pattern

Concept. When one "part" or facet of a person enters into a conflict-causing relationship with another part in such a way that it initiates self-interrupting and self-sabotaging processes, we create an internal "fight" between these two parts. Frequently, people will live for years or even a lifetime with such internal conflict raging within. This, of course, wastes tremendous amounts of psychic energy, sabotages effectiveness, and creates incongruency.

The pattern of "parts negotiation" provides the technology to change that. With it we can put a stop to the conflict between the parts and negotiate a peace settlement. With this approach, we view each "part" as having a valid purpose and function, one that simply gets in the way of, and interferes with, the other part. Accepting this, we then simply construct a way so that both parts can sequence their activities and create a win/win solution for both.

The process involves first finding and accessing each part, discovering their purpose, role, and positive intention, finding out how they interrupt each other, and inviting each of them to sequence their activities so that they don't interrupt the other.

The Pattern

1. *Identify the parts.* "What part of you creates this behavior?" "What part creates this emotion or thought?"

2. *Determine the desired outcome.* What does each part want? And what meta-outcomes do each obtain by the first level outcomes? Specify in VAK terms.

3. *Engage the parts.* Check to see that each part understands and values the role and function of the other part. Assist each part in realizing that the problem lies in how each interrupts the other (hence, a sequencing issue).

4. *Determine the positive intent.* If step 2 did not elicit and identify the positive value of each part, then continue asking each part, "What positive function do you serve?" Do so until each part can see and value the importance of the other part.

5. *Negotiate an agreement.* "Do you value your own function enough, that if the other part will agree to *not* interrupt you, you will do the same in return?" Have the person check to see if he or she has an internal sense of "yes" or "no." Continue until the parts reach an agreement.

6. *Make a deal.* Ask each part if it will actually cooperate for a specified amount of time. If either part becomes dissatisfied for any reason, let it signal you that the time has come to renegotiate.

7. *Run an ecology check.* "Do any other parts play a role in this process?" "Do any other parts interrupt this part?" If so, renegotiate.

#13 The Six-step Reframing Pattern

Concept. As we get "organized" in the way we think, feel, speak, and behave we develop some facet of ourselves (a "part"). These parts operate not only to accomplish outcomes, but they also establish our *meanings.* And when our meanings become habitual, they drop out of our conscious awareness. As we no longer consciously attend them, they begin to operate at *unconscious levels.* So behind every belief, emotion, behavior, habit, etc., we have some "part" organized to accomplish something of value due to some frame of reference (or meaning).

Over time these parts become more and more streamlined or automatic and function as our basic frames of reference. This saves us time, trouble, energy, etc.: an "ecology" of mind (Bateson, 1972). Yet this can also create major problems for us. As things change, our organized "parts" can come become increasingly irrelevant, inaccurate, and sabotaging. If, as a child, we developed a part to "keep our mouth shut" because "kids ought to be seen, not heard," then we might have installed a "non-assertive" program based on those old meanings. Initially, that part functioned appropriately and usefully but, over time, we can simply outgrow those old programs.

The six-step reframing pattern addresses "programs" of behaviors, habits, emotions, etc., that have become so unconscious, automatic, and unyielding to change that we now need to address them at an unconscious level. This technology becomes useful when conscious thought (as in goal-setting, education, or reframing) doesn't work, or when the response continues to operate even against our better judgment. This pattern works well for habits such as smoking, nail biting, phobic responses, etc. If you say to yourself, "Why do I do this?" or "I hate the part of me that..." then try this pattern.

This pattern provides a way to re-align our parts. That, in turn, creates better integration, self-appreciation, and harmony. Our unconscious mind has already established numerous communications with us—we call them "symptoms." This pattern gives us a way to use these symptoms in developing more functional behaviors.

The Pattern

1. *Identify a behavior that you find troublesome.* Find a behavior that fits one of these formats:

> "I want to stop doing X."
> "I want to do X, but something stops me."

2. *Communicate with the "part" that produces this behavior.* Go inside and ask, "Will the 'part' of me that generates this behavior communicate with me in consciousness?" Wait for and notice your internal responses: feelings, images, sounds. Always thank the part for communicating. Say, "If this means *Yes*, increase in brightness, volume, intensity." "If this means *No*, let it decrease." (You may also use idiomotor signals such as designating one finger to move in response to "No" and another in response to "Yes".)

3. *Discover its positive intention.* Ask this Yes/No question: "Would you agree to let me know in consciousness what you seek to accomplish by producing this behavior?" Wait for response.

> If you get a *Yes*, then ask yourself, "Do I find this intention acceptable in consciousness?" "Do I want to have a part that fulfills this function?" If *No*, then ask the part, "If you had other ways to accomplish this positive intent that would work as well as, or better than, this behavior, would you agree to try them out?'"

If you get a *No*, then ask yourself, "Would I agree to trust that my unconscious has some well-intentioned and positive purpose for me, even though it won't tell me at this moment?"

4. *Access your creative part*—the part of you that comes up with new ideas. Anchor it. Now ask the part that runs the unwanted behavior to communicate its positive intention to your creative part. Using the positive intention, have the creative part generate three new behaviors which it would evaluate *as useful or more valuable than the unwanted behavior*, and to then communicate these behaviors to the first part.

5. *Commit the part.* "Will you now agree to use one of the three new alternative behaviors in the appropriate contexts?" Let your unconscious mind identify the cues that will trigger the new choices, and experience fully what it feels like to effortlessly and automatically have one of those new choices become available in that context.

6. *Check for ecology.* "Does any part of me object to having one of these three new alternatives?"

#14 The Aligning Perceptual Positions Pattern

Concept. Sometimes our ability to perceive things from out of our own eyes (first-person perception) and from out of the eyes of another person (second-person perception, the "empathy" perspective), and from an observer position (third-person perception), gets out of alignment. Structurally, each of these perceptual resources can operate as separate "parts."

These *perceptual positions* refer to the ways that we can "look" at the world. Conceptually, we can become stuck in one position or another. The first three refer to *the three perceptual positions* identified in NLP—the last two have arisen within the past couple of years.

First position: Self, from one's own eyes—self-referencing.
Second position: Other, from eyes of another person—other-referencing.
Third position: External view, from any other position—meta-position.
Fourth position: We, from viewpoint of the system, group—group referencing.
Fifth position: Systems, from viewpoint meta to the system, simultaneously referencing all of the positions—integration-referencing.

Those *stuck in first position* can become totally self-referencing in their view of things so that they think-and-feel in highly "narcissistic" ways. They will process things only in terms of themselves. Those *stuck in second position* tend to become totally other-referencing in their perspective and can get stuck in the role of rescuers and caretakers to the exclusion of taking care of themselves. People *stuck in third position* may take a historical view, a cultural view, etc., so that they become so dissociated from their body and emotions that they seem more like robots than people (Satir's "Computer" stance).

Not only can we get *stuck* in one position, but we can experience an out-of-alignment between these perceptual positions. Problems may also arise from having parts of ourselves react from different perceptual positions. When that happens we end up working against ourselves. *Aligning perceptual positions* in all representational systems results in inner congruence and personal power. This pattern also enables us to resolve inner conflict and attain internal alignment.

Use this **triple description pattern** whenever you lack a full awareness or perspective on a given problem. Take all three positions to broaden your thinking-feeling. This can truly enrich perspectives in such situations as conflict resolution, mediation, influencing others, personal flexibility, etc. The technology enables us to gain an expanded perspective on problem situations.

The Pattern

1. *Identify target information.* Specify a limitation, a problem or a situation in which you (or another) feel stuck. Describe the situation in which you would like to have a more congruent response.

2. *Identify the visual, auditory and kinesthetic factors within each perceptual position.*

a) **Visual:** What and how do you see the situation? From what perceptual position? If you have two or more "parts" that reference this same subject, check what perceptual position each part uses. Do some parts see the situation as an observer or from the eyes of another person? Locate the position of each part. Point out (internally or externally) where you find them. Do some of the parts seem closer to the situation than others? How does each part see the situation? What does each part actually see? What differences occur between them?

b) **Auditory:** What sounds and words do you hear about the situation? From what perceptual position do you hear these things? If you have two or more parts, what does each part say? Listen for the pronouns that each part uses. A part in *the observer mode* will have a neutral voice and will refer to "he" or "she." An "other" voice will typically refer to "you" with a more judgmental tone. The "self" voice will use "I" and "me." Where exactly in your body do you hear each part? (Side positions often indicates other or observer, self usually comes from vocal chord area.)

c) **Kinesthetic:** What do you sense about the situation? From what perceptual position? For multiple parts, where do you sense each part in your body? What emotions do you experience with each part? Do you have any neutral parts, as if you only observe and don't experience life?

3. *Realign perceptual positions in all representational systems.* For the observer alignment (third position), go through the VAK checks.

    a) **Visual:** Ask the observer part, "Would you communicate any information you have gathered to the self part?" Continue the dialogue until self and other view the situation similarly.

    b) **Auditory**: Ask the observer part, "Would you shift pronouns to support the self using 'I', 'he,' or 'she?'" Also, please use "self" tone of voice.

    c) **Kinesthetic:** Ask the observer part, "Would you be willing to shift feelings to those compatible with self feelings?" Also move feelings to the place where "self" holds feelings.

4. *Align your self in terms of the VAK perceptual positions.*

Make sure you see from your own point of view and out of your own eyes. Make sure your voice location arises from your own vocal chords and that you use "I" pronouns. Make sure that all feelings come from inside the "self" and reflect resourceful states.

5. *Do an other alignment (2nd position) in the same way.*

"Please adjust your perceptions to make them compatible with the view held by self." Move the location of other to the place occupied by self. Please move the voice you hear to the vocal chord area and have it represent "self" bringing any enriching information to the 'self' position. Align feelings from 'other' to those of "self." Integrate feelings in such a way as to make the "self" more flexible and resourceful.

6. *Run an ecology check.* Do all the parts feel aligned and in harmony?

7. *Future pace.* Allow yourself now to become aware of new behavioral possibilities.

Describe any new abilities and behaviors that now become available to you. And you can notice yourself performing in the future as the "self" part increases in richness and flexibility. If the "other" part objects to integration, you can request that this part return to the person to whom the thoughts and feelings belong.

#15 The Agreement Frame Pattern

Concept. When two people conflict and lack agreement about something, they will continually butt heads. Often disagreements will arise because people look at given situations from different points of view, and they do so in categorical ways. To achieve an agreement frame, both must move to a higher logical level that encompasses all of the concerns, perceptions, and frames of reference. This pattern enables us to facilitate the process whereby people or groups in conflict reach quality agreements with each other.

The Pattern

1. *Identify the current frames.* Ask each person for a specific description of their outcome. "What do you want specifically?" "What values, beliefs, and criteria drive this goal?" "How do you evaluate this as important?" (These questions not only gather important information, but also pace each person so that each feels heard and understood. It also begins to construct meta-outcomes for an agreement frame.)

2. *Identify common elements.* Find a common element (at a higher level) that unites the outcome and see if you have agreement at this level. "Jack wants a blue chair and, Jill, you want a red one. It seems that, at least, you both agree on purchasing a chair, right?" By pacing the higher level want, it moves the parties there.

3. *Identify a higher level category.* If you get a no, then move the parties up to the next category. In the example, you might use "furniture." "Do you both agree that you want to purchase some piece of furniture?" Continue until you find some level (category) of agreement. "So you could both agree on an expenditure for the house, right?"

4. *Utilize the parties' meta-outcomes to formulate the larger level agreement frame.* "By purchasing X, what will that do for you, Jack?" "And if you purchase Y, what will that do for you, Jill?" "When you get that outcome, what does that do for you?" Continue this until the parties agree to the other person's higher level intent. "So you both want a comfortable and attractive home?"

5. *Frame the negotiation using the higher level agreements.* Move back down from the general frame of agreement to specific exchanges. "Would buying this blue chair meet the criteria of purchasing something comfortable and attractive?" "Would letting Jack decide this one and Jill the next meet your joint criteria of having equal input into decisions?"

6. *Confirm agreements.* During the process, continually identify and solidify all levels of agreement reached and their importance to each party.

#16 *The Aligned Self Pattern* (Using Logical Levels)

Concept. As humans, we can become torn and out of alignment with our values and beliefs regarding our identity and our mission in the world. "Who am I?" "What is my mission in life?"

We can also get so caught up in all the details of this or that task that we forget our overall purpose. The Aligned Self pattern addresses these problems. Using this pattern, we can rediscover and reclaim our values and beliefs about our identity and mission. We can then utilize it to integrate all of our experiences in order to operate more congruently. This pattern forms Dilts' Neurological Levels Model which utilizes environment, behaviors, capabilities, values/beliefs, identity, and spirituality as categories of self-definition. While these levels *do not* describe a true logical level system (see Hall, 1997, *NLP: Advanced Modeling Using Meta-States),* they do provide a most useful model of distinctions about beliefs.

The technology in this pattern works to bring renewal and realignment of identity and mission for those who feel that they need a sense of purpose that will transform their emotions and behaviors. It provides a way whereby we can experience an increased sense of self. Use this technology when you feel out of balance.

The Pattern

1. *Identify resources.* Begin by identifying an ability or resource which would aid you (or another) in becoming more congruent and purposeful. You may want more calmness, confidence, assertiveness, centeredness, resilience, etc. Elicit and anchor these resources fully.

2. *Establish six anchors.* Identify a visual space for environment, behaviors, beliefs and values, capabilities, identity, and spirituality.

3. *Anchor the resources (X) into the visual space.*

Focusing on the environment space, answer the question, *"When and where* do I want to act with more X?"

Focusing on the behavior space, answer the question, "What *behaviors* do I need in order to act more X in those times and places?"

Focusing on the capabilities space, answer the question, "What *capabilities* do I have or need in order to perform those behaviors in those times and places?"

Focusing on the beliefs/values space, answer the questions, "What *values and beliefs* do I need to support and guide me to my goal? For what reasons do I want to use these capabilities?"

Focusing on the identity space, complete the sentence, "I am *the kind of person* who X-es."

Standing in the spiritual space, answer the questions, "What *overall life purpose* do I pursue? How would I describe my personal mission?"

4. *Solidify gains.*

Solidify spirituality identity. Allow yourself to fully experience the spiritual space that you have entered and take that physiology and inner experience and step back into the identity space so you experience both states simultaneously. Notice how the experience of *spirituality* enriches your experience in the identity space... .

Solidify capability. Take the experience of both your mission and identity and bring them into your capability space. Again notice how your experience of capability becomes enriched by spirituality and identity... .

Solidify belief. Bring your vision, identity, and capabilities into beliefs and values space. Experience how they all strengthen, change and enrich the beliefs and values you experience within yourself.

Solidify behavior. Bring your vision, identity, capabilities, beliefs and values into the behavior space. Allow yourself to notice how all the manifestations of the higher levels give additional meaning to new behaviors.

Solidify environment. Bring all levels of yourself into the environment space and notice how your experience of today becomes fully transformed and enriched by spirituality, identity, capabilities, beliefs, and behaviors.

5. *Allow the entire process to integrate.* Allow all the new insights, beliefs and qualities from each of the levels to integrate.

6. *Solidify values into capabilities.* Future pace. Now, taking this new reality, imagine yourself moving into your future fulfilling your expanded potentialities...

(Note: You can do this process kinesthetically if you mark off spaces on the floor for each level and use language with lots of kinesthetic predicates. To adapt for auditory representational systems, designate a place for each voice. Then use auditory language.)

#17 *The Resolving Internal Conflict Pattern*

Concept. Given that we can experience and exhibit internal disagreements, this provides yet another pattern to help sort out the polarities involved. We can use it with beliefs or with internal "parts". This offers another pattern to promote personal alignment.

The Pattern

1. *Identify a personal conflict.* Think of some "conflict" that you experience between values, beliefs, roles, goals, parts, etc.

2. *Recall a memory from the observer position.* Remember a time when you experienced the conflict and review that memory from an observer point of view (dissociated).

3. *Take first position with one side.* Now step into the experience and take one side of the conflict. From this position, fully review the opposite side of the conflict. Notice what information (pictures, sounds, sensations, words, values, intentions, beliefs, etc.) you can receive via this process.

4. *Search for positive intention.* Ask the opposite side, "What positive intention do you have in this context?" "What meta-outcome do you seek to achieve by doing what you do?"

5. *Switch roles.* Switch now to the opposite part, step into the experience and repeat this process, identifying the positive intention, belief and goal of the other part. Gather as much information as you can from this point of view.

6. *Repeat.* Go back and forth doing this until each part has a full understanding of the other's beliefs, values, and positive intentions.

7. *Go to a meta-position.* Imagine moving up a logical level and taking a position above both of these parts. From this perspective, ask the parts to come up with an outcome satisfactory to both.

8. *Run an ecology check and integrate.* Once you have checked out the ecology concerns, bring the new belief or the new integrated part into the body and let it become a part of you.

9. *Future pace.*

#18 The Advanced Visual Squash Pattern

Concept. Individuals frequently develop unconscious parts or facets of themselves which disagree with each other. When parts become incongruent to each other and to the rest of our system, we become incongruent. To re-integrate these parts we will first want to identify the positive intent of each part. Originally developed by Bandler and Grinder, this advanced form comes from Dr Bobby Bodenhamer. You can do this also by using a spatial anchor on the floor for each part, observer, and meta-position.

The Pattern

1. *Identify and separate the parts.* "You have a part that responds by generating a certain behavior, do you not?" Identify and separate this part from other parts with which it conflicts. One part may desire food, another part may desire to lose weight. These parts will make different value judgments.

2. *Form a visual image of each part.* Make a full representation of each part. "What does the part responsible for X look like? What does the part sound like? How does the part feel?" Upon doing this, put the images of each part in your palms. "Which hand would this part want to be in? Will it move on to your right or left hand?" Ask the other part to move on to the other hand. When working with another person, observe his or her gestures. This will enable you to identify which hand represents which part.

3. *Separate the positive intention of each part from its behavior.* Every behavior has some use in some context. No matter how harmful a part's behavior, it seeks to do something of positive value. "Go inside and ask this part, 'What positive purpose do you have in producing this response for me?'"

Establish a common positive intention. Find a positive intention that represents the positive outcomes for both parts. (See Agreement Frame.) If you do not receive a positive intention, continue to reprocess the question, "What do you evaluate of value and importance by doing that behavior?"

4. *Transfer resources from one part to the other.* You may say to the person, "Now that you realize that these two parts have a very similar positive intention for you, does each have resources that the other could use?" Most of the time you will get an affirmative answer. (If you don't, continue to work between the parts.) If you get a resource, ask the part to inform your (or another's) conscious mind of the resource(s). Now, form an image of the resource.

Motion with your hand from the hand of the person, up their arm, through their head, down the other arm and into the opposite part in the other hand, then say, "Now, transfer the resource from this part to the other." Calibrate as the person does this. Do this with each resource. "And you can notice how this part begins to look and feel differently..." This procedure facilitates neurological integration through submodality mapping across. The mapping takes place as the image of a resource is transferred across to the other hand.

5. *Form an integrated third image.* Ask the person to form a third image of what the parts would look like with combined resources. Once they form this image, have them place this image in the center of the other two images on their hands.

6. *Turn the images in the hands toward each other.* Ask the person to turn his or her hands to face each other and to create a series of visual images representing a transition of each part to the center image.

7. *Lead by placing your hands in the mirror image of the person's hands.*

"You now know that each of these parts has a similar positive intent for you, and you have exchanged resources from one to the other. Now, allow your hands to come together only as fast as you can permit the integration of these two parts into one super-part, preserving the highest positive intent of each."

Now move the person's hands together just slightly faster than they do.

8. *Complete the integration.* Once the hands come together, allow the person adequate time to experience total neurological integration. When the parts have integrated, ask if the two parts have merged into one image. Ask the person to describe the image. With hands together, lead the person to bring the new integrated part into him- or herself.

Conclusion

These patterns address the all too common phenomena in human experience of incongruity, inner conflict, and the lack of balance between all of the facets that comprise our reality. These parts installed within us can cause us to become very torn and full of conflict when they get out of alignment with our whole system of beliefs, values, decisions, strategies, etc. The technologies within this chapter aim at re-creating balance and wholeness. They aim at integration, completeness, and inner harmony.

What can we expect from these things? A greater experience of congruency which, in turn, makes for greater personal power. And with more power—we have more focus and energy to devote to our dreams and visions.

Chapter 5

IDENTITY

Inventing And Re-inventing "Self"

Patterns For Building Empowering Self-Images

"All man's miseries derive from not being able to sit quietly in a room alone."

Pascal

Some of the difficulties that we struggle with arise from, and concern, an *abstraction*—the paradigm we construct in our mind about ourselves:

- "Who am I?"
- "What value or worth do I have as a human being?"
- "What confidences, skills, or abilities can I own as my own?"
- "Am I a loveable, attractive, and desirable person?"
- Etc.

These "self" questions raise inquiries about (1) identity, (2) self-esteem, (3) self-confidence, (4) self-loveability, etc. From the beginning of life, we embark on *this journey of self-discovery* as we differentiate ourselves from mother and father, family, teachers, and social groups. We do this to *identify* our values, beliefs, skills, etc.

Without such individual awareness, we will not feel or attain a sense of independence nor a sense of being personally response-able (responsible) *for* ourselves. And without that we will lack the autonomy to "know ourselves," and lack the integration that comes from *centering* ourselves in our values and beliefs, *fulfilling* ourselves by finding our aptitudes and skills, and feeling secure with clear and definite boundaries.

The importance of these **self constructs** also shows up in our ability to move on to *inter-dependence.* Healthy relationships flow best from a person who has differentiated him or herself from others, who assumes proactive responsibility for self, and who can extend him or herself for the sake of others. Without such independence, people frequently move from dependence to co-dependence. The following patterns in NLP offer ways of addressing and resolving various "self" problems.

#19 The Belief Change Pattern

Concept. Beliefs develop over time via our experiences, as we entertain thoughts and representations, and then, at a meta-level, say "Yes," to them. Once thoughts have transformed into beliefs, they function as our perceptions about things. These "grown-up" ideas then become habit and drop out of our awareness. Beliefs, as grown-up understandings, become durable maps by which we code *meanings*. Then, as *perceptual filters*, we "see" our beliefs everywhere. This describes how we endow beliefs with a self-fulfilling quality so that "as we believe, so we experience." Thus beliefs function as a central part of our *psychological organization*. Richard Bandler (1982) wrote,

> *Behaviors are organized around some very durable things called beliefs. A belief tends to be much more universal and categorical than an understanding. Existing beliefs can even prevent a person from considering new evidence or a new belief.*

Structurally, beliefs operate as a meta-level phenomenon *about* ideas, representations, and states. This means that while we may try on various "ideas" and "thoughts" about ourselves, a "belief" does not arise until we affirm, validate and say *"Yes"* to those ideas. We "believe" in information at a higher logical level than we represent information. To create a belief, we bring a state and conviction *about* some learning or conceptual understanding. You have to *go meta* in order to experience the phenomenon of belief.

By contrast, a state of doubt refers to a state of disconfirmation, a state of saying *"No!"* to the primary level of thoughts. This also indicates, structurally, a meta-state composition. Indecision, by contrast, generally operates at a primary level. Can we change our beliefs? You bet! Bandler (1985) noted,

> *The process of changing a belief is relatively easy, as long as you have the person's **consent**.* (Emphasis added.)

The technology within **the belief change patterns** offers us a way to change the very structure of a "belief." By using these processes, we can transform, update, and clarify beliefs about our "self" that no longer serve us well. Use this excellent pattern whenever someone wants to change a belief, and especially a "self" belief.

Preparing For Belief Change

1. *Identify a limiting belief* that you would like to change. Use the following sentence stems to evoke beliefs and to get your limiting beliefs. "What I believe about myself is..." "What I believe about X (e.g., people, work, relationships, God, health, responsibility) is..."

2. *Identify your meta-limiting beliefs.* What do you believe about that belief? Step back from your belief and ask about the meaning you give to it.

3. *Note your belief representations.* How do you represent your belief? What representational system? What submodalities drive the belief? What languaging do you use?

4. *Identify your doubt representations.* Think of something you feel in doubt about. How do you represent "doubt" in RS, submodalities, and language?

5. *Contrast your doubt and belief representations.* How do these two sets of representations differ in structure? Identify the submodalities that distinguish them.

6. *Test the submodalities.* Do so one at a time to discover which submodalities most powerfully affect or alter the belief or doubt: location, brightness, clarity, voice, tone, breathing, etc.

7. *Create a new positive enhancing belief that you would like to believe.* What would you like to believe instead of the limiting belief? State it in positive terms as a process or an ability. "I can learn to handle criticism effectively." "I can learn quickly and thoroughly."

8. *Check the ecology of this new belief.* Does any part of you object to having it?

Transforming The Belief

1. *Turn your limiting belief into doubt.* Access your limiting belief and slowly change it into the submodality codings you have for doubt.

2. *Begin to switch the old limiting belief back and forth from belief to doubt.* Continue to do so...repeatedly. Once you get the hang of turning it back and forth, begin to do this faster and faster and faster. Do this until you feel disoriented, dizzy, confused.

3. *Put in the new enhancing belief in the place of the old.* Turn all of the RS and submodalities down so that you can't see, hear, feel the limiting content. Replace with the new enhancing belief— turn up all of the RS and submodalities. Switch this to belief, then doubt, back and forth several times.

4. *Stop with the new enhancing belief coded as belief.* Turn up all of your driving submodalities. Amplify as needed to make a compelling representation. Stop, absorb, consider what this looks like, sounds like, feels like. Future pace into tomorrow... .

5. *Test.* Break state. Think about the subject of the old belief. What happens?

#20 The Dis-identification Pattern

Concept. Sometimes we over-identify with some facet of our life experiences—our beliefs, body, gender, race, etc. Such over-identification can lead to conceptually positing one's self as dependent upon external qualities and actions, thereby constructing the self as a victim, dependent, etc.

Assagioli (1965, 1973) provided a process for discovering one's higher self by creating an *"exercise in dis-identification"* (116) which begins by becoming *"aware of the fact, 'I **have** a body, but **I am not** my body'."*

> *Every time we **identify** ourselves with a physical sensation we enslave ourselves to the body... . I **have** an emotional life, but I **am not** my emotions or my feelings. I **have** an intellect, but I **am not** that intellect. I **am** I, **a center of pure consciousness**.*
>
> (117)

Assagioli used the linguistic environment ("**I have...I am not...**") to apply this dis-identification to our other human powers and expressions ("I **have** a will, I **am not** a will," etc.). Then, using hypnotic language patterns, he wrote out an entire induction for accessing this state-about-a-state:

> *I put my body into a comfortable and relaxed position with closed eyes. This done, I affirm, "I **have** a body but I **am not** my body. My body may find itself in different conditions of health or sickness; it may be rested or tired, but that has nothing to do with my self, my real 'I.' My body is my precious instrument of experience and of action in the outer world, but it is **only** an instrument. I treat it well; I seek to keep it in good health, but it is **not** myself. I **have** a body, but I **am not** my body.*
>
> *I **have** emotions, but I **am not** my emotions. These emotions are countless, contradictory, changing, and yet I know that I always remain I, **my-self**, in times of hope or of despair, in joy or in pain, in a state of irritation or of calm. Since I can observe, understand and judge my emotions, and then increasingly dominate, direct and utilize them, it is evidence that they **are not** myself. I **have** emotions, but I **am not** my emotions.*
>
> *I **have** desires, but I **am not** my desires, aroused by drives, physical and emotional, and by outer influences. Desires too are changeable and contradictory, with alternations of attraction and repulsion. I **have** desires, but they **are not** myself.*
>
> *I **have** an intellect, but I **am not** my intellect. It is more or less developed and active; it is undisciplined but teachable; it is an organ of knowledge in regard to the outer world as well as the inner; but it **is not myself**, I **have** an intellect, but I **am not** my intellect."*
>
> *After this dis-identification of the 'I' from its contents of consciousness (sensations, emotions, desires, and thoughts), I* **recognize and affirm that I am a Centre of pure self-consciousness.** *I am a Center of **Will**, capable of mastering, directing and using all my psychological processes and my physical body.*
>
> (118-119)

What am I then? What remains after discarding from my self-identity the physical, emotional and mental contents of my personality, of my ego? It is the essence of myself—a center of pure self-consciousness and self-realization. It is the permanent factor in the ever varying flow of my personal life. It is that which gives me the sense of being, of permanence, of inner security. I recognize and I affirm myself as a center of pure self-consciousness. I realize that this center not only has a static self-awareness but also a dynamic power; it is capable of observing, mastering, directing and using all the psychological processes and the physical body. I am a center of awareness and of power.

(119)

Over-identifying *with temporal facets of self or with our situation causes us to become "possessed" by the identification. We then become our roles, our masks, our emotions, etc. And, this, in turn, "tends to make us static and crystallized...prisoners.*

(121)

The type of patients for whom the exercise is particularly indicated includes all those who are over-emotional, and all those who are either strongly identified with a particular affective state or linked with an idea or plan or type of action—which may be of a higher or low order—which keeps the patient in a state of obsession. This includes fanatics of all kinds.

(120)

Among some patients, particularly Americans, there is a great deal of resistance to the idea of dis-identifying oneself from one's body, feelings, and thoughts; and a deep fear of becoming split into different parts by so doing. However, on the contrary, many patients like the idea of fully experiencing a center within themselves, a center from which they can find the strength and the wisdom to withstand the stresses of modern life.

(122)

The Pattern

1. *Start with the supporting belief.* Accept the enhancing belief that *you* transcend your powers, expressions of personality and your circumstances.

2. *Dis-identify linguistically.* Use the linguistic environment, "I have... but I am not..." to frame any and all of your powers and functions and circumstances as not you.

3. *Dis-identify in trance.* Access a relaxed and comfortable state and induce yourself into this transcendental state *about* your psychological and physiological powers. "If I lost any of these powers, my core self would remain."

4. *Distinguish self and function while in trance.* As you recognize more fully how each power, function, circumstance, etc., differs from your core self, reframe its meaning as that of a function or tool to use in navigating through the world.

5. *Send your brain up another level to create a transcendental identity.* Specify the You who exists above and beyond these powers—the user of the powers, the state of "pure consciousness." Represent this with a symbol or word to anchor it fully.

6. *Create an image of this higher self as a stable center* out of which you can live and express yourself.

#21 *The Re-imprinting Pattern*

Concept. Traumatic episodes and reactions can arise from traumatic experiences, negative input through stories, movies, and imaginings. As such, once we map out a "trauma," the trauma can come to function as *belief and identity imprints* that lead to limiting beliefs.

"*Imprints*" themselves can involve *positive* experiences as well as negative. Frequently, people abused as children will grow up and make unconscious choices that put them back into situations that seem to repeat the prototype trauma situation. By definition, an "imprint" codes people with a map that seems to function in a very ingrained way—one not so easily affected by conscious methods of cognitive restructuring.

Imprints may involve single experiences or a series of experiences. From them we may come to believe the imprint as reality, "This is the way things are." Imprints can even arise from the beliefs of significant persons, the belief of another person which becomes imprinted in the child. Sometimes the belief operates in a "delayed action" format. Thus, at the time, the person may reject the other's view, but later the other's beliefs (as internal representations) seem to "come alive."

Imprints, as beliefs, also work in a self-fulfilling way. When we try to argue with a belief, the person may have too much data, gathered over time, supporting the belief. By going back to the original imprint, we come to a time before the person's maps became cluttered by later confirmations. In imprint situations, often a person switches positions with a hurtful person and experiences the other's reality. A child in an intense ongoing relationship with parents often imprints or introjects some of the parent's beliefs and behaviors and makes them part of his or her own beliefs.

Children do not have a clear sense of their self-identity. They often pretend to think and act as someone else. Sometimes they take on the role model, lock, stock, and barrel, with very little discrimination about the consequences of what they have accepted. Our adult selves, in many ways, involve an incorporation of the models we grew up with. Our model of adulthood has the features of past significant others. In them we can find family beliefs, precedents, rules, scripts, etc., that have arisen from our childhood.

Introjection of a significant other frequently, although not always, occurs in the imprinting process. When this doesn't occur, we probably just have a problem with a person or certain behaviors. The key lies in what belief(s) a person developed via the imprint experience. Imprints generally operate outside conscious awareness.

The mechanism for discovery of the imprint comes from *anchoring an imprint feeling* (a negative emotion) and using the emotion as a guide to finding past memories. (See Change History for the transderivational search—TDS). Travel back with it to the point where you feel confused, to the point of "I don't know." At the impasse, we have probably come to "the right address." The emotion will lead to the experience out of which we made the limiting belief. If one encounters a "blank," anchor that blank as a dissociated state, and take it back in time to a significant past imprint.

When a person reaches an impasse or imprint, immediately interrupt them and anchor a powerful resource state (courage, power, etc.). Take that resource state back into the impasse to help the person get through it.

By finding the imprint experience and re-coding it with the resources that all the persons involved needed back then, people change their perspectives and the subsequent beliefs that derived from that experience. Re-imprinting creates a multiple perspective viewpoint which serves as the basis for wisdom in making decisions, dealing with conflicts, negotiating, relating, etc.

Re-imprinting helps with the updating of internal maps by highlighting resources one can use to resolve and/or avoid trauma situations. In re-imprinting, we even give (mentally in our minds) the people who perpetrated hurt the resources they needed in order not to have created such hurt. Doing this doesn't excuse or condone the hurtful behavior, but maps out appropriate resources and behaviors. Often, victims of crimes build limiting beliefs that are then maintained by anger and fear. These show up as revenge beliefs and create even more stuckness by creating a "victim" identity. Giving the perpetrator the resources they needed prior to the incident where the imprint occurred helps to resolve the episode in their memory.

Re-imprinting helps a person to update the internal maps. It allows them to hold different beliefs and resources. It allows the imprint experience to mean something resourceful.

The Pattern

1. *Identify the problem.* What belief, behavior, emotion, etc., do you want to change? What associated feelings go along with it? Inquire about what the person has done to change that belief or behavior. Ask, "What stands in the way?" "What stops you?"

2. *Locate the experience.* With the anchored feeling, initiate a TDS using your Time-line, etc., to locate the imprint experience.

3. *Using a Time-line, travel back with the emotion.* Establish a Time-line and go back to the imprint experience. Have the person stay with the feeling (while you hold the anchor) and begin to remember the earliest experience of this feeling. When the person has reached an earlier experience, while associated in this regressed state, have him or her verbalize the beliefs (generalizations) formed from that experience.

> "Take a moment and think about how frustrating (or whatever the negative emotion) everything has been. Take that feeling back in time... . What do you experience? Does it involve anyone else? ...Do you see the person looking at you? ...Go ahead and put yourself inside 'the you back then' for just a moment. What beliefs do you have about this experience? ...What beliefs about others, about the world, about God?..."

Sometimes when the person verbalizes the belief, this will represent the first time he or she has become aware of it. The articulation of the belief itself will cause the misbelief to simply evaporate.

4. *Break state and review the experience.* Ask the person to step off the Time-line and review the imprint experience, identifying the situation and the other participants.

> "I want you to come back here to this room now, and to leave that past memory."

Then have the person experience the episode as if watching a movie of himself.

> "Look back at that experience you had, put it way out there so that it completely leaves, so that you no longer find yourself in it at all...and watch that younger you... . How has that experience affected you since that time?"

Ask the person to verbalize any other beliefs formed as a result of this imprint (those beliefs that arose "after the fact"). Sometimes people don't form beliefs at the time of the imprint, but later. We can build imprint beliefs both during and after the episode.

5. *Find the positive intent in the feeling or belief.* Determine the positive intent. You may have to ask the "character","What positive intent did you have in doing this?" (Note: "Character" represents Robert Dilts' terminology and refers to a real or imagined part.) Did it seek to install this belief that you exist as a worthless person or try to screw you up? Would this part like it if it knew what is now going on with you?

6. *Identify and anchor the needed resources.* Ask the person to identify and anchor the resources and choices that he/she needed back then and didn't have. Do the same for any other parts in the situation.

> "What would you need to give those parts in order for them to respond differently?" "More acceptance." "So they need a realization that different people have different models of the world."

Get those resources. "I want you to vividly recall a time when you fully had that accepting feeling. Find a specific example." Anchor it.

7. *Apply the resource.* Ask the person to review the imprint experience, off the Time-line, from the perspective of each of the parts involved. Holding the anchor, give each part involved in the situation all the resources it would have needed to achieve a desired outcome—back then.

> "Take these resources and give it to this other person. This other person is in your brain right now—that image or memory comes from your brain. So take this and give it to him. What does he or she do differently?... What beliefs do you now build out of this experience?... Just go inside, and allow your unconscious mind to review each experience with this experience knowing that they now have the resources they needed. We know that this person didn't have that resource at that time, although as your resource, you can update that model now..."

"There is a younger self back in that experience that needs resources that he or she didn't have then. What resources do you have now that would have allowed you to build a different set of beliefs then?... What insights, skills, abilities...? What is the closest you have come to having that resource? Now take that light and shine it back through your history. Shine it on that younger you...so that as that younger you begins to feel this resource, you can allow yourself to imagine how that would have changed things. And you can now allow yourself to be relaxed and secure, calm and comfortable with yourself in that memory...see that younger self in front of you building resourceful beliefs and abilities."

8. *Associate and relive the imprint experience.* Becoming each part, have the person step onto the Time-line (holding the anchor) with all the resources previously given to that part. Then have the person update and/or modify the beliefs associated with the experience.

9. *Receive resources.* Ask the person to step onto the Time-line as their younger self and receive the qualities, attributes, they needed from each significant character.

10. *Review and future pace.* Ask the person to step off the Time-line and review the changed experience. When he/she feels satisfied with the outcome, have the person step back onto the Time-line, and then move up quickly into his/her future. Then stop and use the resources to see how they will think-feel and live in a new and different way.

#22 The Time-line Pattern

Concept. Sometimes the problem we struggle with does not concern anything in today's reality, but something that occurred in "the past." Thus the problem exists about *how we keep* our thoughts and feelings from the past in our current awareness.

As we take cognizance of the world via our nervous system with its five central portals, we *input information.* Next we *process* that information with our internal programs. We also go further as we create *abstractions* of those abstractions. Through words and concepts, we start constructing an internal world full of "ideas" that transcend our senses. Immanuel Kant called these *a priori* categories of the mind. Korzybski called them higher-order abstractions. In NLP we call them *non-sensory based symbolic maps*. In everyday parlance, we call them "ideas," "beliefs," "understandings," etc.

"Time" exists as one of these. This term refers to what? Since the *"coding"* of anything determines everything, we need to become aware of how we *represent* this abstract concept. *Source:* Bandler, James and Woodsmall (1988), Hall and Bodenhamer (1997).

"Time" Elicitation Pattern

1. Think of some simple activity you regularly do. Think of some simple thing that you did five years ago, one year ago, this morning, that you will do next week, next year, five years from now (brushing teeth, going to work, getting dressed).

2. Notice your representations. What awareness do you have of this activity that allows you to distinguish having done it? In what modality? With what submodality qualities? Especially notice how you use location: size, detail, space segment of "time": the size of "today," "a week," "month," "year."

3. Step back and identify the overall configuration. Does your time structure look like a line, a boomerang, a spiral, etc.? Do you have some metaphor for it? Do you have more than one Timeline or time-configuration? How many? For what arenas of life (business, personal, recreational, spiritual, etc.)?

Figure 5.1

"Time" Orientations

Past	Present	Future
Memories	Sensory Awareness	Possibilities/Plans
Solid/Real	Flexible	Anticipation
Fixed, Rigid, Stuck	Some Fixedness	Primarily Movement
Limited	Choice	/Opportunities
		/Expansive
Predestination	Responsibility	Visions/Dreams
Consequential	Impulsive Thinking	Anticipatory
Thinking		Thinking
Already	Now	Then, One of these
		Days
Sense of Reality	Sense of Today,	Sense of Hope
	the Now	/Desire

The coding/structure of "time" enables us to tell the difference between events past, present, or future. It affects our personality in major ways since it affects our sense of cause-effect, order, structure, etc.

Figure 5.2

"Time" Styles

Out of Time	In Time	Atemporal
Dissociated	Associated	Timelessness
Out of the Body	In/through the Body	Above the Body
Sequential	Random, Simultaneous,	Meta Position
	Synthetic	
Values and Likes Time	Disvalues and Dislikes	Neutral to Time
	Time	
On time; Punctual	Frequently Late,	
	Non-Prompt	
Aware of Time	Lost in the Now, the Moment,	
	the Memory	

The Pattern

1. *Identify your "time"-line(s).* Having elicited your representations for "time" past, present and future via the metaphor of a "line," now imagine floating above it and looking down upon it.

2. *Float back in "time" along the Time-line.* As you do, notice the You of your "past."

3. *Now go forward in "time",* observing both the events you represent and how you represent those events, remembered or imagined.

4. *What "time" problems* did you notice that you'd like to address? What events exercise too much importance? What events carry too little impact?

5. *How might you like to alter your "time" line?* Identify some of the things you might like to change about the events on your "time" line: shape, configuration, tilt, color, etc.

6. *Using the submodalities,* change the properties of the situation, e.g., distance, size, brightness, etc.

#23 The Change Personal History Pattern

Concept. The "past" only exists "in our mind." Externally, in the world "out there," it no longer exists. It has passed. But we keep it inside us (in our mind and body) and call that "past" our "memory." And yet our memories continually change. With every new understanding, development, learning, and experience we keep revising and updating our past memories. Since our memory only exists as a construction, Richard Bandler has noted that, "It is never too late to have a happy childhood."

Now *what* we remember, *why* we remember, and *how* we use our memories involve our personal response-ability. To carry around "accurate," but hurtful and traumatized memories just because "that's what really happened," only empowers those events. By doing so, we keep cuing our mind-body system to "live in the past" and to keep re-accessing negative emotional states. When we do this, we create ongoing hurt and disempowerment. Not a wise way to run our own brain. Now we can use this pattern to *change our personal histories!*

This pattern offers **a way to recode** the "past" in such a way that it no longer serves as a reference for destructive feelings or for defining self in negative ways. It recodes memories as resources and learnings, and becomes an enhancing orientation for moving into the future with a positive attitude. The process finds a problem memory, traces it to its source, reframes it with resources and then brings that resource state up to the present and into the future.

The Pattern

1. *Access a problematic memory.* Access and elicit the problematic, unwanted, or unpleasant feeling. Find a memory wherein you felt less than resourceful. As you do, establish an anchor for this state. Calibrate to this state in the person.

2. *Invite the person to engage in a transderivational search* (TDS). Utilizing this anchor, assist the person in finding a previous experience when this same feeling occurred. "Take this feeling and let it guide you back in time to help you remember other times when you felt this same kind of feeling. Allow yourself to float back, in your mind, all the way back to previous times and places where you *felt this...*" Whenever you note that the person seems to re-experience the same negative state, have the person stop and re-anchor it. Ask, "What age do you feel yourself in this experience?"

3. *Continue the TDS.* Using the anchor, have the person go back through time and find three to six experiences of this same negative state. Each time ask his/her age while re-anchoring. When you get back to the earliest one, stop.

4. *Break state to dissociate and to anchor resources.* Have the person step out of that "younger him" and watch that younger him from his adult self. Now inquire, "As you look back on those experiences, what specific *resources* would you need in

those past situations for that younger you to have responded in a more effective way?" Elicit and anchor these resource states fully.

5. *Collapse resourceful anchor with the unresourceful anchor.* As the person returns to the earliest experience, simultaneously fire off the negative state anchor and the resource anchor. As you do, ask, "What would that past memory feel like when you know you *have this resource* with you back then?" "How would this resource make that past different?" Then have the person come up through history, stopping at each past experience with the new resource so that his history begins changing, so that each experience becomes more resourceful and satisfying.

6. *Trouble-shooting.* If the person has difficulty changing the past experience, bring him to the present and construct and anchor more powerful resources so that his resource anchor becomes stacked with resources.

7. *Break state.* Once you have changed all of the past experiences, have the person break state. After a little bit, have them think about that problematic or unwanted feeling.

8. *Test.* What happens? Have the memories changed? In what way? Does the person experience the resource as there?

9. *Future pace.* Finally, have them think about similar experiences that may occur in the future. As they do, you may want to fire off the resource anchor.

#23b The Change Personal History Pattern—Adaptation

The following adaptation of this pattern restates it using the Meta-states model. This was developed by Hall and Bodenhamer.

1. *Identify the problem event.* This will serve as the primary state. "Think about a time and place in your history that still troubles you." "How does it trouble you?" "What problem does it create for you?" "When you step into that memory, what emotion arises? What meanings?" Now step out of that problem state.

2. *Take an observer's viewpoint of that experience.* This represents a meta-state about the primary state. Float above your Time-line (dissociate) and go back to the problem event and observe it as a witness to it. From this meta-position, see that *younger* you going through that event. (If you have difficulty staying dissociated, put your representations up on an imaginary screen.)

3. *Gather learnings about the event from the observer position.* This allows you to move into another meta-state about the primary-learning about the event. "What resources did that younger you need?" "What resources did the others in the situation need?" Identify the resources needed that would have changed it.

4. *Return to the present and fully access the resources.* From the position of the here-and-now, access and anchor each and every resource needed. Amplify these and then test your anchors for the resources.

5. *From the observer meta-position, transfer the resources.* When you have returned to the past event, give that younger you each resource as a gift from your present self. Then let the event play out with the resources, and imagine the younger you now acting, thinking, feeling, etc., in a transformed way. From this position, you can also give the others in the movie the resources that they needed.

6. *Come forward through your history with the added resources.* Step into the movie and become that younger you for the moment, and then imagine yourself moving up through your Time-line experiencing the resources so that, as you move through each subsequent year of life, the resources transform your history and enrich your life. Let the resources transform yourself and the others.

7. *Return to the present and run an ecology check.* Does this new edition of your memory provide you with a sense of closure? Does it encode better learnings and responses? Does it enhance your life? Would you like to live with this new edition? Does it provide you a more useable map for navigating life?

8. *Future pace.* Look out into your future from the perspective of having made these changes in your sense of your personal history, and imagine them continuing into your future...

#24 *The Swish Pattern*

Concept. Since "brains go places" and take us to thoughts-and-feelings that may create problematic and limiting states, the Swish Pattern enables us to identify the cues that *swish* the brain to go wherever it goes. Detecting these then enables us to re-direct our brain so that it goes to somewhere more useful and productive. This pattern can change the way we feel and behave.

"Mind" (consciousness) operates as our information processing mechanism with the *languages* of "mind":

   i. our representational systems with their sub-modality qualities

   ii. the *linguistic* map involving the digital symbols of words, sentences, etc.

   iii. the *physiological* system of breathing, posture, facial expressions, etc.

We deal with reality indirectly through *map representations.* Therefore our responses to the world (emotions, behaviors, etc.="patterns") arise from our *model of the world.* Change that model, and we change ourselves, our responses, our emotions, our patterns.

We elicit "states" of consciousness by responding to specific *stimuli* (external or internal; remembered or imagined). Taking charge of our states (state management) involves actively "running our own brain" by using the languages of "mind."

The Swish Pattern represents an especially generative pattern. If you think about "the behavior that would change the old response," you program in a specific action or response. But if you think about *"the me* for whom this would no longer operate as a problem" you send your consciousness to a more powerful, positive, and confident You—or self-image.

The neuro-dynamic principle behind this pattern involves the fact that *brains move away from unpleasantness (pain) and toward pleasure.* So, whenever we attach a *"pleasure"* meaning to a stimulus, we program ourselves to move toward that "pleasure." In this way, we directionalize our consciousness and wire it neurologically. Often these pathways outlast their value. Generally, we always make our best choice at that moment.

The Pattern

1. *Develop a full representation of the cue picture* (or sound, sensation, word). The cue representation "triggers" the person into feeling stuck or unresourceful, or into problematic behavior. "What do you see, hear, feel just before you engage in unwanted behaviors?" Make the cue picture *an associated image*.

2. *Develop a fully represented desired self image.* Develop a representation of a desired self that no longer has these problems. Put into this image all of the qualities and attributes (not behaviors) that you believe necessary to the desired outcome. Make this picture *dissociated*.

3. *Check for objections* and see that all parts want the desired self. Quiet yourself and go inside and ask, "Does any part of me object to this new image of myself?"

4. *Link the two representations.* We now want to create a linkage between the representations so that the cue always leads to the resourceful picture. In building this mechanism, we will use the person's *driving modalities*. Start with a cue picture big and bright, in front of the person and construct a small dark future self in the corner or in the middle of this picture. Always start with the cue image and then add the future self image.

5. *Swish.* As the cue image gets smaller and darker, have the future self image grow bigger and brighter until it fills the whole screen. Do this very, very quickly, in just a couple of seconds. Do it as fast as it takes to say, "Swwiissshhhhh." After this, ask the person to clear "the screen."

6. *Repeat* this swish five or six times, allowing your brain to go quicker and quicker with each swish.

7. *Test.* Ask the person to think about the cue image (or behaviorally test by creating the external cue for the person!).

8. *Future pace.*

Distance/Color Swish

1. *Establish the cue image.* And as before, make sure you have it close, full and associated.

2. *Create and establish a future self image.*

3. *Ecology check.*

4. *Link the pictures.* Have the cue image close and full of color. Have the self image far away and black and white.

5. *Swish:* Move the cue image out while the ideal self image comes in closer and full of color. Ask the person to hold this image for a few seconds.

6. *Repeat* five or six times.

7. *Test.*

#25 *The Circle Of Excellence Pattern*

Concept. This pattern provides a marvelous resource for becoming more centered and balanced as a human being. We have also found it especially useful in encouraging performance excellence or any task expressing mastery.

The thoughts-and-feelings that we hold as we move through the world affect tremendously whether we operate from a "center of strength" or from a vacuum of weakness. By building and anchoring a *state of excellence,* we can operate from our best. Using the subconscious mind, this strategy anchors desirable patterns of behavior into the physiology which we can then use in all aspects of our lives.

The Pattern

1. *Identify an excellent state.* Name a state that you would like to have available to use, a state which allows you to act with full capacity.

2. *Imagine a circle on the floor.* As you place the circle in front of you make sure that it has enough size for you to step into.

3. *Endow the circle with color.* Pick a color to symbolize the resource and then begin to notice the qualities of the circle in terms of color, texture, material, size, etc.

4. *Take a meta-position.* As you stand outside the circle, recall a time when you had all the qualities you would like to have available now and in the future. You may pretend you have these qualities or you may copy the qualities someone else has. Recreate a full experience including how you feel, what you say to yourself, what you see and how you hold your body when you possess these abilities. Decide on an anchor, so that you can recreate this state instantly by firing the anchor.

When working with another person and he/she experiences these qualities and abilities, anchor them with a touch on the shoulder. Reinforce this by asking the person to think of a number of instances or ways in which he or she can feel excellent. Anchor each one.

5. *Image yourself in the circle* possessing all the qualities and abilities you want. Hear what you say to yourself, see what you look like and notice what you now feel.

6. *Fire your anchor.* While holding the resource anchor, step into your circle of excellence. Move into that picture of yourself. Allow yourself to totally experience your thoughts, memories, awarenesses, and feelings—associatedly—and to make these representations even bigger. See what you see as you have all these abilities fully available. Talk to yourself in a powerful way. Allow yourself to believe that all these qualities have become yours and that they will grow and increase... .

7. *Future pace.* While you continue to experience the circle, think about what it looks like and feels like to have these qualities or states... . See, hear and feel yourself performing exactly as you would like to in these special situations... . After you become fully aware that this state belongs to you and that you can call on it anytime you want to use it, step out of the circle.

8. *Break state and test.* Think of something you did yesterday. Now test by firing your anchor to recreate this "excellent state." If you need to reinforce it, simply recycle back through the exercise.

#26 The Decision Destroyer Pattern

Concept. Sometimes, as we move through life, we make some poor decisions. Afterwards, those decisions become part of our mental map and begin to operate as a major psychological force in our life (as a Meta-state). This pattern *destroys* such limiting, destructive, and unenhancing decisions.

"Decisions" function as part of our mental maps that provide specific instructions about what to do. And, while a decision in one context and at one time may function very well for our benefit, as contexts and times change these decisions can become outdated and unuseful. This pattern allows us to alter the decisions that we have constructed.

The Pattern

1. *Identify a limiting decision that you still live with.* What did you decide? Fully express the decision and its meanings. When did you adopt this decision? How long have you lived with it? How has it become limiting to you? Fully elicit this information.

2. *Identify an enhancing decision you'd like to live life by.* By using the criteria of the well-formedness conditions (the first meta-pattern)—access fully a more enhancing decision that would serve you better now and in the future. As you access this decision state, anchor it fully.

3. *Float above your Time-line back to when you made the limiting decision.* Observe it dissociatedly from above your Time-line. Float down into the experience—and observe it associatedly. Anchor this experience.

4. *Repeat.* Float back to other instances of this limiting decision until you get to the earliest experience of using this limiting belief.

5. *Now float back up above your Time-line and fully re-access your enhancing decision.*

6. *Go back fifteen minutes prior to the decision.* Once you have your enhancing decision fully accessed from above the Time-line, float back to fifteen minutes prior to the earliest decision, then float down into that younger you, bringing with you that Enhancing Decision fully and completely.

7. *Experience the old situation with new resources.* As you do, bring these enhancing resources with you, letting them (in your mind and internal experience) completely change your awareness and feelings as you experience the effects of this new decision.

8. *Then quickly zoom up through your Time-line to the present.*

9. *Stop at the present.* Fully integrate the experience and future pace.

#27 The Core Transformation Pattern

Concept. Creating a transformational change that operates out of one's core values, beliefs, and identity moves one to a state of congruence and wholeness.

This first pattern plays upon the term "Core" as a metaphor of "depth", suggesting going "down" to one's core and identifying or discovering one's core values and states. It presupposes that all of one's parts *works out of that core*. The next pattern does the same thing, but plays upon the term "Meta" and so takes us up to our highest, most transcendent values.

The purpose of each pattern involves developing and maintaining an inner sense of well-being, wholeness, and connection with those traits and qualities with which we most want to identify. By doing so, we can then integrate them so that we will operate in a centered and balanced way even when experiencing times of trouble or distress.

This pattern takes us to our "deepest levels of being" and uses these resource states (core states) to transform our emotions, behaviors, and responses with an ongoing sense of well-being. Use this pattern to address inner conflict or disharmony with yourself, a lack of integration between parts, and/or just a desire for a more resourceful center. *Source:* Andreas and Andreas (1991) *Core Transformation*, developed from the six-step reframing model.

The Pattern

1. *Choose a part to work with.* "What part (a behavior, feeling, etc.) would you like to work with today?" Think about any part of yourself that you have which you might not yet appreciate.

2. *Experience and welcome the part.* "Where do you feel the part in your body?" Welcome and receive the part. "What difference do you feel in your body as you do this?"

3. *Discover the purpose and intention of the part* Ask the part what it wants for you that it values as positive.

4. *Discovering the outcome chain.* "Ask the part, 'If you have the outcome from the previous step fully and completely, what do you want through having that, that you value as even more important?'"

5. *Repeat.* Repeat step 4 until you reach your core state which will involve a state of consciousness similar to "love, peace, oneness, or being-ness," etc. Once you access your core state, take some time and enjoy experiencing it fully and completely.

6. *Reverse the outcome chain with the core state.* Begin by gently inviting your part to notice, "When you have this core state (name the one elicited from step 4) as a way of being in the world, how does already having (core state) make things different?"

Then more specifically, ask, "How does already having this core state (name it) as a way of being transform, enrich, radiate through X, Y, and Z (name the intended outcomes from step 4)?"

Finally, transform the original context with the core state: "How does already having this core state as a way of being in the world transform your experience of (name the context where you wanted a change)?"

7. *Grow up the part.* To do this, ask your part the following questions: "How old are you?" "Do you want to have the benefits that come from evolving forward in time to your current age, with this core state fully present?" Evolve forward through time, from whatever age you find this part, all the way forward to your current age, having this X (core state) there through every moment of time.

8. *Bring the part fully into your body.* Notice where you have the part now located in your body and allow it to flow fully in and through your body, through the "outcome chain," with the grown-up part fully in your body (general, specific, original context).

9. *Check for objecting parts.* "Is there any part of you that objects to your having X as a core state now as a way of being in the world?" Bring any objecting parts, and any additional parts associated with this issue, through steps 1-9 before going on.

10. *Time-line generalization.* Begin by envisioning your Time-line and floating back over it to just before your parents conceived you. Now, with your core state radiating through your being, allow yourself to move forward through "time," letting this core state color and transform every moment of experience up to the present. Next, envision yourself moving forward on that

same trajectory into the future, noticing how it becomes colored by the fact that you have this core state. Finally, cycle back through the Time-line generalization several times, faster each time.

(Note: You will find it helpful to write down each intended outcome and core state so that, when you begin the process of cycling back through this series of states, you will remember and name the outcome states in the order in which you elicited them from the person.)

#28 The Meta-Transformation Pattern

Concept. We can create generative transformation that will permeate all of our personality if we make a change at a higher logical level—a meta-level. The primary difference between this pattern and Core Transformation lies in the operational metaphors. In Core, we use the idea of "going down" to our "core," to identify and access deep "core" states. Here we turn the metaphor around, and go **up** (meta) to a higher logical level to access desired transcendental meta-states. By finding the positive intent of each state, we get to our highest transcendental Meta-states, hence *meta-transformations.*

This pattern fully develops our desired outcome and elicits a desired chain of states. Continue to ask the exploration question, "**What** do you seek to experience, accomplish, feel, etc., and, when you get that, what does it get for you?"

Generally, in NLP, we do not ask the "why" question or go exploring the past for *explanations or causes.* Such *why* questions tend to focus us on problems, the past, and on causations. And the answers we get to such questions usually only keep us *in the problem.* Instead, we focus primarily on *how* and *what* questions. "What do I seek to accomplish by these current actions?" This question orients us toward our objective, purpose, and our desired state(s). Once we know our chain of desired states, we can then ask the *how and what* questions. "How can I best get there? What resources will help me?"

Because we try to accomplish something of value as we discover these desired states, we can then allow these answers to become *the basis of our inner life!* In other words, we can "just step up into these desired outcome states." We can use them as *our way of being* in the world. *Source:* Hall (1996).

The Pattern

Four Going-Up Steps:

1. *Identify a behavior.* Consider some behavior, state, experience, or habit that you do or engage in, but which you do not evaluate as effective or pleasant. What behavior or state do you experience that you don't appreciate about yourself? (You can also use this pattern with positive behaviors that you do like and appreciate.)

2. *Explore your 'what' of intention and design.* "What do you seek to gain by doing this?" "How does this hold value or purpose for you?" "What do you want to achieve by this?"

3. *Keep repeating.* "And what do you seek to accomplish, experience or gain when you do this?" Continue this line of questioning until you begin to loop. "What do you want, through obtaining this, that you deem even more important?" "If you get this desired state, in just the way you want it, what would you like that is even more important to you?"

4. *Continue until you loop.* Eventually you will generate a string of desired states. You'll know when you've reached the top when you begin to loop among the highest states.

Four Going-Down Steps:

5. *Fully describe your ultimate transcendental Meta-state (TMS).* Describe what this ultimate transcendental Meta-state would look like, sound like, feel like, the language you use to talk to yourself about it, etc.

6. *Step into the TMS.* Use all of your descriptive cues to help your brain-body create the desired state and then just *step into it.* Use the "as if" frame if you need to: what would it look, sound, feel like to fully and completely experience the TMS?

7. *Experience the state fully.* After you step into the TMS, allow yourself to *experience* it fully so that you can absorb it throughout your body.

8. *Use the TMS to relate its resources downward.* How does already having this state transform your experience? How does it enrich it? How does it change the way you think-and-feel? Take the TMS and let it organize, modulate, alter, and drive the lower states.

#29 *The Making Peace With Your Parents Pattern*

Concept. Sometimes our "self" image results from having adopted the same view of ourselves which we believe our parents held about us. If we believe a parent labeled us as "stupid," we often keep that belief as part of our self image. This pattern helps to identify these dysfunctional introjects and to shift them into a resource. It operates from the pre-supposition that all behavior, physical and emotional, has a positive intention. When we can identify this intention, we can use it to change our beliefs.

So when, as an adult, we have not "made peace" with our parents, but continue to expend a lot of mental-emotional energy on their hurtful parenting, or blame our parents, or excuse ourselves based on our childhood experiences, we need to "get over it," and get on with life. This pattern will allow us to amplify and integrate the positive qualities that we can receive from our parents and "finish the business" that may have caused us to get stuck in our development. *Source:* adapted from Robert McDonald.

The Pattern

1. *Identify a conflict with your parents.* Identify an area of conflict or negative feelings associated with your parents that you would like to resolve.

2. *Get "mother" representations.* Think about your mother and notice where in your mind and/or body you hold negative feelings, images, or sounds. How do you represent her? Where? What other submodality qualities?

3. *Intensify your "mother" representations.* Intensify the feelings, images, sounds even more and allow them to stream from their location in your body into the open palm of your left hand. Let the feelings, images and sounds flow into your left hand until you have all of them represented there.

4. *Solidify into a visual shape.* Now allow the feelings, sounds, images to take a visual shape. Ask the feelings and sounds to come together into a shape you can see.

5. *Break state.* Look at the ceiling, tie your shoe—or do anything that enables you to break state.

6. *Repeat with your "Father" representations.* Think about your father and notice the feelings, sounds and images associated with him. Where do you feel him in your body? Intensify these feelings, sounds and images even more and allow the feelings, images and sounds to stream from their location in your body into the open palm of your right hand. Let the feelings flow into your right hand until you have all of these representations there. Allow these elements to become a visual shape. If you could mold all these elements into a shape, what would it be? Afterwards, break state again.

7. *Probe for the positive intention.* Ask your mother, "What did you try to do for me that you evaluated as positive?" Repeat the question until this part of you (your internalized mother) identifies a meta-outcome that you find positive and valuable. She may have sought to protect you from disappointment or to equip you to handle the world's hurt, etc. Repeat by probing

the positive intention of your father. Ask your father, "What did you try to do for me that you evaluated as positive and valuable?"

8. *Thank and validate these parts.* Thank both your "mother" and "father" internalized parts for their concern for you.

9. *Let these parts appreciate each other.* Allow both your "mother" and "father" representations to appreciate each others' intentions and positive purposes.

10. *Combine into a single part.* When both parent representations accept the other's positive intentions, explain that they can now combine to create an even more powerful positive intention. Ask them if they would feel willing to become more influential by combining their wishes for you into one positive force. Then, slowly bring both hands together and watch and feel the two parents mix, mingle and merge together. Pause... . Give the person some time for integration if working with someone else. Then ask them to open their hands to discover a new image which represents a full integration and synthesis of these parts. The positive intentions of both parents now combine into one powerful resource.

11. *Store inside.* "Now where would you want to store this integrated image inside you so that it can become an integral part of you? In your heart? Beneath it? In your lungs? Let it come in, and you can touch that spot to anchor these new resourceful feelings, now... .

"And while you hold this anchor, let the feelings you have, as you bring this integrated image into yourself, take you all the way into your past, to just before you came into this world, at birth. Imagine yourself fully and completely in your mother's womb feeling all these positive feelings. Now with these resources deeply within your body and cellular structure, rapidly grow up through all the years of your life to this present moment.

12. *Future pace.* Keeping the anchor, step into the future and image what your life will become from now on as you walk into the future with these integrated resources totally within you.

#30 The Loving Yourself Pattern

Concept. Not infrequently, we speak and behave in a way that doesn't demonstrate healthy self-love, but self-contempt. This pattern works very effectively for building a more complete identity. By increasing a sense of worthiness, the self becomes more integrated. Then other abilities such as self-appreciation become possible. Designed to use for ego strengthening and self-esteem enhancement. *Source:* Suzi Smith and Tim Hallbom.

The Pattern

1. *Comfortably think of a model of loving.* Put yourself in a comfortable place where you can do something that you thoroughly enjoy. When you find that place, allow your mind to identify someone who has cared about you intensely, even if it only occurred for a moment.

2. *Describe this "loving" model.* Begin identifying and describing this person's qualities and attributes so that you obtain a full sense of all the components that go into conveying to you a person who loves you.

3. *Take second position.*

Now leave your body and float into the body of the person watching you. Once you take this second position, begin to describe the you that this person sees from out of his/her eyes.... Notice the things that this person particularly loves about that you. How do you feel as you watch this person love and appreciate you? What words would he/she use to describe the inner loving feelings toward this you? How does this you look when seen through the eyes of someone who loves you? Allow yourself to become aware of how looking at yourself lovingly from another point of view enriches the experience of knowing yourself as a loveable person.

4. *Anchor this feeling.* As you go into the state of feeling completely loved by this person, set an anchor for yourself with some stimulus (a visual image, word, sound, touch, etc.).

5. *Experience the loving.*

Now receive the love sent to you by this person who really loves you. Experience the feelings you have as this person looks at you with love. Appreciate your loveable qualities also. Hear what you say to yourself when you enter into the presence of someone who really loves you. What do you see as you look out of your eyes knowing this complete love and acceptance?

6. *Anchor.* Notice how you created the state of feeling lovable. Anchor it. Recall all the new information about yourself and take it in to enrich your sense of self.

7. *Test and future pace.*

#31 The Self-Sufficiency Pattern

Concept. This pattern works well to connect a person to his or her internal resources. So often we look outside ourselves for answers to problems instead of relying on our own inner strengths. This pattern enables us to increase our self-efficacy and self-confidence. *Source:* Suzi Smith and Tim Hallbom.

The Pattern

1. *Identify resources.* Identify a feeling you would like to get from yourself instead of looking to others or to activities, such as support, understanding, love, etc.

2. *Identify a person to model.* Think of someone (or pretend you know someone) whom you can "always count on." As you do, make a picture of this person with this resource. Notice the location where you see him or her. What size of a picture do you make of them? Notice the size and shape as well as any other submodality factor that drives this representation of trustworthy, stable, solid, etc.

3. *Receive the model's resources.* Imagine seeing this model person giving you all of the resources for self-efficacy and confidence. Vividly imagine getting the emotional resources you want for yourself. Enjoy receiving them.

4. *Map over to your own self representation.* Now take (or create) your own self image and put it in the same location as your model. Make your picture the same as the picture of "the person you can count on" in all of the ways that make a difference to you. Become that ideal self loving and supporting you.

5. *Move this other you in even closer.* Increase the feelings of comfort, support, and connectedness coming from your ideal self. Enjoy the feeling of counting on yourself as you imagine having become that ideal self loving you. Feel the love you can have toward yourself. Enjoy this feeling of loving you.

6. *Reorient and test.* Now, move back into yourself and take this loving person into yourself. Notice what a difference it makes having this support. You now have an internal self that you can always count on.

#32 The Receiving Wisdom From Your Inner Sage Pattern

Concept. The root idea in the term "education" describes a "drawing out" process, thereby suggesting internal resources, understandings, and wisdom within. This process assists drawing out such built-in wisdom or learned wisdoms which we sometimes forget to access, or learnings that we have made in other areas that we need to transfer over—this pattern offers us that technology.

Further, the concept of "an Ancient Sage" with whom we can converse and from whom we can gain knowledge provides a marvelous metaphor about how to use our internal wisdom. Doing so gives us a moment to think before acting—a very wise way of moving through the world.

The Pattern

1. *Induce a relaxation state.* Use any process that enables you or another to relax fully and completely.

2. *Imagine a sage.* Then allow yourself to imagine a wise person sitting in a chair or floating in the air before you. See this wise person smiling graciously, looking at you with love and acceptance.

"And this wise person has much wisdom to share because as you can see, he/she radiates that wisdom in his/her demeanor with dignity, joy, good health..."

3. *Initiate a dialogue with the sage.*

"This sage has come to work with you as an advisor in your decision-making. So, allowing yourself to feel accepted and understood, you can begin to ask questions of this inner sage... questions that you feel as important...and wonder, really wonder, what insights might come to mind as you do..."

4. *Identify with the sage.* As you look and interact and talk and think out loud in the presence of this wisdom, you can begin to feel yourself more and more attracted to this wisdom, knowing that, as you do, the wisdom there will flow easily and gracefully into you... . And, as it flows into you, you also can flow into it. Because, as you imagine floating in wisdom itself and connecting with wisdom, you can experience more and more of it."

5. *Appreciate and integrate.* "Thank this sage wisdom for your expanded perspective and a more resourceful state, and ask that wisdom to live more and more intuitively in you every day..."

Conclusion

With these patterns we can empower ourselves (and others) to truly *re-invent ourselves.* Our constructed mental map (or ideas) of our "self" (i.e., our "identity") arises from how we have used our experiences to map out understandings of ourselves. Many people suffer from a poorly mapped-out "self" concept. Others have accepted toxic definitions that lock them into a world of pain.

"Personality," as a meta-level construct, exists as a piece of subjectivity with much plasticity that we can alter and recreate so that...
   we align our differing values and beliefs, so that...
   we can balance our multiple perspectives, so that...
   we can transform from higher level understandings so that...
   we create a "self" that motivates and encourages.

Chapter 6

Emotional States

The Art Of Managing
Neuro-Linguistic States

Emotions—sometimes we love them, sometimes we hate them! Sometimes they put us in some highly resourceful and creative places; sometimes they make life a living hell. *Emotions*, probably more than anything else, typically drive us to seek help. Life may be "going to hell in a handbasket," but many (perhaps the majority of us) don't do anything about it until we *feel* the need! Typically, we let things go, and keep trying the same solutions that don't work(!), allowing the problems to continue to grow to unmanageable proportions. By then, we usually have put ourselves into some very negative, and self-reinforcing, *emotional states*. Does this sound familiar?

The patterns in this chapter address the subject of our **emotional states**. Here we will especially focus on the negative ones (e.g., stress, anger, fear, regret, guilt)—those *primary emotional states* that, when they become too intense, prevent good thinking, problem-solving, presence of mind, etc. These emotional states represent the very opposite of *resourcefulness*; they represent **unresourcefulness.**

The NLP model centrally addresses these "states" of consciousness (or mind-body states). And because *states* involve both thoughts-and-emotions—and indeed we cannot have one without the other—we describe them as *neuro-linguistic* states. This reminds us of the two "royal roads" to state: mind (linguistics) and body (neurology, physiology). In this chapter, you will discover some cutting-edge human technology for recognizing, managing, and transforming emotional states.

#33 The Visual-Kinesthetic Dissociation Pattern (Phobia Cure)

Concept. We can process information in two central ways: *analytically and experientially.* When we "think" or read something experientially, we feel as if we have *entered into* the story, so to speak. To do that we representationally *encode* it in such a way that we cue ourselves to *experience* it *neuro-linguistically.* Conversely, when we "think" or read something analytically, we hold the material at "arm's length," so to speak. We analyze it, think *about* it, and take a spectator's point of view regarding it. In the first instance, we **associate** *with and in* the content; in the second, we **dissociate**.

A caveat *about this language:* In using the term *"dissociation,"* we do so with caution inasmuch as we do *not* (and cannot) literally step out of our body and *not* experience an emotion. Thus, even "dissociation" involves our body, and occurs *in* the body, hence our somatic sensations and feelings. More accurately, we *conceptually* step aside from our emotions and *think* about them from a *meta* position. As embodied neuro-linguistic beings, we **cannot** actually or literally *dis*sociate from our bodies.

Each of these perceptual styles has its strengths and weaknesses. *Association* empowers us to take the first perceptual position of self, to enter into a story, and to "know" it from within. *Dissociation* allows us to take the second and third perceptual positions, to apply scientific or personal analysis, to learn from it, to not let it activate our emotional responses, to know it from without. Too much association and we become emotional cripples, hysterical, unable to "think," having emotional reactions, etc. Too much dissociation and we become intellectual eggheads, emotional incompetents, unable to relate emotionally and personally, etc.

With regard to hurts, traumas, and unpleasant realities, many people can't *even think about* such information. To do so re-traumatizes. Typically, such individuals eventually lose their willingness to even entertain painful thoughts; those in helping professions frequently burn out. Others develop PTSD (Post Traumatic Stress Disorder). Because they cannot "think" without going into negative painful emotional states, they experience "thinking" as distressing and unpleasant. This robs them of an important resource: the skill of *thinking comfortably* **about** *unpleasant events.* So "reality" pains them. So they repress, suppress, deny, avoid, etc.

The *V-K dissociation pattern* offers a marvelous technology for recovering from trauma states and from PTSD. It empowers us in learning how to "think" about unpleasant things *without* re-associating and re-experiencing the situation. We can stop signaling our body to respond to "thoughts" as if actually in the trauma again. By stopping the ongoing re-traumatization, we resolve the pain and move on in life.

The technology within this pattern works by moving, mentally/conceptually, to a different frame of reference (other position, third position, dissociated viewpoint) and viewing the information from a position of distance. This stops us from associating into the experience and accessing negative emotional states. This allows us to bring new resources to bear on the situation.

To recapitulate, *the V-K dissociation pattern* works by moving us to a different frame of reference (a spectator viewpoint) where we can view the "painful" information comfortably. This interrupts our trauma thinking and prevents us from processing the information in such a way that we collapse into a negative emotional state.

This constructivist understanding of human subjectivity ultimately identifies the source of experience as how we code it in our mind-body. As you code information—so you experience. Human subjectivity lies almost completely in the coding. When you change that coding, you change your experience at the neurological level.

So, with our two categorical ways of "thinking" (*associatedly and dissociatedly*), we can now develop the *flexibility of consciousness* to choose which to do when. We can decide **how** to code and experience information—analytically, "objectively," and un-emotionally, or experientially, "subjectively," and "emotionally." We can remember old events as a spectator to the experience—as a movie goer, rather than as an actor in the movie. Use this technology for effectively managing "emotions", so that you learn from the past rather than feel bad about it. Use it to "switch off" any scene that you don't need to play any more in your inner theater.

A final *caveat*: if you use this pattern on pleasant experiences, you will thereby neutralize them—and that will work to your detriment. Doing so will rob you of *the feeling of being alive and vital.* It will eliminate good feelings, motivation, emotional understanding, etc.

The Pattern (e.g., *The Phobia Cure*)

1. *Create a dissociated representation.* Create a dissociated image by imagining yourself sitting in a movie theater. On the screen in this mental theater, put a black-and-white picture of the younger you in the situation *just before* the traumatic event occurred.

Freeze-frame, as a snap-shot, a scene prior to the movie. Now sit back to watch it, aware that you have taken a spectator's position to that younger you. Notice that you have stepped out of the picture, and have a position from outside. This will change how you feel *about* it.

As you gain this psychological distance, anchor this dissociative response, delighted that you can feel glad for this ability to step aside even further. Because taking this spectator position to your old memories enables you to *begin to learn* from them in new and useful ways.

You might notice that your younger self in that memory thought and felt from a less resourceful position than you do now, sitting here and observing that younger you with your adult mind. And this can give you a new and different perspective, can it not? Now.

2. *Identify your driving submodalities.* As a spectator to your movie, notice your VAK codings and their submodalities (another meta-level state). Play around with altering them.

Since you have taken this new position to your younger self, you can now look at the ways you internally represent that memory...and notice the submodalities your brain has used, up to now, to code this memory.

As you begin with the visual system, just notice whether you have the picture in color or black-and-white? A movie or snapshot? Bright or dim? Close or far? And as you make these distinctions, you can begin to choose which coding would enable you to *think comfortably about* that memory so that you can stay resourceful and thoughtful in a relaxed and comfortable way.

Begin to check out the auditory system of the sound track of your memory. Do you even have a sound track? What sounds do you hear coming from that movie? What quality of tones do you hear? At what volume, pitch, and melody? Now check out your language system. What words do you hear from that younger you? From where do you hear these words coming? Notice their tone, volume, and location.

As you notice how that younger you feels, what sensations does that you have in your body up there on the screen? Where and at what intensity, weight, pressure?

What shifts in these submodality codings enable you to *think comfortably about* that old memory? As you make these alterations in your coding you can relax in the growing sense of distance and control that this gives you.

Notice the effect it has for you when you dim the picture of your unpleasant memory. Now turn down the brightness, further, further, until it doesn't bother you anymore. Send the picture off into the distance... . Soften the tonality of the sound track.

3. *Move to a second-level dissociation.*

Now imagine yourself floating out of your body in the tenth row of the theater and float back to the projection booth. From this point of view you can see today's self (in the tenth row) watching the younger you on the screen. As you note the adult you sitting in the theater, let yourself also see beyond to the still picture on the screen.

At this second-level dissociation, if at any time you feel uncomfortable and need to remind yourself that you are not in the picture, but merely watching it, put your hands up on the plexiglass to remind yourself to feel safe and secure in the control booth.

4. *Let the old memory play out as you watch it from the projection booth.*

Let the initial snapshot play out as a black-and-white movie as you watch the memory from the projection booth. Watch it from the beginning to the end. Then let it play beyond the end to a time when the bad scene disappears and you see that younger you in a time and place of safety and pleasure. As you keep watching after the passing of the trauma, move to a scene of comfort...either at that time or, if necessary, fast-forward your memories to some future event of comfort. When you get to that place, stop the action, and freeze frame the picture. [If the experience becomes especially intense, dissociate to a third level.]

5. *Step in and rewind.*

The next step will occur really fast. So don't do it until you get all of the instructions about what and how to do it. In a moment, *rewind this memory movie* in fast rewind mode, as you have seen movies or videos run backwards. Now rewind this movie backwards at high speed. This time, rewind it while **inside** it. From that vantage point, you might see a confusion of sights and a jumbling of sounds as everything zooms back to the beginning.

Now associate yourself into the comfort scene at the end of the movie and feel those feelings of comfort and okayness fully and completely.

Do you feel that comfort scene? Good. Now push the rewind button and experience it rewinding...zooooooommmmmm. All the way back to the beginning. It only takes a second or two to do that fast rewind, and how did that feel...rewinding from inside the movie?

When you experience the fast rewinding, all the people and their actions go backwards. They walk and talk backwards. You walk and talk in reverse. Everything happens in reverse, just like rewinding a movie.

6. *Repeat this process five times.*

Having arrived back at the snapshot at the beginning, clear the screen in your mind. Take a break. Shift your awareness. Open your eyes and look around.

Now, go to the situation of comfort at the end again and, *as soon as* you step into it, feel, see, and hear it fully...rewind the movie even faster. As you do this over and over your brain will become more and more proficient and the rewind will go faster and faster until the rewind takes only a second each time. Zoommmm!

7. *Test your results.*

Break state from this exercise. Then after a minute or two, call up the original memory and see if you can get the feelings back. Try as hard as you can to step into the scene and feel the full weight of the emotions.

Other Editing Tools

From the double dissociation position of the projection booth you can not only rewind, you can do numerous other things to change your codings. You have many other choices. You can program your brain to process the film in ways to give you a great range of perspectives and reframes on the memory.

1. *Associate a resourceful memory.* Recall the memory of a time when you felt creative, confident, powerful, etc., from the past. See what you saw at that time. Now turn up the brightness on that memory. When you are fully associated into this resourceful state, bring into that scene the negative stimulus (dog, spider) that you fear, or the traumatic memory, and merge the two memories until they integrate and you see yourself handling the situation with your resources.

117

2. *Alter your sound track.* Re-process the way you hear yourself and others talk. How would you want to make your voice different? Or the voice of someone else? What qualities would make the memory less intense? What voice would you like to have heard? Install an internal voice to help you through this situation.

3. *Add tonal qualities to the sound track to make it better.* Take an unpleasant memory and put some nice loud circus music behind it. Watch the movie again. How do you feel now? Put circus music to other memories of anger and annoyance.

4. *Apply your spiritual faith.* If, in your spiritual belief system, you can bring in your guardian angel, a loving heavenly Father, etc., then split your screen and see through the eye of your faith, your guardian angel hovering over the earthly scene of your memory. See and hear your angel caring for and loving you. Perhaps you hear, "I am with you." "I will help you." See Jesus touch you with his healing hand.

5. *Symbolically code the memory.* For instance, you might want to make the people in your memory transparent. Color them according to how you think/feel about them. Draw a line around the three-dimensional persons in your memory, make them two-dimensional and color them according to your evaluation of them.

6. *Humorize your memory.* Since laughter gives us a great distancing skill, use your humor so that you can laugh this emotional pain off. How far in the future do you need to transport yourself before you can look back on a memory and laugh at it? What difference lies between a memory you can laugh at and one that you can't? Do you see yourself in one, but not in the other? Do you have one coded as a snap-shot and the other as a movie? What difference lies in color, size, brightness? Imagine the hurtful person talking like Donald Duck. Turn your opponent into a caricature cartoon character with exaggerated lips, eyes, head, hands, etc.

#34 *The Accessing And Managing Resourceful States Pattern*

Concept. Whenever we don't *have* our states (i.e., own them, control them), but our states *have* us, at that point we need to develop the skills for taking ownership over them so that we can manage them. This pattern empowers us to do just that, to *take charge of our own life.* Here we have some basic tools for changing our states.

Mind and physiology comprise the tools for working with states:

i. **Mind:** the content of internal representations about things: what we see, hear, smell, feel in the "theater of our mind," plus the words we say to ourselves about those sights, sounds, and sensations.

ii. **Physiology:** the state of our health, body, neurology, and all the factors that make up and affect our physiological being. State-dependency refers to the fact that our states govern our learning, memory, perception, behavior, etc. State-dependency leads to *"emotional expectational sets"* and *"conceptual expectational sets"* which also determine what we see and hear. Two persons with entirely different emotional or conceptual expectational sets will experience the same event in radically different ways.

The Pattern

1. *The memory access.*

Think about a time when you thought-felt, talked or behaved in such a way that you had the resource of X (confidence, assertiveness, calmness, gentleness, etc.). Fully access that memory by seeing what you saw then, hearing what you heard, smelling and tasting what occurred in that experience, and feeling what you felt. Allow yourself to go back there fully and completely until you have entered that experience... .

2. *The imagination access.*

Think about what it would look like, sound like, feel like if you stepped into X (the resource)...imagine it fully and allow yourself to experience it.

3. *The modeling access.*

Think about somebody you know, know about, or someone you've seen or heard in the movies, etc. who has the resource of X. See, hear and feel them having this state completely and fully. Take second position so that you see, hear, and feel from out of their eyes, ears and body.

Anchoring The Resourceful States Pattern

Once we have experienced a resourceful state of mind-body, we can use the anchoring pattern to fully re-access the state. When doing it for ourselves, we will want to set up some self-anchors. This gives us the ability to re-trigger the state at will.

#35 The State Of Consciousness Awareness Pattern

Concept. If a person lacks awareness of their mind-body states of consciousness, of how they shift, of what contextual cues trigger them, of how they think-feel that puts them into those states, etc., then they could benefit from developing more awareness. The following provides a way to increase "state" awareness. As a psychotherapist, I (MH) often use it as a homework assignment or as a workshop tool.

Our states can become so habitual that they become automatic. When that happens we experience them without awareness. To bring our states to consciousness and attend to them necessitates a willingness and a commitment. We have numerous ways to do this.

i. We can constantly monitor our states throughout a day. "What state of mind or emotion or body do I now experience?" "What state would I call this one?"

ii. We can ask one or more persons to assist us in cuing and monitoring our states. "What state are you now experiencing?"

iii. We could journal our states every day for a month or more. The following chart offers one such format that only requires five minutes per day.

iv. We could analyze our states at the end of each day—our journal for just a particular state over which we want to gain more control over. The second chart provides a format for this.

Figure 6.1

Chart For Journaling States (Bubble Journaling)

Instructions: Draw a circle to represent *the states* that you have experienced today from the time that you first woke up to the present time. Inside the state: draw a smile or frown to indicate a positive (+) or negative (-) emotional quality of the state. Put a number (0 to 10) for intensity. Underneath the states identify the content of your *Internal Representations* and factors of your *physiology* that play a role. You can use an * to indicate things that triggered the state (the natural anchors in your world). The design of this is to develop more state awareness of when and how you shift states and the composition of states.

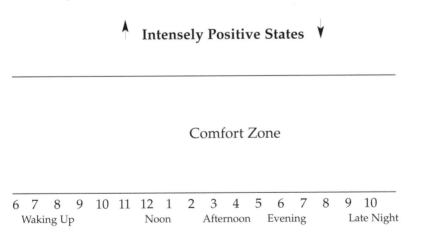

↑ Intensely Positive States ↓

Comfort Zone

6 7 8 9 10 11 12 1 2 3 4 5 6 7 8 9 10
Waking Up   Noon   Afternoon Evening   Late Night

↑ Intensely Negative States ↓

Figure 6.2

Chart For State Identification And Analysis

In column 1, make a list of all the *states* you experienced this past week. In column 2, evaluate intensity of these states from 0-to-100. In column 3, evaluate the state as a **P**rimary **S**tate (PS) or **M**eta-**S**tate (MS), as Normal, Dragon or Royal State. How did the dragon states feel/operate as a dragon to you? In column 4, specify the content of the state—what **I**nternal **R**epresentations run the state? What beliefs? Meanings? If a MS, identify the state-about-a-state structure. In column 5, specify the structure of the state using the VAK model and the driving submodalities.

State Identify	Intensity 0 to 100	Primary State, Meta-State Dragon/Normal/Royal	Content Ideas/IR/Beliefs	Structure Form in MD and SBMD

#36 The "As If" Frame Pattern

Concept. The **"as if"** frame refers to the idea of *pretending to experience* a state, emotion, behavior, way of operating in the world, etc. Developed from Vaihinger (1924, *The Philosophy of "As If"*), this process provides us with a way to use our constructive imaginative skills in order to instruct our brain-body about what a particular "reality" would look like, sound like, feel like, etc. The process works inasmuch as we do not deal with reality as such, but only with our models of reality. When we expand our maps of reality, we expand our repertoire of choices.

If a person seems unable even to "imagine" a particular experience, have them model another person. Utilize this technology if you (or another) need to practice by pretending until you construct and install the resource. This pattern offers a very generative pattern—a kind of new behavior generator pattern.

The Pattern

1. *Identify the desired experience.* What way of thinking, feeling, speaking, behaving, relating, etc., would you like to obtain for yourself? Fully describe this desired experience in descriptive (see, hear, feel) terms.

2. *Give yourself full permission to step into the desired frame and pretend to experience it fully.* This step plays a crucial role for those who have set the frame (in terms of believing, valuing, deciding) that somehow "pretending is a bad thing," "pretending is a fake thing," etc.

3. *Construct the "as if" frame and step into it fully.* Pretend that you can step into that experience. What would you hear...feel... say to yourself... ? How would you experience that state physiologically? What would someone else see as they look at you? What submodalities operate in that experience?

4. *Run an evaluation check.* At this point don't worry about your emotions, i.e., what it feels like. It will feel "weird, strange, uncomfortable, not-me, etc. Evaluate the experience in terms of its usefulness, what you can learn from it, how it might empower some aspect of your life, etc.

5. *Future pace.* Suppose you took this way of thinking, feeling, acting, etc., into your future, and go out a year, five years... .

6. *Permit yourself to use the "as if" frame until it becomes installed.* If you like the benefits and consequences of the experience, give yourself permission to keep trying it on and experimenting with it and to do so until it habituates as your style of responding.

#37 The Chaining States Pattern

Concept. Our states of consciousness move, change, transform throughout a day. Yet sometimes going from one state to another represents too big an alteration to do all at once. Sometimes we have to *more gradually* veer from state to state. Every day we move from one state to another. Such state changes occur naturally. On any given day, we typically experience anywhere from eight to thirty discrete states of mind-and-body. The "state" journaling method develops awareness of our state changes.

Because we constantly move from one state to another, direction-alizing our mind-emotions provides a *tool* for us to create pathways to resourceful states. This chaining-states pattern involves several pieces of preparation work with lots of breaking state, and testing.

Sometimes we get stuck, because we don't seem to have a path from a limiting or distressful state to a more resourceful state. So when we get into a state of frustration, for example, we may only have a map to go into deeper emotional pits: anger, resentment, revenge, fight/flight, etc. With this pattern, we now have the technology for building bridges (or pathways) to more resourceful states.

The Pattern

1. *Identify an unresourceful state.* Think about a state from which you almost always go to deeper levels of unresourcefulness. What state do you have the most difficulty recovering from? (e.g., frustration, self-contempt, stress overload, etc.)

2. *Design a plan for developing a new direction.* Where would you like to end up when you experience that negative state? Obviously, moving from frustration to pure ecstasy would feel nice, but in most contextual situations where you experience a blocking of your goals ("frustration"), to immediately feel ecstasy would not serve to bring out your skills and resources that enable you to effectively cope with the blocking of your goals. What would you like to feel? Presence of mind, calmness, problem-solving ability, curiosity, creativity, etc.?

3. *Specifically identify a pathway.* Once you know the negative state (e.g., frustration) and your desired state (e.g., presence of mind), plan for a series of two to four intermediate stages whereby you can veer from the problematic emotion to an ever-increasing resourceful state. For instance, you might want to plan to move from *frustration* to *endurance* to *calmness,* to *acceptance, and* then to *presence of mind.*

4. *Access and anchor each state.* First establish an anchor on the skin between the thumb and index finger on the back of your right hand for *frustration* (or on the hand of someone you are working with). Then set an anchor for *endurance* on the knuckle of the index finger, then an anchor for *calmness* on the knuckle of the middle finger, then one for *acceptance* on the knuckle of the next finger, and finally an anchor for *presence of mind* on the knuckle of the little finger. Test each anchor.

5. *Chain the states together.* When you have completed all of this preparation, begin with the first state and **slowly** have the person access it, helping by firing off the first anchor. *When* the person gets to the peak of that state (ask them to nod their head), *then* fire the next anchor *while* holding the first. Hold *the first* for a couple of moments while holding *the second.* Then release the first and maintain the second. Repeat five times. Then fire the second, and when it gets to its peak, fire the anchor for *the next state.* Use same process, hold both, then release the first. Repeat five times. Continue through the chain.

6. *Test the chain.* Fire the first anchor for the person to move quickly and automatically to *the outcome state.* If so, you have successfully set up a chain so that the person has a neurological pathway whereby he or she can move from frustration to presence of mind.

7. *Future pace.* "Imagine some time in the next week when you may feel frustrated (fire anchor) and you can feel this (fire the chain of anchors, holding on "presence of mind") as you go smoothly and easily to...[the desired state]."

#38 The Submodality Overlapping Pattern

Concept. Sometimes we have difficulty using a particular representational system (RS) to generate a particular resource. At such times, we may first need to start with our favorite RS, with which we have plenty of skill, and *overlap* to the weaker system. In doing this we learn to develop a less favored RS.

A public speaker or presenter can engage in submodality overlapping by simply using all of the RS, and alternate between them. (Great literature that uses all of the systems, and which alternates using one to begin and then another, provides the same pattern. The Judeo-Christian scriptures provide a great example of this.) This pattern follows the general pattern of "pace, pace, lead."

The Pattern

1. *Identify targeted modality.* Perhaps someone does not make internal pictures very well or to his or her satisfaction, yet would like to develop the ability to relax by visualizing peaceful scenes and/or do other meditative processes.

2. *Begin with favored representational system.* If auditory: "...and imagine listening to the sound of the wind rustling in the leaves of a tree on a fall day, and you can hear that wind blowing ever so gently..." If kinesthetic, "...feel the gentle air blowing in the trees and hear it rustle and begin to catch a vague glimpse of the tree limbs moving... ."

3. *Then overlap to the new modality*. "And as you can hear these things you can begin to see the brown and red and yellow leaves blowing off the trees... ."

#39 *The Threshold Pattern or Compulsion Blowout*

Concept. Sometimes a way of thinking-and-feeling that doesn't serve us well continues to work simply because (at some level) we still believe it will if we just work at it long and hard enough. So we stay in dysfunctional relationships, patterns, organizations, etc.

Yet patterns of thinking, emoting, talking, and behaving can "threshold." They can accumulate over time to the point that one has an internal sense of "Enough!" "No more!" We can experience "the last straw" phenomenon about things. When we do, suddenly we find ourselves "going over the top." Then "something snaps" in a sudden and irrevocable way, just as, if we bend a piece of metal back and forth, back and forth, eventually it reaches an internal "threshold." Then it snaps. At that point, something "breaks" and, like Humpty-Dumpty, we can't put it back to its previous state.

Sometimes a person will hit threshold with a habit pattern such as smoking, drinking, cussing, putting up with a mate, enduring a job, etc. Then something snaps. Therefore, the old pattern cannot cohere in that person's life. They can't stand even the smell of a cigarette. The taste of alcohol no longer holds any appeal. The thought of a particular person repulses them! They've hit threshold. *Source:* Andreas and Andreas (1987).

The Pattern

1. *Identify your compulsion state.* What do you feel compulsive about? What do you obsess about mentally, emotionally, and behaviorally? Identify the problem.

2. *Identify a non-compulsion state.* Think about something similar to the compulsion, but unlike it in the sense that you don't become obsessive-compulsive about it. For instance you may feel compelled about pistachios but not about peanuts, about ice cream, but not about yogurt.

3. *Run a contrastive analysis.* Compare the differences between these two items in terms of their *driving* submodalities. How do you *code* the thing you feel compulsive about? How do you code the similar thing about which you do not feel compulsive?

4. *Blow it out.* Take the quality of the representation (the submodality) that drives the compulsion (size, closeness, color, etc.) and make it more and more so (bigger and bigger, closer and closer, brighter and brighter, etc.) until you blow it out! Exaggerate it until the experience cannot exist in that form.

When you do this, expect that the feelings of compulsion will increase at first, and will get stronger and stronger...then as it thresholds, it will pop, snap, blow out, etc.

5. *Test.* Think about the item. How do you feel? Is the item blown out?

6. *Ratchet the experience.* An alternative method for getting an experience to threshold involves ratcheting it like you would a car jack, making it go higher and higher. Take the experience and the driving submodality qualities that pump it up and ratchet it again and again. Do so repeatedly until you get it beyond threshold. Then pause for a few minutes and test.

7. *Swish to a new resourceful you.* After you have changed the compulsion, invite the person to think of the "you" for whom these contexts offer no problem. Then use the Swish pattern (# 24) to move from the old cues that triggered compulsion to the new states of resourcefulness.

#40 Transforming "Mistakes" Into "Learnings"

(First "Mistakes" Pattern, see also #74 for a second one)

Concept. As with various obsessive-compulsive patterns, sometimes we find ourselves repeatedly falling into "the same old pattern" again and again. Did we not learn anything? Maybe we did not!

Sometimes we organize our thinking, emoting, and behaving to accomplish an outcome, and then *just get into a pattern of repeating it mindlessly.* If the pattern even partially worked, we may subsequently simply have failed to update it. We don't reality-test it anymore. *Source:* Dilts and Western States Training Association.

The Pattern

1. *Identify the over-used pattern.* Identify any pattern or cluster of negative responses that happens over and over, (i.e. remarrying alcoholics, repeating a particular self-defeating behavior, etc.)

2. *Identify supporting limiting beliefs that keep the pattern operating.* Identify the limiting beliefs which you have developed that contribute to or support this pattern. Believing in persevering without considering the context, the particular situation, ongoing feedback, etc., can operate as such a limiting belief.

3. *Identify an experience of similar structure.* Select a negative experience that exemplifies this response.

4. *Worst-case scenario comparison.* Compare the negative experiences to something worse that could have happened, but which did not. We may feel thankful that what occurred was only that bad and that "something worse" did not happen!

5. *Explore positive side-effects.* Identify how the negative experience actually caused, or contributed, something positive at some later point in time. Perhaps some of the most useful things in your life would never have happened without these seemingly negative events.

6. *Find the positive intentions behind the negative events.* Identify the positive intention behind the negative event. Also become aware of the positive intentions of any other people involved.

7. *Find positive meanings to negative events.* An event that may mean something negative on one level may mean something positive on another level. The fact that we experienced a problem on one level may mean that we have solved it on another level.

8. *Re-edit.* Go back to before all the negative events happened and relive them using the positive insights you now possess.

9. *Go to the place you keep information, insights, etc.* Mark these new "learnings" so that you can find and use them again.

#41 Becoming Intentionally Compelled: The Godiva Chocolate Pattern

Concept. This pattern links very strong, even compulsively positive feelings, with behaviors which we want to continue and for which we need more motivation. This pattern therefore becomes especially useful for installing a desire to do those things which we know we should, but which we do not feel committed to doing. With this technology, we can change our motivation and feelings. *Source:* Richard Bandler.

The Pattern

1. *Identify a compulsion.* Think of something you feel wildly excited about or compelled toward—such as eating good luscious chocolate.

2. *Experience yourself doing the compulsion.* Recall the experience associatedly in all of the RS (VAK) in such a way so that you immediately step back into a memory and re-experience the situation fully. Let's call this picture 1.

3. *Identify a desired experience.* What do you want to have more and stronger compulsive feeling about? Allow yourself to picture yourself doing that which you, intellectually, need or want to do. Make this a dissociated image. Let's call this picture 2.

4. *Run an ecology check.* How would "feeling compelled about this activity" serve you? Would it help or hinder you? How would it enhance your life?

5. *Connect the two pictures.* Put picture 1 of your compelling activity at the back of picture 2 (the picture of the desired activity). Visually see these two pictures inter-connected, one at the front, the other at the back.

6. *Quickly open up a small hole in the center of picture 2* and do so in such a way that you can see picture 1 through that hole.

7. *Rapidly link the two.* In a very, very rapid way, make the hole as big as you need to in order to bring picture 1 through. Have it cover picture 2. Feel the excitement.

8. *Reverse.* Now shrink the hole as rapidly as possible while keeping the positive feelings.

9. *Repeat three times.* Repeat this process at least three times, or as many times as necessary until thinking about the activity has become completely associated with the desired feelings.

#42 The Decision-Making Pattern

Concept. Sometimes we struggle with indecisiveness as we attempt to make a decision. Yet because our experience of "making a decision" involves using our VAK modalities, producing better decisions will involve using the appropriate representational systems in the most efficient sequence. We generally find it difficult to "feel" a good choice and to make good decisions without comparing alternatives visually. With this pattern we can produce decisions of higher quality.

Additionally, a *decision* (linguistically) exists as a nominalization of the process of *deciding* between alternatives. Yet to move back and forth between alternatives necessitates moving to a higher logical level (a meta-position) in order to have a larger perspective. This highlights the fact that *effective decision making*, of necessity, involves meta-levels, hence meta-states.

The Pattern

1. *Identify a decision area.* What decision would you like to make? Do you have a well-formed outcome regarding the result of the decision? If not, use the pattern for Well-Formed Outcomes.

2. *Access one visual possibility.* First allow yourself to see one possible decision and the solution that follows from it. (When using this pattern with another person, as you make this

suggestion, gesture up to the right and track to make sure the person follows visually.)

3. *Meta-comment about the option.* Invite the person to language the thoughts and emotions that come to mind about that option. "As you think about that possible alternative, what thoughts come to mind?" (Here you may want to gesture down and to the right as you express this to enable the person to more easily follow. Or, you may want to gesture up to a meta-position.)

4. *Access a kinesthetic response.* Next, get a feel for how much you like the option. Ask the person to get a feel for how much he or she likes the option by looking down and to the left.

5. *Repeat steps 2 through 4.* Having elicited these responses about the first option, do the same for the other alternatives. Invite yourself or the other person to create another possibility and repeat steps 2 through 4. Do this repeatedly until you consider all of the significant options or can think of no other option.

6. *Go meta and select the best.* Move to a meta-position above all of the individual options that you considered. At this level, specify the essential criteria by which you will make your decision. *Prioritize* these standards. Now *select* the option that meets most of the criteria.

7. *Future pace.* Having selected the most desirable solution and using all of the sensory modalities, experience living out and using this option as you imagine, fully and completely, moving out into your future with it.

8. *Check for objections.* Does any part of you object to that option? Can you integrate that objection into the option? What price will you pay for this choice? What price would you pay for another choice?

9. *Troubleshoot.* If no solution seems adequate, contact the creative part and ask that part to generate several new options. Recycle.

#43 *The Pleasure Pattern*

Concept. "Pleasure" differs from happiness as a primary state differs from a meta-state. **Pleasure**, as a primary state experience, operates as a function of our senses—the pleasures of sight, sound, sensation, movement, smell, and taste. From that we move to a higher level and experience **enjoyment or happiness** *about* that pleasure (a pleasure of a pleasure).

To experience *pleasure* one needs sensory equipment: eyes, ears, nose, skin, etc. We experience *pleasure* purely and simply as the stimulus of our sense receptors. But to experience *enjoyment*, we need consciousness or "mind." We then bring pleasant, validating, *thoughts-feelings* to bear on the sights, sounds, sensations, smells, and tastes. This explains why our enjoyments differ so greatly. We vary in our thoughts *about* the sensory experience. One person gives it pleasant meanings, another says that he finds it boring, dull, unpleasant, nasty, obnoxious, etc.

The structure of happiness involves bringing "happy thoughts" to bear on some pleasure. For this reason, we can learn to feel "happy" about almost anything! Happiness results *not* from primary level experiences but from *the ability to appreciate*, to see value, to endow with meaning, to give more importance and significance to something. The more significance one gives to an experience—the more pleasant and enjoyable we make it, so we experience it. This technology works well for anyone who seems incapable of enjoying the experiences of life, especially the pleasurable experiences.

The Pattern

1. *Make a "fun" list.* Begin by making a list of all the things that "make you happy." Include anything that gives you a sense of enjoyment, happiness, thrill, pleasure. "What I have fun doing, experiencing, seeing, etc., consists of..."

2. *Pick out one item of pleasure* —one that you really like. Use it to begin eliciting your structure of happiness. First, test it to make sure it exists as a sensory-based referent: can you see, hear, feel, smell or taste it? (Examples: taking a hot bath, watching a sunset, playing with a kitten, reading a book, etc.)

3. *Discover your pleasuring.* Once you have a primary state "pleasure", relax and generate as many answers as come to your mind to the question: *"What positive meaning of value and significance do I give to this pleasure?"* To create a diagram of the meta-levels of meanings about that pleasure, draw a circle designating your P-S (primary state) pleasure with each answer to this question as a "state" of meaning and feeling *about* (@) that pleasure (see chart).

4. *Repeat.* Repeat step three for the higher-level pleasurable meanings that you give to the P-S pleasure. For each, ask the question again: "What positive meaning of value and significance do I give to this pleasure?" Sketch out your full enjoyment/happiness structure with all of its meta-levels.

Figure 6.3

Meta-Level Structure Of "Pleasure"

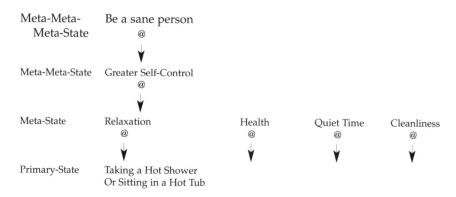

5. *Appreciate the gestalt.* Now sit back and notice all of the meanings, beliefs and states that you have generated *about* that initial primary pleasure. Allow yourself to recognize that these meanings *drive* your pleasure. They give it its meaning, energy, motivation, and power. Now you know **why** it "holds so much pleasure for you."

6. *Use your highest pleasuring.* Go to your highest meta-pleasure state and access it fully and completely. Step into it and "be there" now. Allow yourself to become fully aware of this transcendental meaning of pleasure (happiness) and imagine taking this perceptual state into some other everyday activities.

Now inquire of yourself: What other everyday sensory-based activities can I use to anchor this high level state? Imagine being in this state in some particular context doing X (future pace). "If I had this state, in just the way I want to, how would this affect and/or alter my experience of...(work, relationships, learning, etc.)?" This enables you to spread your pleasuring around and connect it to other behaviors.

#44 *The Reducing Enjoyment Pattern or Anti-Addiction Pattern*

Concept. We can develop and experience too much enjoyment about some things. Our *neuro-semantics* (the *meanings* incorporated into our *neurology*) can get out of balance. We can endow smoking, drinking, eating, etc., with *so much meaning* that we use those behaviors to trigger our "happiness" even when we have to pay the price in various forms of unhappiness, in the long run!

The following pattern represents the happiness pattern applied to over-used pleasures. To start this pattern, begin with a sensory-based primary state "pleasure" that you want to decrease so that it does **not** function in an overly pleasurable mode. This technology works with addictions, obsessions and compulsions around some pleasure that we over-use and which undermines other important values in life.

The Pattern

1. *Identify the disliked pleasure* (smoking, over-eating, drinking, relaxing, etc.)

2. *Identify the meta-state levels of meaning* that drive it as in the Happiness Pattern. "What positive meaning of value and significance do I give to this pleasure?" Draw a circle designating your P-S pleasure with each answer as a "state" of meaning and feeling *about* that pleasure.

3. *Repeat.* Repeat step two for the higher-level pleasurable meanings. For each ask the question: "What positive meaning do I give to this pleasure?" Sketch out a diagram of your full enjoyment/happiness structure with all of its meta-levels. (See chart in previous pattern).

4. *Appreciate the enjoyment gestalt.* Notice all of the meanings, beliefs and states that *drive* this undesired pleasure. This will provide you with insight as to **why** this pleasure has such power over you.

5. *De-meaning/de-enjoy.* Put your hand over one set of meta-level meanings. Inquire: If I took away this line of Meta-states about the pleasure, *how much would that reduce my enjoyment?* Continue to do this until you know which meanings you need to eliminate in order to reduce the power of this pleasure. Inquire: How many of the meanings do I need to take away before it starts to exist as whatever it "is" at the primary level— eating for health and nutrition rather than for comfort, to de-stress anger, to overcome loneliness, etc.?

6. *Future pace the de-enjoyment.* Imagine yourself fully engaged in the primary pleasure, for example, eating. When fully "there," hear yourself say, "This is *just* food. It nourishes my body—a nice pleasure for the moment, but no more. I refuse to over-load it with meaning. If I love it too much—I see globs of ugly fat growing at my mid-section" (attach whatever *displea*-sure works for you!).

7. *Access your highest meta-pleasure state fully.* Allow yourself to step into that highest level meaning and to be there completely. As you step into this state and experience it fully then *realize* that you can do so without engaging in that behavior anymore. Now allow your creative part to identify other behaviors that will allow you to experience this meta-level meaning in everyday life.

Summary. With this pattern you can sort and separate primary pleasures and meta-pleasures (enjoyments). You can discover those neuro-semantic meanings that drive your behaviors and you can change that structure so that it serves you better. With this pattern you can amplify your happy states of enjoyment, and de-energize pleasures to which you don't want to give away your power.

#45 *The Breaking Up Limiting Synesthesias Pattern*

Concept. At times we can get several modalities combined, confused, and stuck together in our representing of information. We call this merging, linkage, or synthesizing of two RS a *synesthesia.* This refers to an *overlap between the senses* of seeing, hearing, feeling, smelling, etc. And sometimes this can create problems. For example, when a person sees blood and automatically feels horror, he or she has a V-K synesthesia (see-feel). As such, it can amplify traumatic memories.

The following pattern provides a method for breaking up such synesthesias. Our overall purpose here involves adding behavioral choices in such contexts by creating new patterns of response. Doing so increases personal flexibility and adds basic resources quickly and easily. This technology enables us to add various neurological traits to existing synesthesias. *Source:* Tim Hallbom.

The Pattern

1. *Identify a problem context.* Find a specific person, time, and/or place where you experience the problem behavior.

2. *Access, anchor and calibrate the problem.* As you access the problem behavior and state, anchor it to a specific location on the floor. When you do this, notice the physiology, breathing, eye accessing, voice tone, etc. in that problem state.

3. *Identify and step into a resource space.* As you specify a resource that would make the problem unnecessary, or prevent the problem, step into it and anchor that resourceful experience to a specific place on the floor. Calibrate by noticing the changes involved in becoming more resourceful.

4. *Step back into the problem space.* While you remember the problem situation again, take on the physiology of the resourceful state fully...including voice, breathing, body positions, etc. Continue to hold the image of the problem while making the physiological changes.

5. *Adding more options.* Next, add an auditory, digital and visual construct to this resourceful state by tapping the left foot and moving the right finger to the chin. As you do, look up and to the right while saying "Mmmmm..." as if thinking of something profound. As you do this, **step back into the resource space**.

6. *Check out all representations.* Now think about the problem by moving your eyes through all of the accessing positions in a figure eight configuration always moving up from the center. Then reverse the direction again moving up from center.

7. *Test and run an ecology check.* Break state, and test to see if you have a different reaction to the problem. Run an ecology check to determine if any part would object to using this more resourceful choice.

#46 Filing Away Memories As Part Of One's Learning History

Concept. Sometimes the things we remember, and how we remember them, cause us problems—torturing us with unpleasant sights and sounds, reminding us to feel bad, guilty, a sense of loss, etc. To de-energize such memories, make positive learnings from them and store them into the inner library of references. *Source:* Dr. Maralee Platt.

The Pattern

1. *Identify a memory.* Think of or identify a traumatic experience that still 'bugs' you.

2. *Identify the submodalities.* Notice the sub-modalities of how you remember it (in color, black-and-white, still photograph, movie, etc.).

3. *Create and work with a symbol representation.* Look over the frames of your memory and let one frame of the movie represent the whole experience. Allow it to become a symbolic representation...as you do, push that picture back to the horizon of

your perceptions and, as you do, let it become black-and-white. See that "younger you" in the picture. Let the picture become smaller and smaller until it becomes the size of a slide. When it does, put a frame around it.

4. *Treat it as a memory to learn from.* Now allow yourself to reach out with your left hand and take hold of the slide, and bring it to your left side (reverse this if the person stores his or her memories on the right side). With the slide sitting there at your left side, begin to extract from it all the learnings that it offers you for your future. You don't even need to know consciously what these learnings may consist of. You can just represent them metaphorically or symbolically. As you do, begin to put the learning into your own personal internal library.

5. *Store it as a valuable memory.* Now take your left hand and push the slide behind you so that your mind-body system will know that the experience has indeed passed and no longer exists, thus allowing you to put the past behind you.

6. *Generalize this process.* You can now ask your subconscious to make the same kind of slides out of any and all memories that have to do with the painful incident, and place them to your left for storage. Continue to repeat this process, allowing it to generalize even more.

7. *Replace with happy memories.* In contrast to the kind of memories that you had, put happy experiences on videotapes in full color with a sound track and place these to your right. Then, with your right hand, push them behind you since they also have finished, and they can stay there... in a place where you can easily access them anytime you want to.

Additional Patterns for Emotional States

> The Re-imprinting Pattern
> The Forgiveness Pattern
> The Collapsing Anchors Pattern

Conclusion

As a cognitive-behavioral (rational-emotive) model, in NLP we view *emotions* as derivative and holistic rather than foundational or elementalistic. This point of view differs radically from the more emotive therapies. "Emotions" arise from the combination of body kinesthetics and evaluative thoughts (values, judgments, beliefs, etc.). The overall gestalt generates an emotional (mind-body) state.

"Emotions," like behaviors, result from a mind-body state of consciousness. By addressing *the component pieces* of internal representations (including kinesthetics), NLP offers patterns for changing, transforming, amplifying and reducing "emotions." With this model we can directly decompose the structure of emotions. This frees us from demanding that people repeatedly feel the feeling until they get over it. Thus in NLP we do not have to track down the history of emotions to deal with them effectively.

Chapter 7

Languaging

Patterns For Languaging Reality
With Precision, Clarity, And Empowerment

How we talk about things, *the language forms* that we use as we define, describe, and symbolize our experiences, powerfully affect **how we experience** life. They also crucially govern the *quality* of our experiences and our overall effectiveness.

What explains why *language* plays such a powerful and pervasive role in our lives? Why would our languaging have this kind of effect? What explains this? It occurs for several reasons, not the least of which involves the fact that, when we use language, we set *frames of reference*. Then those frames establish our "reality" (or models of the world, paradigms, world views, etc.).

The founder of General Semantics, Alfred Korzybski, an engineer by training, analyzed language and found that it functions in the human nervous system like a map or blueprint *of* reality. This means that, as a symbolic system, language itself can never exist as the territory itself; it never "is" the territory. It only represents and stands for the territory. Korzybski described this neurological mapping, which our brain and nervous system does, as *"abstracting."* In other words, to deal with the world, we *abstract* from it to create a facsimile of the world by which we then navigate our way through the world.

Our very nervous system does this to create various *neurological maps*—such as our sensory-based visual, auditory, and kinesthetic maps. After that, as we continue to abstract, we develop *language* as a true symbol system *of* the sensory representational maps. Now words "stand for" and reference the earlier abstractions.

So what? If we do not deal with the world directly, but indirectly, through the mediation of various levels of mental mapping, then false-to-fact mapping and language structures will mislead us, mis-direct our energies, and prevent us from adjusting ourselves to reality. To describe a poor adjustment, Korzybski utilized the term "unsane." And Korzybski felt that the primary source of human unsanity arises due to the Aristotelian language structure that we have inherited over centuries and millennia. To address this deficiency, he wrote *Science And Sanity* (1933/1994) to present an entirely new, functional, dynamic and non-Aristotelian way to language things. This began what he later designated as *neuro-linguistic training*.

From Korzybski's beginning formulations, numerous writers have brought his language technologies (or "extensional devices") into popular awareness (S.I. Hayakawa, Gregory Bateson, Noam Chomsky, Abraham Maslow, Karl Pribram, Jerome Bruner, etc.). Bandler and Grinder also tapped into the most fundamental General Semantic formula. In their first NLP book, *The Structure Of Magic* (1975), they quoted Korzybski:

> *A map **is not** the territory it represents, but, if correct, it has a **similar structure** to the territory, which accounts for its useful-ness. ... If we reflect upon our languages, we find that at best they must be considered **only as maps**. A word **is not** the object it represents; and languages exhibit also this peculiar self-reflexive-ness, that we can analyze languages by linguistic means. ... Antiquated map-language, by necessity, must lead us to semantic disasters, as it imposes and reflects its unnatural structure... .*

> *As words are **not** the objects which they represent, structure, and **structure alone**, becomes the only link which connects our verbal processes with the empirical data. ...That languages all have some structure...we unconsciously read into the world the structure of the language we use... .*

> (58-60)

Talking Our Way To Sanity

What we call *psychotherapy* essentially involves a *conversation*. Via talking about our experiences (primary level or state) and about our mental maps of our experiences (meta-levels), we somehow come to experience therapeutic effects. We experience a clarifying of our mind, an expressing of our feelings, we engage in problem-solving, develop insights and understandings, experience a validation of our person, etc. Effective languaging does all of that, and more.

A century ago, Sigmund Freud's patient, Anna O., labeled the process of psychotherapy as *"the talking cure."* Since then therapeutic talk has taken a significant role in assisting people in recovering from distresses to live life more fully. Since George Miller and the Cognitive Psychological movement began (1956), we have also come to realize that we can *heal* people through language, but also that language can equally wound, hurt, damage, and traumatize people. Ellis and Beck popularized the power of *cognitive distortions* which show up in irrational language structures: must-ing, should-ing, awfulizing, catastrophizing, personalizing, emotionalizing, etc.

NLP also initially focused on the power of therapeutic languaging. Bandler and Grinder observed two key figures in the therapy field (Fritz Perls and Virginia Satir) who "just said words" and who communicated exquisitely both verbally and non-verbally, thereby making what seemed like "magic" happen. From the way these therapeutic wizards talked and interacted with people, their clients developed new understandings, their emotions became healthier and more vigorous, and their behaviors and actions became more effective in moving them toward their desired outcomes.

As Bandler and Grinder analyzed and modeled the language behavior of these and other highly successful therapists, they developed **the Meta-model of language in therapy**, codified in their books, *The Structure Of Magic, Volume I & II* (1975 and 1976). Here they developed twelve linguistic distinctions which they used to indicate how a person's language shows ill-formedness. As they modeled the therapeutic wizards, they noted the linguistic distinctions that they paid attention to, and responded to, in their clients as they told their stories. These wizards also seemed to have a way of "challenging" these distortions, generalizations, and deletions so that it assisted the client in recovering valuable information and mapping out more accurate and precise understandings.

The Meta-model simply summarized the key patterns in Satir's and Perls' way of interacting therapeutically with their clients. It highlighted the linguistic structures they chose to address and offered specific *questions* that they used to challenge the person's way of mapping. These questions about the person's experience and way of languaging it enabled the person to "go back in" to their internal references to thereby re-map their understandings in more useful and accurate ways. By re-connecting the person to his or her remembered experience, a context was provided for them to create a more complete and enhancing map. Doing this, people found their cognitive mental worlds expanded, which then transformed their emotions and behaviors.

While language and language use *obviously* play an essential role in psychotherapy, **languaging** plays just as central a role in business, personal relationships, negotiating, health, law, education, etc.

The patterns in this chapter summarize the *linguistic patterns* of NLP. Here you will find "the structure of magic" (Bandler and Grinder, 1975), and some of "the secrets of magic" (Hall, 1998). This **language technology** enables us to bring more accuracy and precision to our mental mapping. It empowers us to become more professional and conscious in our use of language. And it provides us with enhanced ways to language ourselves and others.

#47 The Meta-Modeling Pattern

Concept. When we speak, we produce what the old Transformational Grammar model of linguistics (Chomsky, 1965) calls "Surface Structure" statements. Such statements have *transformed* our "meaning" from numerous prior abstractions (called the Deep Structure). This refers to a fuller linguistic and neurological model of our awarenesses.

Korzybski (1933/1994) earlier established General Semantics founded on making a basic distinction between *map and territory.* He also identified the processes by which we *"abstract"* from the territory of the world via our neurological mechanisms and then internalize those abstractions (neurologically) into our very nervous system. From there we abstract again and again, summarizing, deleting, generalizing, distorting, etc., until we create, first, neurological maps and, later, linguistic maps *of* reality. Out of this understanding of human neurological information processing (or mapping) developed an understanding of how to enable all of us to better use and handle our map-making skills.

Conceptually, we then begin with the understanding that we often experience problems and distress not because the world lacks richness of resources or opportunities, but because *our maps do.* Yet we so often either don't know this or forget it. What we say *about* the world, our experiences, the events that occur, *seem* so "real" and obvious. How could they exist as anything else?

Korzybski referred to this as *"identifying."* The first unsane form of identifying occurs when we forget that all of our "thoughts," representations, words, etc., only exist as *symbols*—symbols **of** some territory, and not the territory. Yet in our language use, we can so easily and so quickly forget this.

With the *Meta-model,* we start with the map of the world presented to us. We listen to the Surface Structure statements, and then enter into that world by exploring and questioning from the attitude of curiosity, interest, and respect. We begin by *pacing* the person so that he or she will feel validated and understood. This elicits "trust," rapport, and transformation. As we then converse, asking questions of specificity, this process co-creates a state of understanding and encourages the other to expand his or her individual maps.

Meta-modeling (as a verb) *refers to the process of listening and then questioning another's map* (or one's own, if applied to oneself). This process elicits the places of ill-formedness in our maps and simultaneously evokes an expansion of our models. When used in "therapy," most people never notice the *Meta-modeling.* It just seems like "talk." Most get so caught up in *content,* they seldom notice the structure of language.

The following twelve distinctions present *the Meta-model of language.* They do so using the three map-making processes: deletion, generalization and distortion, thus highlighting the fact that we make our models of the world by leaving characteristics out (deletion), by summarizing or generalizing features (generalization), and by altering/distorting other features (distortion).

Figure 7.1

The Meta-Model Of Language

Patterns/Distinctions   Responses/Challenges

Deletions:

1. Unspecified Nouns or Referential Index (simple deletions):

They don't listen to me.	Who specifically doesn't listen to you?
He said that she was mean.	Who specifically said that?
	What did he mean by 'mean'?

2. Unspecified Relations (comparative deletions):

She's a better person.	Better than whom?
	Better at what?
	Compared to whom, what?
	Given what criteria?

3. Unspecified Referential Index:

He rejected me.	Who specifically rejected you?
People push me around.	Who specifically pushes you?

4. Unspecified Verbs:

She rejected me.	How specifically did she reject you?
I felt really manipulated.	Manipulated in what way and how?

5. Nominalizations (hidden or smothered verbs, ambiguous words):

Let's improve our communication.	Whose communicating do you mean?
	How would you like to communicate?
What state did you wake up in	Use Co-ordinates to index:
this morning?	Specifically what?, when?, who?, where?, which?, how?, etc.
	De-nominalize the nominalization to recover the hidden verb.

Generalizations:

6. Universal Qualifiers (allness, generalizations that exclude exceptions):

She never listens to me.	Never?
	What would happen if she did?

7. Modal Operators (operational modes of being):

(necessity, possibility, impossibility, desire).

I have to take care of her.	What would happen if you did?
I can't tell him the truth.	What wouldn't happen if you didn't?
	...Or what? What would happen if you did?

8. **Lost Performative** (An evaluative statement with the speaker deleted or unowned):

It's bad to be inconsistent.

Who evaluates it as bad?
According to what standard?
How do you determine this label of "badness?"

Distortions:

9. **Mind Reading** (meaning attributions and cause-effect assumptions about others):

You don't like me...

How do you know I don't like you?
What evidence leads you to that conclusion?

10. **Cause—Effect** (causational statements of relations between events, stimulus-response beliefs):

You make me sad.

How does my behavior cause you to feel sad?
Counter example: Do you always feel sad when I do this?
How specifically does this work?

11. **Complex Equivalence** (the "is" of identity, identifications):

She's always yelling at me; she doesn't like me.

How does her yelling mean she doesn't like you?
Can you recall a time when you yelled at someone you liked?

He's a loser when it comes to business; he just lacks business sense.

How do you create this equation in an absolute way between these things?

12. **Presuppositions** (silent assumptions):

If my husband knew how much I suffered, he wouldn't do that.

This statement presupposes that she suffers, that her husband's behavior causes her suffering,
that he lacks knowledge about her suffering,
that his intentions would shift if he knew.
How do you choose to suffer?
How is he reacting?
How do you know he doesn't know?

The Pattern

1. *Listen for ill-formedness or vagueness in representation.* As you listen for the surface sentence statements, cue yourself to stay in sensory awareness. Do this by noticing if the words themselves permit you to see, hear, feel, taste and smell the referents. Continually *track over* directly from the words to creating your own internal representations. Do this without adding anything to the words. As you do, continue to ask yourself:

> When I track over, do I have a complete understanding of the person's referents and meanings?
> Have they left something out? (Deletion) What? Unspecified nouns, verbs, relations, etc.? If so, inquire.

Continue also to check for other problems (generalizations and distortions.)

> Have they generalized something so that it lacks specifics?
> Have they distorted some process so that I don't know how it works (cause-effect), what it means or how it came to mean that (complex equivalence), have they information about another person (mind-reading), etc.?

To Meta-model, a person has to stay in *sensory awareness* and *not* project their own meanings, references, definitions, etc., onto the other person's words. To do this, adopt a "no-nothing" frame of reference.

2. *Challenge the ill-formedness.* Any time you don't know *what* the person has reference to or *how* a mental map works, inquire about it.

> "How do you represent this 'rejection?'"
> "Where did you get that information?"
> "Does it always work that way?"
> "What have you presupposed?"

Learn and utilize the Meta-model questions that call for more specificity, precision, and clarity.

3. *Continue checking for areas of unclarity and asking for more precision until you have a sufficient adequate representation of the other's meanings.*

For the newest development regarding the Meta-model, see *The Secrets Of Magic* (1998). This work surveys the twenty-five year history of the Meta-model regarding its evolution and development. It also adds nine new distinctions from General Semantics, refers to current developments in the field of linguistics and to the effect of the demise of Transformational/Generative Grammar on the Meta-model, and much more.

#48 The Pattern Of Meta-Model III

Concept. Tad James (1987) developed a specific use for the Meta-model by packaging it as a way to do "detailed questioning for a specific result." He initiated this use of the Meta-model by asking,

> *What question can I ask which, by the very nature of the presuppositions in the question itself, will enable a person to make the greatest amount of change by accepting the presuppositions inherent in the question?*

The following pattern starts with a problem and invites a person (1) to articulate the problem content, (2) its cause, (3) failed attempts at solutions, (4) and possibilities for solution.

Then, things flip around and the following questions orient the person towards thinking about the solution. It invites the person (5) to first make specific the content of the change and (6) the time for the change (along with an embedded command) , (7) an invitation to generate suggestions (with a temporal shift), and finally (8), a confirmation of the beginning of a change. Source: This particular shortened format came from Bodenhamer (1996) who says that this pattern necessitates "deep rapport."

The Pattern

———>

1. *"What do you evaluate as wrong?"*

2. *"What has caused this problem?"*

3. *"How have you failed to resolve this problem up to this point?"*

4. *"What would it look, sound, feel like if you went out in time out beyond the solution to your problem?"*

Flip

<———

5. *"What would you like to change?"*

6. *"When will you stop it from functioning as a limitation to you?"*

7. *"How many ways do you know you have solved this?"*

8. *"I know that you have begun changing and seeing things differently."*

#49 The Denominalizing Pattern

Concept. Within the Meta-model, we have a linguistic distinction known as a **nominalization**. This refers to both deleting *a process or a set of actions* and over-generalizing the process as we summarize it into *a static noun form* (hence the term *nominalization).* This *naming* of the actions distorts things. As a result we have *a nominal- ization* which thereafter sends several false signals to the brain. For example, when we use nominalizations, we cue our brain that our referent exists as a static thing rather than as a dynamic process ("decision," rather than deciding, "motivation" instead of "motivating," etc.). By implication, this typically suggests that we have no participation in the process. And if we don't play a part in the process, we consequently lack any ability or power to affect it. This represents some big-time unsane mapping of reality (e.g., "self-esteem" instead of self-esteeming, "relationship" instead of relating to someone, etc.)

Since so many of the words by which we report our experiences involve nominalizations, learning to **de-nominalize** empowers us to change "the frozen universe" back into processes and actions (a strong emphasis in General Semantics). Doing so empowers us to respond within, and to, the processes, and to recognize the choices available to us. Glasser (1983) noted the importance of this in his ongoing development of Reality Therapy when he began to disallow emotion and psychosomatic words to stand as nouns. He insisted on turning them into verbs: angering, guilting, depressing, headaching, etc.

The Pattern

1. *Identify the nominalization.* We can make a picture of a true noun (a person, place or a thing). Not so with a nounified verb. You can't make a picture of "motivation," "self-esteem," etc. These verbs-turned-into-nouns describe an ongoing process. The stem, **"an ongoing..."** offers a way to flush out true verbs cloaked in a noun form. Hence, "an ongoing relationship" makes sense, but "an ongoing chair" does not.

2. *Find the hidden verb lurking inside.* When the term fits into the structure of "an ongoing..." then look inside it for a hidden verb. Inside "motivation" we have "motivate" or "move." Inside "self-esteem" we have the verb "esteem," which means to appraise. With some nominalizations, we may have to go back to the language out of which they came or back to the context from which they originated. Hence, inside "religion" or "religious" we have the verb "to bind back." Inside "soul" we have "breathe."

3. *Put the term back in verb form and restore the representations of action, movement, and process.* "Who relates to whom?" "What do you feel motivated or moved to do?" "How much would you like to accomplish that?" "What else appeals to you?"

#50 *The Problem Defining/Formulating Pattern*

Concept. When we construct a "problem" that we conceptually have no way out of, or when our problem formulation prevents a realistic solution, we can use this pattern to transform these limiting, constricting, and unsane maps. After all, "problems" only exist as linguistic constructions. Neither you nor I have ever seen a "problem." This represents another nominalization. And this one lures us to think of our "problem" as a thing, does it not? The map-language does not empower us to see, hear, or feel the specifics of any particular process. As a result, it seems so solid, permanent, unchangeable, etc. This describes the case with so many of the things with which we have difficulty.

Since such words refer to nothing "in the world," but everything "in the mind," first we have to recover the see-hear-feel referents. Then we have to move to our conceptual world of meaning (semantics). This enables us to recover our behavioral *complex equivalence* for "the problem."

For example, suppose someone complains about low "self-esteem." The Meta-model teaches us to **not** respond with "Yes, I know what you mean!" Instead, we might inquire about what see-hear-feel references they used in referencing this abstraction ("self-esteem") and what criteria, rules, values, etc., they used to make that determination. Look for the process. If the person meets their criteria, they will language themselves as "valuable, successful, right," etc. If they don't meet those criteria, they language themselves as "worthless, failure, without dignity and respect," etc.

Ultimately, *the person* (and only the individual person) makes the decision to *esteem or contempt* his or her "self". "I value myself when I drive a new car." "I devalue myself when I get poor grades." "I value myself when I get a raise." etc. Either way, the person **constructs** this semantic reality by defining, equating, and attributing meaning to certain experiences. With this strategy, people can de-construct the old formats and re-construct newer and more enhancing ones.

The Pattern

1. *Examine the "problem" in terms of the Meta-model distinctions.* Check for violations to well-formedness. These will show up as lack of precise terms (vagueness), over-generalizations (abstract words and terms), and distortions in meaning, causation, presupposition, etc.

With "low self-esteem" the person states the "problem" as a thing, as something he or she does not "have." This frames it as outside their area of control or response. Denominalize to recover the self-esteem-ing process, then explore that process. "For what reasons do you low self-esteem yourself? What would it feel like if you esteemed yourself? What stops you?"

2. *Run an ecology check on the "problems" formulation.* "Does it serve you well? Do you find low self-esteeming useful? How? In what way? How might it undermine your experiences? Does it make your life more of a party? Less of a party?"

3. *Examine the presuppositions in the "problem."* "Does the 'problem,' as defined, offer any solution? Or has it put you in a corner?" Languaging problems as static things, beyond anything you can affect or control, constructs a map for disempowering. Challenge dysfunctional presuppositions.

4. *Use the "as if" frame to explore possible new formulations of the problem.* "Suppose you act as if you have high self-esteem— how would that affect your life? Would that enable you to have a higher likelihood of success?"

Conclusion

NLP exists as *a model* of other models that provide specific content to "the structure of psychotherapy" (the "talking cure"). Accordingly, NLP highlights *how* language crucially and centrally affects human consciousness (thinking, emoting, experiencing, etc.). NLP also highlights the field of psycholinguistics through its central and originating model—*the Meta-model.*

The Meta-model offers an explanatory scheme for *how language works* and, more importantly, how to work with our own and others' languaging. NLP began with the Meta-model as its central methodology. Almost all of its technologies grew out of this core.

This model informs us about how we use language to create our mental maps of the world—and the mapping problems that we sometimes generate. Recognizing these mapping processes (deletion, generalization, and distortion) gives us a pathway to facilitate change in our model of the world, as well as the models of those with whom we communicate. Even more crucially, this model installs within us *a tentativeness about language.* As a consequence, we can overcome our "semantic reactions" to words and ideas, we can develop a "thoughtful" response to language as symbolic or semantic reality, and we can begin to use language as *only a map* and not reality.

Most of the patterns in this chapter depend upon an understanding of *the Meta-model of language.* In human affairs, *"magic"* can and does occur when people talk. This becomes especially true in the therapeutic context. It also holds just as true for the communication that occurs in close and intimate relationships where people talk about the things that really matter to them. With this model, we can now work more methodologically and systematically with our languaging as we communicate.

For more "magic" utilizing developments in General Semantics, see my (MH) recent work, *The Secrets Of Magic* (1998), which revisits *The Structure Of Magic.* In *Secrets,* I have updated the Meta-model by extending it with additional "missing" Meta-model distinctions gleaned from General Semantics and Cognitive-Behavioral psychology.

Afterword For Chapter 7

In the years since the appearance of the Meta-model, a great deal has changed in the field of linguistics. Grinder and Bandler originally developed the Meta-model from *the language patterns* that they heard and modeled from Fritz Perls and Virginia Satir, and later from Erickson. They did so in their original work using the tools of Transformational or Generative Grammar (TG)—hence the lengthy Appendix A on TG in their book, *The Structure Of Magic, Volume I.* They even noted the newer developments then occurring in Generative Semantics (p. 109, Note 6).

Actually, prior to that 1975 publication, TG had suffered what Harris (1993) called *The Linguistic Wars.* There he detailed the wars in Linguistics as newer "schools" arose to defeat Chomsky's (1957, 1965) Interpretative or TG. Harris also noted the death of Generative Semantics in the early 1980s.

Lakoff (1987) later explained why TG failed as a linguistic model. He described it in terms of the philosophical difference between a formal mathematical model and the way people actually think and process information—a constructivistic embodied grammar. Earlier, he, McCawley, Ross, Postal, et al., had taken Noam Chomsky's model and sought to find meaning in the Deep Structure. However, the more they pushed in that direction, the more they found irregularities, anomalies, and exceptions. And the more they moved in that direction, the more Chomsky backed off, went on the attack, and ultimately reformulated TG. He eventually eliminated Deep Structure as an explanatory device as he sought to explain all transformational rules exclusively in Surface Structure devices.

As TG became more problematic, both it and Generative Semantics gave way to other theories and models: Fauconnier's (1985) space grammar (later "mental space"), Langacker's massive two-volume *Foundations Of Cognitive Grammar* (1987, 1991), etc.

Where does this leave NLP and the Meta-model? *How* much does the Meta-model depend upon TG? To what extend does the Meta-model need the Deep and Surface Structure format?

Interestingly enough, the Meta-model actually does *not* depend on the TG model at all. Bandler and Grinder certainly did bring over much of the terminology of the Meta-model from TG (modals, universals, nominalizations, transderivational search, etc.—all come from linguistics). They also brought over the general two-level model of Deep and Surface Structure. Yet no subsequent author in NLP ever repeated the TG Appendix in *The Structure Of Magic.* This actually indicates how little NLP depends on TG.

The NLP Meta-model needs only a concept about "levels of abstraction" as postulated by Korzybski (1933/1994) in order to operate. Korzybski constructed his *levels of abstraction* from his studies of human neurology. His levels refer to the fact that the nervous system abstracts first at the sense-receptor level as it transforms the energy manifestations of the world and codes them into various neurological processes. Yet the nervous system does not stop there. It abstracts again from the cell activation at the end receptors and transmutes that "information" into bio-electric impulses which it sends to the central nervous center (the brain). Next it abstracts from those neurological processes and translates the impulses using various neuro-transmitter chemicals.

The Meta-model assumes such abstraction levels—that surface expressions differ from deeper or prior expressions by the abstracting processes. In this way, the Meta-model actually never had a marriage with TG—only an affair! In that fling, it only appropriated the language of linguistics.

Today in Cognitive Linguistics we see many new developments that I find much more fitting for the NLP model of representation, logical levels, frames and contexts. Langacker's (1991) work, *Image, Metaphor, and Concept* speaks about three central processes of mental representation.

Chapter 8

Thinking Patterns

Sorting Patterns That Govern Thinking

I could have had a moment of meta-thinking.

Michael Hall

Sometimes *the problems* that we struggle with, or that another person experiences, or that we experience with another person, occur in that invisible realm prior to, and "meta" to, *thinking itself.* In other words, the arena of tension, conflict, or difference involves our very **thinking patterns.** This raises several questions about this dimension of human experience, namely:

- **What** controls and determines *the way* we think in the first place?
- **What** governs our *style and mode* of thinking prior to the moment we actually "think?"
- **How many** *thinking or sorting styles* exist?
- **How** can we learn about and discern these invisible thinking styles?
- Once we identify them, **what** can we then do about them?

The form or structure of our thinking, as our *thinking style*, exists at a level above (or *meta*) to our thinking itself. In NLP, we designate these thinking styles as **Meta-programs**, i.e., programs above the content programs. These "programs" arise in human development as we use our consciousness in sorting, paying attention to, and processing information.

For example, we can pay attention to the *size* of a piece of information from the tiniest detail to the largest level meaning (detail —global). Those who regularly and systematically use the "detail" mode think from details to general understandings, use inductive thinking (they "chunk up" on the scale from specificity to abstraction). Those who typically think about "the big picture" (global meanings), move conceptually from "global" to specific. They reason deductively, rather than inductively. They "chunk down" the scale.

Another thinking pattern involves *matching or mismatching*. When some people process information, they sort for things that match. "What fits?" "How does this match what I already know?" Others mismatch. "How does this differ from what I already know?" "What doesn't fit here?" This Meta-program offers two different styles of thinking and leads to two ways of orienting oneself in the world. Now imagine how these two styles interface when people who use them marry! Though they may talk, they will probably each feel unheard and not validated. They will probably feel as if they don't talk "on the same wavelength" or channel.

Metaphorically, Meta-programs operate in human consciousness isomorphically to a computer's *operating system*. This suggests that the same inputted data will "mean" and evoke different things depending on the operating system of the computer (Windows, DOS, etc.). In human functioning, this leads to such questions as:

- What operating system does this particular person typically use?
- What other operating systems does this person sometimes revert to?
- What operating systems *drive* this person?
- What operating system would provide a better fit for this information?

Because we can "think" on several different levels, we develop Meta-programs. *Content* thinking describes **what** we think about— the details and context of our concern, "Where will we go for Thanksgiving this year?" *Process* thinking describes a higher logical level of thinking—the **way and style** of our thinking. See Figure 8.1 for a list of the NLP Meta-programs.

#51 Identifying And Pacing A Person's Meta-Programs

Concept. We all have, and use, various *sorting mechanisms* (i.e., Meta-programs) at a meta-level for paying attention to and processing information. By simply learning to notice and match the person's Meta-programs in our own communications, we have an express road for getting "on the same channel." Doing this will enable us to more effectively "enter into their world" and "speak their language." This will undoubtedly increase understanding, empathy, and rapport.

When we identify and pace Meta-programs in such contexts as teaching, presenting, training, selling, persuading, etc., we make our communication maximally effective. Why? Because we, in essence, *use the other person's style of thinking and reasoning* to package our message. This makes it easier for them to hear and understand. It allows us to adapt to their way of "making sense" of things.

The Pattern

1. *Move to a meta-position and notice the structure or style of the other's processing.* Use the Meta-program lists (Figure 8.1) and "run a diagnostic analysis" on the other's processing style. Check which Meta-programs the other person uses.

2. *Package back your words, ideas, and suggestions using the other person's Meta-program.* If you detect that the other person sorts for the global picture, match them by using global and general statements, rather than specifics and details. If they use the visual channel—use visual words, terms, and predicates, etc.

3. *Take into account your own Meta-programs.* Every one of our *driver* Meta-programs supports not only our strengths and skills, but also our weaknesses and blind spots. This arises because, as we tend to over-use our *driver* Meta-programs, we lose the flexibility of consciousness to shift to the other side of the continuum.

#52 *Recognizing And Challenging Limiting Meta-Programs*

Concept. If the way we interact in a conversation seems problematic and unproductive, it may indicate *mis-matched Meta-programs* or some cognitive distortion. We find cognitive distortions in the twelve distinctions of the Meta-model. These show up as "ill-formedness" in expression, structure, or meaning. Typically, these become especially unproductive when we over-use them. We have noted some of the Meta-model "violations" in the list of cognitive distortions (Figure 8.3).

Because the *Meta-programs* describe how we think (or sort), they refer to our *thinking styles.* As such, Meta-programs create difficulty for us when we over-use them or use them in inappropriate contexts (e.g., when they become *driver* Meta-programs).

The Pattern

1. *Move to a meta-position and listen for style or structure of someone's thinking (yours or another's).* By directing our consciousness above the content level of the messages, we will (or can) begin to notice the various styles and processes that we and others use in thinking and communicating. Identify the operating Meta-programs by "going meta" and using the Meta-program list (Figure 8.1).

Keep going meta. Almost everybody has problems *staying out of content,* especially at first. When this happens, rest yourself comfortably in the knowledge that this indicates your humanity, not that you have something wrong with your meta-thinking skills! Most of us find content juicy. It easily captures our attention. Resist it with grace by floating above the content.

2. *Evaluate the effectiveness of that Meta-program given the content, context, or subject.* Not all Meta-programs work equally well in all contexts. Music appreciation necessitates using an auditory modality, whereas in art appreciation we need the visual modality.

Whenever we run a "quality control" analysis, this by necessity calls on the Meta-program of sorting for differences— mismatching what doesn't fit. But that meta-program will not work very efficiently for bonding with a loved one!

3. *Invite the person* (yourself or another) *to a Meta-position to run an ecology check on the use of that Meta-program in that context.* "How useful does it seem to you to use this Meta-program of Association when you think about traumatic memories?" "How effective does it make you to run an other-referent authority sort when you need to center yourself in your own values and beliefs?"

Figure 8.1

NLP Meta-Programs (Processing/Sorting Styles)

Chunk Size:
 __ General: gestalt; deductive thinker—the big picture, general principles.
 __ Specific: detail; inductive thinker—the specific details of something.

Match/ Mismatch:
 __ Sameness: what does it match and seem similar?
 __ Difference: how does it differ? How does it mismatch with what I already know?

Representation System:
 __ Visual: pictures, movies, images.
 __ Auditory: sounds, volumes, tones, pitches.
 __ Kinesthetic: sensations, feelings, movement, temperature, pressure.
 __ Auditory digital: words, language, specific statements.
 __ Gustatory/olfactory: taste, smell.

Value Direction:
 __ Toward: future possibilities, values one feels drawn towards.
 __ Away From: past assurance. Dis-values that one feels repelled from.

Information Gathering Style:
 __ Sensors: uptime. Empiricism, pragmatism. Sensory-based information accessible by the senses.
 __ Intuitors: downtime. Visionary, rationalism, meanings, values, internal knowings.

Adaptation Style:
 __ Judgers: wanting to make life and events adapt to oneself, to take charge.
 __ Perceivers: wanting to adjust and adapt to life and events, to float through.

Operational Style:
 __ Options: alternatives, other ways to do things, choices; random.
 __ Procedures: the rules and steps for doing something the right way, sequential.

Reactive Style:
 __ Inactive: not acting much at all in response to something.
 __ Reflective: acting by reflecting, thinking, meditating on it.
 __ Active: taking action, jumping to do something.

Reference Frame: (Authority Sort):
  __ Self-referent (internal): referencing from what one thinks, feels, and wants oneself.
  __ Other-referent (external): referencing from what others think, feel and want.

Modal Operator (modus operandi)
  __ Necessity: must, should, have to. World of rules and constraints.
  __ Possibility: could, would, might, may, will. World of options, choices.
  __ Desire: want, desire. Mode of operating according to wants.
  __ Impossibility: can't, shouldn't, must not. World and mode of constraints.
  __ Choice: want, will, choose. Mode of personal choice and will.

Experience of Emotion/Body:
  __ Associated: emotionally experiencing the information, in state, first person.
  __ Dissociated: thinking *about* the information, second person, objective, computer mode.

Convincer Sort (Believability):
  __ Visual: looks right (observer).
  __ Auditory: sounds right (hearer).
  __ Kinesthetic: feels right (feeler).
  __ Auditory digital: makes sense (thinker).
  __ Experiential: experiencer (doer).

Preference Filter (primary interest):
  __ People (who): enjoys people, wants to spend time with people.
  __ Place (where): sorts for environment.
  __ Object (what): thing and task oriented.
  __ Activity (how): sorts for achievement, accomplishment.
  __ Time (when): highly conscious of when.

Goal Sort:
  __ Optimizing: does best one can and leaves it at that. Easy on self about errors.
  __ Perfectionism: demanding and pushing self to do better, never satisfied.
  __ Skepticism: refuses to set goals, disbelieves in its value.

Value Buying Sort:
  __ Cost: money.
  __ Convenience: ease, comfort.
  __ Time: speed, quickness.

Time Tenses
__ Past: back then.
__ Present: now.
__ Future: one of these days.

Time Experience:
__ In Time: random, spontaneous, lost in time.
__ Through time: sequential, high level of awareness about time.

People Preference:
__ Extrovert: recharges personal batteries socially, around people.
__ Introvert: recharges personal batteries by oneself.

Affiliation Filter:
__ Independent.
__ Dependent.
__ Team player.
__ Manager.

Satir Stances (communication mode):
__ Blamer (accusatory).
__ Placator (pleasing).
__ Computer (dissociating).
__ Distractor (crazymaking).
__ Leveler (assertive).

Response Style:
__ Congruent: response fits with stimulus.
__ Incongruent: response does not fit with stimulus.
__ Polarity: response goes to the opposite pole, complete mismatch.
__ Competitive: response tries to win.
__ Meta: response takes meta-position and relates to or about the stimulus.

More Meta-Programs

In this work we have only given a very brief description of the Meta-programs and the significance of the distinctions. Several books provide a much more thorough presentation. See James and Woodsmall (1988), Shelle Rose-Charvet (1995), Woodsmall and Woodsmall (1997), and Hall and Bodenhamer (1997). I (MH) have recently written a major work on Meta-programs with Dr. Bob Bodenhamer, *Figuring Out People: Design Engineering Using Meta-Programs*, and extended the list to fifty-one, and have included that list here.

Figure 8.2

Meta-Programs And Meta Meta-Programs

| **Processing** | **Feeling** | **Choosing** |
Cognitive/Perceptual	**Emotional/Somatic**	**Conative/Willing**
#1 Chunk Size *General/Specific* *Detail/Global*	#13 Emotional Coping *Passivity/Aggression/* *Dissociated*	#20 Motivation Direction *Toward/Away From* *Approach/Avoidance*
#2 Relationship *Matching/Mismatching* *Same/Difference*	#14 Frame of Reference *Internal/External* *Self-Referent/Other-Referent*	#21 Conation Adaptation *Options/Procedures*
#3 Representation System *VAKOG* A_d	#15 Emotional State *Associated/Dissociated* *Feeling/Thinking*	#22 Adaptation *Judging/Perceiving* *Controlling/Floating*
#4 Information Gath. *Uptime/Downtime*	#16 Somatic Responses *Active/Reflective/Inactive*	#23 Modal Operators *Necessity/Possibility/Desire* *Stick/Carrot*
#5 Epistemology Sort *Sensors/Intuitors*	#17 Convincer/Believability *Looks, Sounds, Feels Right*	#24 Preference *People/Place/Things*
#6 Perceptual Categ. *Black-White/Continuum*	*Makes Sense* #18 Emotional Direction	#25 Adapting to Expectations
#7 Scenario Thinking *Best/Worst* *Optimists/Pessimists*	*Uni-directional/* *Multi-directional*	*Perfection/Optimitizing/* *Skepticism*
#8 Durability *Permeable/Impermeable*	#19 Emotional Exuberance *Desurgency/Surgency* *Timidity/Boldness*	#26 Value Buying *Cost/Convenience/* *Quality/Time*
#9 Focus Quality *Screeners/Non-Screeners*		#27 Responsibility *Over-Resp/Under-Respon.* *Balanced*
#10 Philosophical Direction *Why/How Origins /Solutions*		#28 People Convincer Sort *Distrusting/Trusting*
#11 Reality Structure Sort *Aristotelian/ Non-Aristotelian* *(Static/Process)*		
#12 Communication Channel Sort *Verbal-Digital/Non-Verbal-Analogue/Balanced*		

Responding
Outputting/Behaving

#29 Battery Rejuvenation
Extrovert/Ambivert/ Introvert

#30 Affiliation/Management
Independent/Team Player/Manager

#31 Communication Stance
Blamer/Placator/Distracter/
Computer/Leveler

#32 General Response
Congruent/Incongruent
Competitive/Cooperative; Polarity/Meta

#33 Somatic Response
Active/Reflective/Both/Inactive

#34 Work Preference
Things/Systems/People / Information

#35 Comparison
Quantitative/Qualitative

#36 Knowledge Source
Modeling/Conceptualizing
Experiencing/Authorizing

#37 Completion/ Closure
Closure/Non-Closure

#38 Social Presentation
Shrewd-Artful/Genuine-Artless

#39 Hierarchical Dominance Sort
Power/ Affiliation/ Achievement

Conceptualizing/Semanticizing
Kantian Categories

#40 Values
List of Values

#41 Temper to Instruction
Strong-Willed/Compliant

#42 Self-Esteem
High SE/Low SE

#43 Self-Confidence
Specific Skills

#44 Self-Experience
Body/ Mind/Emotions/Roles/Choices

#45 Self-Integrity
Conflicted Incongruity/Integrated Harmony

#46 "Time" Tenses
Past/Present/Future

#47 "Time" Experience
In Time/Through Time

#48 "Time" Access
Sequential/Random

#49 Ego Strength
Stable/Unstable

#50. Morality
Strong/Weak Superego

#51 Causational Sort:
Causeless/Linear CE/Multi-CE/
Personal CE/External

Meta-Programs Elicitation

One common and very powerful way to use Meta-programs involves asking questions that elicit a person's Meta-programs. In the following list, we have reproduced the elicitation questions from *Figuring Out People* (1997).

1. "When you pick up a book or think about attending a workshop, what do you pay attention to first—the big picture, book cover, or specific details about its value?"

    Chunk Size
    __Global
    __Specific

    "If we decided to work together on a project, would you first want to know what we generally will do or would you prefer to hear about a lot of the specifics?"

2. "How do you 'run your brain' when you first attempt to understand something new to you? Do you look first for similarities and match up the new with what you already know? Or do you first check out the differences? Or do you first do one pattern and then immediately do the other?"

    Relationship Sort
    __Matching/Same
    __Mismatching/
    Differences

3. "When you think about something or learn something new, which sensory channel do you prefer?"

    Representation Style
    __Visual
    __Auditory
    __Kinesthetic
    __Language A_d

4 & 5. "When you listen to a speech or conversation, do you tend to hear the specific data given or do you intuit what the speaker must mean and/or intend?" "Do you want to hear proof and evidence since you take more interest in your intuition about it?" "Which do you find more important —the actual or the possible?" "Upon what basis do you make most of your decisions—the practical or abstract possibilities?"

    Epistemology Sort
    __Sensors/
    Uptime
    __Intuitors/
    Downtime

6. "When you think about things or make decisions, do you tend to operate in black-and-white categories or does your mind go to the steps and stages that lie in between? Which do you value most?"

    Perceptual Style
    __Black-White
    __Continuum

7. "When you look at a problem, do you tend first to consider the worst case scenario or the best?...the problems and difficulties or the opportunities and positive challenges?"

    Attribution Style
    __Optimist
    __Pessimist

8. "As you begin to think about some of your mental constructs, your ideas of success and failure, of love and forgiveness, of relationships and work, of your personal qualities...do you find the representations of what you know permanent or unstable? How can you tell?" "Think about something that you know without a doubt—about yourself." "Now think of something that you know but with doubts and questions..."

    Durability
    __Permeable
    __Impermeable

9. "When you think about the kind of places where you can study or read, can you do this everywhere or do you find that some places seem too noisy or have too many of some other stimuli?" "Describe your favorite environment for concentrating on something?" "How distractible do you find yourself generally in life?"

Focus Quality
__Screening
__Non-Screening

10. "When you think about a subject (whether a problem or not), do you first think about causation, source, and origins (why), or do you think about use, function, direction, destiny (how)?"

Philosophical Direction
__Origins/ Why
__Solutions/ How

11. "When you think about reality, do you tend to think about it as something permanent and solid made up of things or do you think of it as a dance of electrons, fluid, ever-changing, made up of processes?"

Reality Structure Sort
__Aristotelian- Static
__Non-Aristotelian Process

12. "When you think about communicating with somebody, what do you tend to give more importance to—*what* they say or how they say it?" "When you communicate, do you pay more attention to the words and phrases that you use or to your tone, tempo, volume, eye contact, etc.?" "When you hear someone say something that seems incongruent with how they express it, and you don't know which message to go with, which do you tend to favor as the more 'real' message?"

Communication Channel Sort
__Verbal/ Digital
__Non-Verbal/Analogue
__Balanced

13. "When you feel threatened, or challenged, by some stress... do you immediately respond, on the emotional level, by wanting to get away from it or to go at it?" Invite the person to tell you about several specific instances when he or she faced a high stress situation. Do you detect a "go at" or "go away from" response to it?

Emotional Coping
__Passivity
__Aggressive

14. "Where do you put most of your attention or reference: on yourself or on others (or something external to yourself)?"

Frame of Reference
__Self-Reference
__Other-Reference

15. "Think about an event in a work situation that once gave you trouble..." "What experience surrounding work would you say has given you the most pleasure or delight...?" "How do you normally feel while at work?" "When you make a decision, do you rely more on reason and logic or personal values or something else?"

Emotional State
__Associated
__Dissociated

16. "When you come into a new situation, do you usually act quickly after sizing it up or do you do a detailed study of all the consequences before acting?"

Somatic Response
__Active
__Reflective
__Inactive

17. "What leads you to *accept* the believability of a thing? Something about it *looks right* (V⁺), *sound right* (A'), *makes sense* (Ad), *feels right* (K⁺) to you?"

Convincer Sort
__Looks Right
__Sounds Right
__Feels Right
__Makes Sense

18. "When you think about a time when you experienced an emotional state (positive or negative), does that bleed over and affect some or all of your other emotional states, or does it stay pretty focused so that it relates to its object?"

Emotional Direction
__Uni-directional
__Multi-directional

19. "When you think about a situation at work or in your personal affairs that seems risky or involving the public's eye, what thoughts-and-feelings immediately come to mind?"

Emotional Exuberance
__Desurgency
__Surgency

20. "What do you want in a job (relationship, car, etc.)? What do you want to do with your life?"

Motivation Direction
__Toward Values
__Away From

21. "Why did you choose your car?" (or job, town, etc.).

Conation Adaptive
__Options
__Procedures

22. "Do you like to live life spontaneously as the spirit moves you or according to a plan?" "Regarding doing a project together, would you prefer we first outline and plan it out in an orderly fashion or would you prefer to just begin to move into it and flexibly adjust to things as we go?"

Adaptation Style
__Judging
__Perceiving

23. "How did you get up this morning? What did you say to yourself just before you got up?"

Modal Operators
__Necessity
__Possibility

24. "What would you find as really important in how you choose to spend your next two-week vacation?" "What kinds of things, people, activities, etc., would you want present for you to evaluate it as really great?" "Tell me about your favorite restaurant."

Preference Sort
__People
__Place
__Things
__Activity
__Information

25. "Tell me about a goal that you have set, and how did you go about making it come true?" "If you set a goal today to accomplish something of significance, how would you begin to work on it?"

Adapting to Expect.
__Perfection
__Optimizing
__Skepticism

26. "What do you tend to primarily concern yourself with—the price, convenience, time, or quality, or some combination of these, when you consider making a purchase?"

Value Buying
__Cost
__Convenience
__Quality
__Time

27. "When you think about having and owning responsibility for something in a work situation or personal relationship, what thoughts and emotions occur to you?" "Has someone ever held you responsible for something that went wrong that felt very negative to you?" "What positive experiences can you remember about someone holding you responsible for something?"

Responsibility
__Over-Respons.
__Under-Respons.

28. "When you think about meeting someone new, do you immediately have a sense of trust and openness to the person, or thoughts and feelings of distrust, doubt, questions, jealousy, insecurity, etc.?"

People Convincer
__Distrusting
__Trusting

29. "When you feel the need to recharge your batteries, do you prefer to do it alone or with others?"

Battery Rejuvenat.
__Extrovert
__Ambivert
__Introvert

30. (i) "Do you know what you need in order to feel and
function more successfully at work?"
(ii) "Do you know what someone else needs in order to feel and
function more successfully?"
(iii) "Do you find it easy or not to tell a person that?"

Affiliation Sort
__Independence
__Team Player
__Manager

31. "How do you typically communicate in terms of
placating, blaming, computing, distracting, and leveling?"

Communication Stances
__Blamer
__Placator
__Distracter
__Computer
__Leveler

32. "When you come into a situation, how do you usually
respond? Do you respond i) with a sense of feeling and acting in a
congruent and harmonious way with your thoughts-and-feelings or,
do you respond with a sense of not feeling or acting in a congruent
and harmonious way with your thoughts and feelings?
Do you respond ii) with a sense of cooperation with the subject
matter, or a feeling of disagreement? Or iii) do you prefer to
go above the immediate context and have thoughts about the situation?

General Response
__Congruent
__Incongruent
__Competitive
__Cooperative
__Polarity
__Meta

33. "When you come into a situation, do you usually act
quickly after sizing it up or do you engage in a detailed study of all
of the consequences, and then act, or how do you tend to typically
respond?"

Somatic Response
__Active
__Reflective
__Both
__Inactive

34. "Tell me about a work situation (or environment) in which
you felt the happiest, some one-time-event."

Work Preference
__Things
__Systems
__People
__Information

35. "How would you evaluate your work as of today?" "How would
you evaluate things in your relationship?" "How do you know the
quality of your work? "Upon what basis do you say that?"

Comparison
__Quantitative
__Qualitative

36. "What source of knowledge do you consider authoritative and
most reliable?" "From where would you gather reliable information
that you can trust?" "When you decide that you need to do
something where do you get the information to do it from?"

Knowl.Source
__Modeling
__Conceptualizing
__Experiencing
__Authorizing

37. "If, in the process of studying something, you had to break
off your study and leave it, would this settle well or feel
very disconcerting?" "When someone begins a story but doesn't
complete it, how do you feel about that?" "When you get involved
in a project, do you find yourself more interested in the beginning,
middle, or end of the project?" "What part of a project do you enjoy most?"

Closure
__Closure
__Non-Closure

38. "When you think about going out into a social group or out   *Social Present.*
in public, how do you generally handle yourself? Do you really   __Shrewd/Artful
care about your social image and want to avoid any negative   __Genuine/Artless
impact on others so that they recognize your tact, politeness,
social graces, etc.? Or do you not really care about any of that and
just want "to be yourself," natural, forthright, direct, transparent, etc.?"

39. "Evaluate your motives in interacting with others in   *Hierarchy Dominance*
terms of your motivational preferences between Power   __ Power
(dominance, competition, politics), Affiliation (relationship,   __ Affiliation
courtesy, cooperation) and Achievement (results, goals, objectives) __ Achievement
and, using 100 points as your scale, distribute those hundred points
among these three styles of handling "power.""

40. "As you think about this X (a thing, person, event, experience,   *Value Sort*
etc.), what do you evaluate as valuable, important, or significant   List Values
about this?"

41. "Can someone 'tell' you something?" "How do you   *Temper to Instruction*
think and feel when you receive 'instructions?'" "How well can   __Strong-Will
you 'tell' or 'order' yourself to do something and you carry it   __Complaint
out without a lot of internal resistance about it?"

42. "Do you think of your value as a person as conditional or   *Self-esteeming*
unconditional?" "When you esteem yourself as valuable,   __Unconditional
worthwhile, having dignity, etc., do you do it based upon something __Conditional
or do you base it upon the fact of your humanity or that God made
you in his image and likeness?"

43. "As you think about some of the things that you can do well   *Self-confidence*
and that you know, without a doubt, you can do well and may even   __High SC
take pride in your ability to do them well, make a list of those   __Low SC
items." "How confident do you feel about your skill in doing these things?"

44. "How do you experience yourself in terms of your mind,   *Self-experience*
emotions, body, roles?"   __Mind
                                                                     __Emotions
                                                                     __Body
                                                                     __Roles

45. "When you think about how well or how poorly you live up to   *Self-integrity*
your ideals and in actualizing your ideal self, do you feel pretty   __Conflicted
integrated, congruent, doing a good job in living true to your values __Integrated
and visions or do you feel torn, conflicted, un-integrated, incongruent?"

46. "Where do you put most of your attention—on the past, present,   *Time Tenses*
or future? Or, have you developed an atemporal attitude so that you __Past
don't attend to 'time' at all?"   __Present
                                                                     __Future

47. "Do you represent 'time' as coming into you and intersected   *Time Experience*
with your body, or outside of yourself and body?"   __In Time
                                                                     __Through Time

48. "Do you represent 'time' as coming into you and intersected   *Time Access*
with your body, or outside of yourself and body?"   __Sequential
                                                                     __Random

49. "When you think about some difficulty arising in everyday life, a disappointment, problem, frustrating difficulty that will block your progress, etc., what usually comes to mind?" "How do you typically respond to internal needs or external hardships?"

Ego Strength Sort
__Unstable
__Stable

50. "When you think about some misbehavior that you engage in, what thoughts-and-feelings come to you when you realize that you had acted in an inappropriate way that violated legitimate values?" "When you think about messing up, doing something embarrassing, stupid, socially inept, etc., what thoughts-and-feelings come to mind?"

Morality Sort
__ Weak Super-ego
__ Strong Super-ego

51. Ask any question that evokes some kind of causational presupposition. "When you think about what caused you to work at the job that you work at, how do you explain that?" "What brought the current situation of your life to exist as it does?" "What makes people behave as they do?" "How did your relationship get in that state?" "Why did you get divorced?"

Causation
__Causeless
__Linear C-E
__Multi- C-E
__Personal C-E
__External C-E
__Magical
__Correlation

#53 *The Meta-Programs Change Pattern*

Concept. Our Meta-programs do not come "written in stone." We *can* change them. In fact, in the normal process of growing and developing over our life span—we do change some of them. These stabilizing ways of thinking develop over time in various life contexts and become habitualized. So as we learn them, we can also unlearn them and develop more effective thinking styles.

Robbins (1986) says that one way to change a Meta-program involves "consciously deciding to do so." Yet most of us never give a thought to the mental software, and so we simply don't change it. This highlights the fact that we must first recognize and detect our operational system, and then use that awareness as an opportunity for making new choices.

Since Meta-programs inform our brain about *what to delete*—if we move toward values, then we delete awareness about what we move away from. If we sort for the details, we delete the big picture. By directing our awareness to what we normally delete, we can shift focus and change our operating systems. The following comes from Hall and Bodenhamer (1997).

The Pattern

1. *Identify the Meta-program* that currently governs your sorting, processing, and attending. Specifically identify when, where, and how you use this Meta-program that does not serve you well. How does it undermine your effectiveness?

2. *Describe fully the Meta-programs you would prefer to use as your default style of sorting in a given context.* What meta-level processing would you prefer to "run your perceiving and valuing?" Specify when, where, and how you would like this Meta-program to govern your consciousness.

3. *Try it out.* Imaginatively adopt the new Meta-program and pretend to use it in sorting, perceiving, attending, etc. Notice how it seems, feels, works, etc., in described contexts where you think it would serve you better. It may seem a little "weird" at first, but consider its strangeness due simply to your unfamiliarity with looking at the world with that particular perceptual filter. Notice what feelings you experience while using this.

If you know someone who uses this Meta-program, explore with them their experience until you can take second position to it. Then step into that position fully so that you can see the world out of that person's Meta-program eyes, hearing what he or she hears, self-talking as he or she engages in self-dialogue, and feeling what that person feels.

4. *Run an ecology check on the Meta-program change.* Go meta to an even higher level and consider what this Meta-program will do to you and for you in terms of perception, valuing, believing, behaving, etc. What kind of a person would it make you? What effect would it have on various aspects of your life?

5. *Give yourself permission to install it for a period of time.* Frequently, a person can "install" a Meta-program filter by granting oneself permission to use it. After you give yourself such permission, go inside and see if any part objects. If no, then future pace. If yes, then reframe using the objection.

For example, suppose you have typically used the other- refer-encing Meta-program (#14) and have given yourself permission to shift to self-referencing, yet, when you do, you hear an internal voice that sounds like your mother's voice in tone and tempo, "It's selfish to think about yourself. Don't be so selfish, you will lose all of your friends."

This voice objects on two accounts: selfishness and disapproval that leads to loneliness. So rephrase your permission to take these objections into account. "I give myself permission to see the world referencing centrally from myself—my values, beliefs, wants, etc., knowing that my values include loving, caring, and respecting others and that this will keep me balanced by considering the effect of my choices on others."

6. *Future pace the Meta-program.* Practice, in your imagination, using this Meta-program and do so until it begins to feel comfortable and familiar.

Troubleshooting. If you have difficulty, then do this procedure on your Time-line. Float *above* yourself and your line to your meta Time-line, then *float back* along the line into your past until you come to one or several of the key experiences wherein you began using the old Meta-program.

Then ask yourself, "If you knew when you originally made the choice to *operate from the other-referent (name the Meta-program you want to change)*, would that have been before, after, or during birth?

Use one of the Time-line processes to neutralize the old emotions, thoughts, beliefs, decisions, etc.: the visual-kines-thetic dissociation technique, decision destroyer pattern, etc. Once you have cleared out the old pattern, you can install the new Meta-program.

#54 *Identifying And Disputing Cognitive Distortions*

Concept. Another set of distinctions comes from Rational-Emotive Behavioral Therapy (REBT). Albert Ellis and Aaron Beck have specified *thinking errors* or *cognitive distortions*. These specific and unproductive ways of reasoning (at the process level) inevitably lead to problematic responses. We have made a list of the REBT cognitive distortions in Figure 8.3 with a brief description of each.

The field of Cognitive-Behavioral psychology has devoted much attention and interest in specifying these cognitive distortions. The following list of cognitive distortions identifies thinking patterns similar in some ways to the Meta-programs and to the ill-formedness of thought in the Meta-model in Figure 8.3. Yet these differ in some significant ways. Ellis and Beck emphasized how these cognitive distortions create *mapping blindness and dysfunction*. Again, we do not plan to take the time here to fully explain each pattern, so we refer you to Ellis and Harper (1975) and Beck (1983) for fuller reading. We list them here as suggestive of other distinctions to make with regard to recognizing and challenging them when they contaminate our thinking processes.

Figure 8.3

Cognitive Distortions As Disempowering Thinking Patterns

Patterns Of Generalization

1. **Over-Generalizing:** Jumping to conclusions on little evidence or without facts.

2. **All-Or-Nothing Thinking:** Polarizing at extremes—black-and-white thinking. Either-or thinking that posits options as two-valued choices.

3. **Labeling:** Name-calling that uses over-generalizations which allow one to dismiss something via the label, or to not make important distinctions, or that classifies a phenomenon in such a way that we do not engage in good reality-testing.

Patterns Of Distortion

4. **Blaming:** Think in an accusatory style, transferring blame, guilt, and responsibility for a problem to someone or something else.

5. **Mind-reading:** Projecting thoughts, feelings, intuitions onto others without checking out one's guesses with the person, over-trusting one's "intuitions" and not granting others the right to have the last word about their internal thoughts, feelings, intentions, etc.

6. **Prophesying:** Projecting negative outcomes into the future without seeing alternatives or possible ways to proactively intervene, usually a future pacing of fatalistic and negative outcomes.

7. **Emotionalizing:** Using one's emotions for filtering information. This style assumes an over-valuing of "emotions" as an information gathering mechanism; involves reacting emotionally to things rather than seeking objective information and using one's reasoning powers.

8. **Personalizing:** Perceiving circumstances, especially the actions of others as specifically targeted toward oneself in a personal way, perceiving the world through ego-centric filters that whatever happens relates to, speaks about, or references oneself!

9. **Awfulizing:** Imagining the worst possible scenario and then amplifying it with a non-referencing word, "awful" as in, "This is awful!"

10. **Should-ing:** Putting pressure on oneself (and others) to conform to "divine" rules about the world and life, then expressing such in statements that involve "should" and "must."

11. **Filtering**: Over-focusing on one facet of something to the exclusion of everything else so that one develops a tunnel-vision perspective and can see only "one thing." Typically, people use this thinking style to filter out positive facets, thereby leaving a negative perception.

12. **Can't-ing:** Imposing linguistic and semantic limits on oneself and others from a "mode of impossibility," and expressing this using the "can't" word.

Empowering Thinking Patterns

To counter the ways that cognizing (thinking) can go astray and become *distorted* (ill-formed) so that we create poor, inaccurate, and dysfunctional maps of the territory, the following list suggests more empowering cognitive ordering. A thorough grounding and training in the meta-model leads to these kinds of thinking patterns. These patterns forecast a more scientific way of thinking.

Figure 8.4

Empowering Thinking Patterns

1. **Contextual thinking (Index thinking/ Inductive thinking):** Inquire about the context of information and index it according to what, when, where, which, how, who, and why. Use the Meta-model challenges for unspecified nouns, verbs, relational terms, etc.

2. **Both-and thinking:** Reality-test to determine if a situation truly functions in an either/or way. If not, then process information in terms of a continuum. Inquire whether the two seemingly contradictory options actually exist as they represent different ways, times, circumstances, etc.

3. **Reality-testing/Appreciative thinking:** Test the reality of the experience: to what extent, in what way, etc., does someone deem something "bad, undesirable, and unwanted?" Meta-model the criteria/value words. Denominalize the words to find the hidden verbs and the evaluative process within. Consider the things that you do appreciate and enjoy.

4. **Denominalizing thinking (Deductive thinking):** Reality-test to determine how a label functions: accurately, usefully, productively, too generally. Denominalize the nouns and pseudo-nouns that make thinking and language fuzzy. Identify the evaluative process that turned the action into a noun.

5. **Systemic thinking (Responsibility to/for thinking):** Reality-test to determine the pattern of causation. Distinguish linear causation from the multifaceted nature of systemic causation. Access a person's "ability" to respond, in what way, under what circumstances, etc. Distinguish between each person's responsibilty **for** (personal accountability) and **to** (relationships).

6. **Information-gathering thinking:** This involves using one's thoughts, feelings, and intuitions to gather information to find the facts and then to check the conclusions. Use the basic Meta-model question, "How do you know?"

7. **Tentative predictive thinking (Consequential thinking; Outcome thinking):** Gather high quality information about the factors, causes, forces, trends, etc., that come together to create an event or phenomenon. Keep an open mind about ways of intervening and altering that destiny. Look at consequences of certain actions, etc.

8. **Critical thinking and meta-thinking:** Think critically and analytically about the multi-causational nature of human emotions and back-track to the thoughts out of which the emotions arose. Think above and beyond the immediate content to the patterns, processes, and structures of the content.

9. **Reality-test thinking about the "shoulds":** Challenge the word "should" by discovering what rule or law orders or demands such. If you can find no law, invite the thinker to shift to desire thinking, "I would prefer that..." "I would like..."

10. **Depersonalizing thinking (Dissociative thinking; Responsibility to/for thinking):** Reality-test to see if the content or context truly deals with and references you in a personal way. If not, then code information in a third-person perspective rather than in first-person. Learn to empathize without sympathizing.

11. **Possibility thinking (Reality-testing; Indexing thinking):** Reality-test the term "can't" to distinguish physical or psychological can'ts, then shift to possibility thinking. Meta-model by asking about the constraints, "What stops you?" "What would it feel like, look like, or sound like, if you could?"

The Pattern

1. *Identify the cognitive distortions in a presentation of a difficulty or limitation.* Use the list in Figure 8.3 to check for cognitive distortions. Specify all of the ones that create problems and difficulties for you or another person.

2. *Check out the cognitive distortion by reflecting it back to the person.* "It sounds as though the way you have thought about this involves awfulizing. Does it seem accurate as you step back from it and examine it?" "How would you characterize this pattern of thought?"

3. *Invite the thinker/processor to a meta-position.* Does this pattern of thinking reflect one that you (or I) typically use? How long have you used this cognitive distortion in sorting through things? Has it served you well? In what way? In what way may it have undermined your sense of well-being and accurate processing? What more useful way of processing this information would you like to use?

4. *Challenge and dispute the distortion.* Argue against personalizing, awfulizing, should-ing, etc. By identifying and arguing against these cognitive patterns, we bring them out into the light where we can deal with them. This breaks their power of working outside our consciousness.

5. *Replace the cognitive distortions with some empowering thinking patterns.* Use Figure 8.4 to prompt you with some of these more enhancing ways of thinking.

Conclusion

We all have problems "thinking." And so we should. After all, as long as we live and function as fallible beings, we will experience fallibility, limitations, irrationality, etc. in our thinking and reasoning skills. Further, as long as we exist as somatic and emotional beings, we can expect our emotions, drives, and impulses to frequently rise up and get in the way of clear thinking, problem solving, and decision making.

Yet this very awareness of our fallibility provides a tempering grace. It enables us to take a meta-position to our thinking—to meta-think about our thinking. From this perceptual position, we can then run an ecology test, do some reality testing, and thereby check out our thinking. In this way, we can have our thinking— rather than it having us!

Chapter 9

Meanings And Semantics

Patterns For Enhancing Neuro-Semantic Reality

The greatest revolution of our generation is the discovery that human beings, by changing their inner attitudes of their minds, can change the outer aspects of their lives.

William James

Having explored our "parts," our identity, our mind-body states of consciousness and the language that drives them, we now move to the weird and wonderful, zany and neurotic world of *meaning*. As **a semantic class of life** (Korzybski) we live, emote, experience, rejoice, and suffer because of meanings.

Yet **meaning**, as such, does not exist in the world. It never has, it never will. In fact, it cannot. *Meaning* (another nominalization) arises from the interaction of the human mind with things (or with other meanings). It takes a "mind" for meaning to emerge (meaning results from "minding"). And in human affairs, it takes a human mind or consciousness to create meaning. The original term from which *meaning* arose goes back to a German term that designated "holding" something like an idea or representation "before the mind."

The Cognitive-Behavioral model quotes as a proverb a saying uttered in the first century by the Stoic philosopher Epictetus as he wrote in *Enchiridion*.

Men are not disturbed by things, but by the views they take of them.

Epictetus

The great majority of our experiences, distresses, joys, neuroses, ecstasies, etc., arise from the experience of "meaning." We attribute this or that meaning to something: to ourselves, others, the world, etc., and via that attributional process we create our semantic reality—nay, our *neuro-semantic reality.*

In this chapter, we separate the dimensions of *meaning* for special attention. The map that codes meaning may need changing, or reframing. Accordingly, we begin with the reframing patterns.

#55 The Content Reframing Pattern

Concept. Meaning arises in the following way. After birth we begin to move through the world. As we do, we first encounter empirical see-hear-feel things and events. We then represent them in our minds using our sensory-based RS. But we don't leave it at that. We inevitably bring *higher level abstractions* (coded in language and higher-level symbols) to bear upon our representations. And when we do, we create a frame.

This *frame of reference* then creates and defines our meanings. Thus begins neuro-semantic reality. What does "meaning" *mean?* Since meaning does not occur in the world, but only in a human mind-body, meaning refers to **the linkage between things external** (or internal) **with internal "thoughts-and-emotions."** What does anything mean then? It all depends. It depends upon...

- the person making the linkage
- the context within which the person makes the linkage
- the mind-emotions evoked in the linkage
- the person's learning history
- the meanings/messages sent by others or set up in the environment by others (cultural meanings)
- the state the person immediately comes from
- etc.

This highlights the complexity of meaning, does it not? Who would have thought that *meaning* could mean so much and could depend upon so many contingencies and upon so many different contexts? Normally, we don't even think about such things. More typically, we tend to think that a thing "means what it means." No one ever explained all of this to us. We might have even assumed that "meaning" somehow existed in the dictionary apart from a meaning-maker!

Yet because **meaning** actually emerges from our thinking, evaluating, explaining, attributing, believing, interpreting (coded in our neuro-linguistics) along with numerous contexts (cultural, personal, somatic, etc.), *meaning functions as one of the most plastic processes around.* In other words:

- anything can mean almost anything
- nothing can mean nothing
- whatever meaning you attribute to anything exists as unique, idiosyncratic, and not precisely shared
- we have to codify our meanings to preserve them
- we can never give anything the exact same meaning twice.

What does all this mean? It means that the *significance* you give to something, you do neurologically-conceptually. You link the external world with your *meanings* and associations. It also means that *nothing inherently means anything.* It always depends.

Given all this, the basic reframing principle simply involves taking a behavior, an external behavior (EB), and a perspective (an internal representation), and putting them together. This creates a *frame* of reference or association.

Changing this formula transforms the meaning. And when *meanings* transform, so do responses, behaviors, and emotions. This explains how reframing transforms meaning. Thinking about this via a formula, we have:

$$\textbf{EB = IS}$$

External Behavior = Internal State
(See-hear-feel stimuli)   (Internal thoughts, connections, emotions, etc.)

Understanding meaning in this way enables us to appreciate that *whoever sets the frame runs the show* (or determines/creates the "reality"). This holds true for the frames in our mind. It also holds true for the frames that we use and operate within us when communicating with others.

When we can't change the external world, we can still change our meaning **about** that world so that we can have new/different internal experiences and therefore new/different responses and emotions. Reframing broadens perspectives, gives more choices, more flexibility, and more sense of control. *Source:* Bandler and Grinder (1982).

Identifying Frames

Identify a subject, then its *content* (the details), then its *structure* (VAK, form and syntax), then step back to ask the *presuppositional questions*: What do we have to assume as true for this to make sense? What perspective does this come from? What assumptions? What beliefs? What values? (Meta-thinking skills).

Content Reframing: Identify a subject then ask *the content* question: **How** can I view this as beneficial or of value?...as having a positive function?

The Pattern (Conscious Reframing)

1. *Identify a behavior* (habit, mental, emotion) *you don't yet like or appreciate in yourself.* Begin at the primary level with any disliked behavior.

2. *What part of you produces this behavior?* Some part or facet of you produces this. As you identify that part, give it a name.

3. *Search out the part's positive intention.* "What do you seek to accomplish for me that you deem as positive? What useful objective do you seek to achieve using this behavior?"

4. *Identify the frame.* What frame (or frames) of reference runs this part? What does this behavior or response mean to you? Why do you value it? What do you seek to accomplish?

5. *De-frame.* What submodality change would effectively alter this frame? What language shift would change this referent?

6. *Reframe* **the content**: How could you view this behavior as valuable for you? What can you appreciate about this part and its intention?

7. *Reframe* **the context:** Where could you use this behavior as a valuable response? When would you find it useful?

8. *Integrate this new frame:* "I give myself permission to use this new understanding/attribution to consciously think about this behavior..." Any internal objections?

9. *Test:* What happens inside when you now think about the part of you that generates that behavior?

#56 *The Context Reframing Pattern*

Identify a behavior, emotion, belief, state, etc. and then ask *context questions*:

- **Where** could I use this as a positive value?
- **When** would I find it useful?

Once you have identified the context, then vividly imagine yourself using the behavior in the appropriate context. This describes the traditional NLP approach to context reframing. In addition to this, we can also take a response and develop greater flexibility by shifting it from its usual frames and exploring its effects and results when we put it in new, strange, and different contexts.

For example, what if we took *playfulness* and moved it to the context of work? Or put it into the context of relationship, negotiating, learning, etc.? Responses take on new and different meanings in different contexts. Suppose we take an attitude of *love or spirituality*, which we usually connect to contexts of relationships and religion, and put them in the context of conflict resolution?

#57 *The Submodalities Reframing Pattern*

Throughout many of the patterns in this book we have already worked with the simplest form of reframing—*Representational Reframing*. This refers to changing or altering sensory-based facets within, and around, our VAK representations. When we change the quality or property of how we have something coded, we frequently alter its very frame of reference.

For example, our frame of reference changes when we take one of our mental pictures and view it with a black border rather than seeing it as panoramic. Or, notice the change that results when we view it as a black-and-white snapshot rather than one with full and bright colors. When we change some of the qualities and properties within our representation coding, it can alter the very *structure* of the information so that it seems re-framed. And, as with all reframing, doing this thereby transforms subsequent thinking, feeling, and responding.

#13 *The Six-step Reframing Pattern* (Repeated here from chapter 3)

Concept. Whenever we have, so to speak, a "part" of ourselves that carries out some set of behaviors which we do not seem able to stop with our conscious mind, that part then operates outside our conscious awareness and may not accept a conscious reframe of meaning. We then may need to use an unconscious reframing model, namely, the six-step reframe.

This pattern provides a method for reprogramming a part which produces behaviors that no longer serve us well, and aligns that part so that it will produce more useful and enhancing behaviors, automatically and systematically. This represents a technology whereby we can develop new behavioral choices which we don't seem to generate from our conscious understandings.

Whenever *meanings* become habitual, they become *unconscious*. Over time, they become so streamlined, that they drop out of awareness, and become the unconscious *frames* of reference that we use—our default frames. This saves time, trouble, energy, etc. **But** it can also create problems, particularly if the meaning (program) becomes unnecessary, untrue, or unproductive.

Sometimes we ask ourselves things like, *"Why do I do this?"* At other times we say, "I hate the part of myself that..." This model provides a way to re-align all of our parts which, in turn, creates better integration, self-appreciation, and harmony. We sometimes fail to update our meanings so that they stay current with our ever-changing situations. *Source:* Bandler and Grinder (1979, 1982).

The Pattern

1. *Identify a troublesome behavior.* "What behavior would you like to change?" Think of something that you want to do, but some part of you prevents you from doing. Or, think of something that you don't want to do but, no matter how hard you try to stop it, you do it anyway. Find a behavior that fits one of these linguistic environments: "I want to stop X-ing." "I want to X, but something stops me." (Yes, actually *you* stop yourself —or some facet of you.)

2. *Establish rapport.* Validate the part that carries out these behavior "programs" so automatically. Also validate the frustration and discomfort you feel (or a person feels) about not feeling able to stop the behaviors. "I want you to go inside and acknowledge the part of you that produces these behaviors."

3. *Communicate with the part that produces this behavior.* Go inside and ask, "Will the part of me that generates this behavior communicate with me in consciousness?" Wait for and notice your internal responses: feelings, images, sounds. Then say, "If this means *Yes* increase in brightness, volume, intensity." "If this means *No*, let it decrease." If "No", increase the rapport with this part. You may also, if working with another, ask the person to allow one finger to move in response to "Yes." Wait for a "Yes" signal. Ask for one finger to move in response to "No," to establish a "No" signal. Always thank the part for communicating.

4. *Discover its positive intention.* Ask the Yes/No question, "Would you feel willing to let me know in consciousness what you seek to accomplish for me that I could deem as positive by producing this behavior?" Wait for response. If you get a "Yes" response, then say, "Do I find this intention acceptable in consciousness?" "Do I want to have a part that fulfills this function?"

5. *Obtain permission for change.* Ask the part that creates this behavior if it would like even more and powerful choices. "If you had other ways to accomplish this positive intent that would work as well as or better than your present behavior, would you feel willing to try them out?"

If you get a "No" response, ask the person: "Would you feel willing to trust that your unconscious has some well-intentioned and positive purpose for you, even though it won't tell you at this moment?"

6. *Access your creative part*—the part of you that creates, innovates, and comes up with new ideas. "Now have the part that runs the unwanted behavior communicate its positive intention to your creative part. Have the creative part generate three new choices and communicate them to the first part. Let that part give a "Yes" signal each time it selects one that it deems as good as, or better than, the original unwanted behavior.

If the part exhibits any resistance to accepting new behaviors, say, "In a moment I will reach over and take your hand and it will not lower any faster than your unconscious mind will generate and begin to use three new ways of behaving that you consider better than those you have previously used and which you find acceptable to all of your parts. And you may not have any conscious awareness of the three new behaviors, but at some point you will find yourself simply using these new behaviors."

7. *Future pace the change*. Address the part and say, "Now become willing to take responsibility for using one of the three new alternative behaviors in the appropriate contexts." Let your unconscious mind identify the cues that will trigger the new choices. Use the cues to experience what it feels like to effortlessly and automatically have one of those new choices become available in that context.

8. *Check for ecology*. "Does any part of me object to having one of these three new alternatives?" If "Yes," repeat steps three through eight.

(Note: Your unconscious mind has already established numerous communications with you—we call them "symptoms." Now you have a way to use these symptoms as barometers for change.)

#58 The Six-step Reframing As A Meta-States Pattern

Concept. The Meta-state model refers to bringing one "state" of consciousness (a mind-body state) to bear upon another state. This moves us to a higher logical level so that our thoughts-and-feelings refer to another state of thoughts-and-feelings. Thus sometimes we experience fear or anger, guilt, shame, or joy. These states refer to **primary** states (as we might refer to primary colors). But, when we fear our anger or fear our fear, we have moved to a higher level and created a more complex and layered form of consciousness (see Hall, 1995, 1996).

The Pattern

1. *Identify the meta-part.* The pattern speaks about some "part" of us that generates an unwanted behavior (either by inhibiting the response or creating a counter-response that conflicts with it) which operates at a meta-level to ourselves. "What part of you refuses to allow you to X (speak assertively, finish a task, feel motivated, etc.) or what part of you produces Y (gets defensive, takes offense, jumps to conclusion) which prevents you from X?"

2. *Identify the positive intention of the part.* As we engage in the discovery process of finding the part's positive intention, this also moves us to a Meta-state about that Meta-state; naming that "part" identifies the state or construct. What does this part of you do for you that you consider of positive value and importance?

3. *Access and apply your creative part.* Asking for our creative "part" to speak to the positive intention essentially describes the process of how we Meta-state our positive intention state to generate better choices. Think-and-feel creatively about the choices that you can produce to attain this desired outcome.

The "unconscious" factor (living without awareness of the part, the positive intention state that has driven this part and is aware of the creative alternatives that we invent via our creative state) describes the unconscious barrier that also makes us unaware of our meta-states and how they drive our experiences...apart from consciousness.

4. *Future pace.* Future pacing the new choices, using the "symptoms" and other signals of the "unconscious mind", shows how meta-levels (in this case the meta-meta-state of "applying the resource to the 'future'") always drives and modulates lower levels. With your new understandings, experience using this new preferred response.

5. *Check ecology.* Running a final ecology check activates an ecology-check state to make sure that the process works holistically for our welfare.

#59 The Pulling Apart Belief Synesthesia Pattern

Concept. If a person experiences a problematic state in several representational systems and in such a way that it seems to "happen all at once" (so the person has no sense of their strategy that creates the state) then we can consider this process functioning as a synesthesia pattern wherein two systems have become so linked together that a stimulus will seemingly fire them both off together.

Robert Dilts (1990), in working with changing belief systems, described the synesthesia pattern of some beliefs which occur quickly and automatically, using the metaphor of a molecule. He pictured the end result as a molecule of many elements (VAK and A_d) all glued together. To help a person separate (or de-frame) this construction, he suggested pulling apart the component pieces and putting them back in the NLP eye accessing cue spaces (See Eye Accessing Cue Chart, Appendix A). This pattern separates and sorts out the representational pieces of an experience in order to de-frame the construction and provide more choice. *Source:* Dilts (1990).

The Pattern

1. *Identify the belief that functions like a synesthesia.* What belief immediately and automatically whoops you into a state? What stimulus suddenly causes you to experience a whole set of VAK representations?

2. *Individually identify the component pieces and sort them out into the eye-accessing positions.* Use your hand to indicate where to put the pieces of the synesthesia. "Do you see anything when you experience this belief? Okay, I want you to look up (remembered or constructed) and see it here. Do you hear anything? Okay, I want you to put that sound over here... . What feelings are you experiencing? Put them here." Etc..

3. *Break state and check the ecology.* Think about the experience now and see if you can do so without the old synesthesias.

#60 *The Establishing Your Value Hierarchy Pattern*

Concept. Our *criteria* refers to our standards of evaluation by which we make decisions about the importance of things, events, ideas, people, etc. Our values and criteria provide an organizing structure to our lives as well as a motivating force. As we add more and more values and criteria, the values themselves can begin to conflict with each other putting us at odds with ourselves. Also, we can over- or under-value some criteria. When this happens, internal conflict can also occur so that we become out-of-balance.

The shift of values and criteria usually involves an analogue shift—adjusting the relative importance of the criteria instead of accepting or rejecting them wholesale. This technology becomes useful when we feel indecisive, can't make up our mind, experience lots of confusion, ambivalence, and inner conflict. We can also use it for resolving interpersonal difficulties, improving our decision making strategies, and before doing agreement frames. *Source:* Andreas and Andreas (1987).

The Pattern

1. *Identify an area.* Think of one realm of life where values seem confusing (relationships, work, etc).

2. *Elicit a hierarchy of criteria.* Think of something trivial that you could do, but you wouldn't (e.g., standing on a chair, throwing a piece of chalk across the room). "Doing the dishes.

What do you accomplish by not doing this?" "I save time."
(Always get the criteria stated in the positive—what the person
wants.)

"What would get you to do this even though it would violate
that particular criterion?" (i.e., saving time, though a waste of
time). "If someone came for a visit."

"So what do you find important about that?" (As they keep
adding more context, find out what the person values in that.)

Behavior	Context	Criterion
(-) Could do dishes, but won't	& few dirty dishes	Save time
(+) Would do dishes	& visiting stranger	Neutral impression
(-) Wouldn't do dishes	& cooking a meal	Excellence (of cooking)
(+) Would do dishes	& unhygienic dishes	Hygiene
(-) Wouldn't do dishes	& crisis in building	Safety of persons

Continue this process of doing or not doing the particular
behaviors by adding more and more context that gets a person
to do the behavior or disengage from it. With each step, identify
the criterion it exemplifies. "What seems important enough to
get you to violate the previous criterion?"

Doing this will *elicit an outcome chain.* When you reach the first
criterion (A), inquire, "What stops you?" This will elicit some
reverse or negative criterion (B).

Then recycle, "When would you do A even through it causes
B?" This brings in the next higher level criterion (C). *Negative
examples* in this process elicit more highly valued criteria.
"When would you not do A even though it results in B or C?"

3. *Identify the highest criterion and construct a hierarchy.* Continue
until you have the most important criterion. Make a continuum
from the least to the most important criteria.

4. *Identify submodalities.* Find the submodality differences between the least and the most important criteria. How do you represent "saving time," "excellence," "safety of others," etc.? Elicit see, hear, feel descriptions and especially the analogue submodalities that vary.

5. *Put your criteria on a continuum.* Determine how much you want to reduce a particular criterion, where you want it to be on the scale. Then shift the submodalities of that criterion so that it matches the submodalities of those at that lower place. Adjust the submodalities so that the criterion becomes coded for the degree of importance that you want it to have.

6. *Ecology check.* Take a meta-position and evaluate your hierarchy of values. Do they serve you well? Do they fall into an order that enables you to make good decisions, to create inner harmony? Any problems or mis-alignments? Identify the criterion you would like to change.

7. *Shift criterion.* Identify the criterion to be shifted and determine where you want it to end up. What order of values will get you where you want to go?

8. *Change submodalities.* Slowly change the criterion to the appropriate place on your continuum. Give it the submodalities according to the importance you wish it to have. Notice the submodalities of the criterion before and after it. Code it appropriately.

9. *Test.* How does your value hierarchy look to you now? Will it help guide you into right behaviors and decisions?

10. *Future pace.* Think of a situation where the new criterion will make a difference to you and put yourself into that context and notice your experience.

#61 The Kinesthetic Hierarchy Of Criteria Pattern

1. *Location 1.* In this location, identify a behavior that the person wants to do, but does not do (e.g., to stop smoking).

2. *Location 2.* In this location, elicit the criteria and meta-outcomes that motivate the person's wants toward his or her desired outcome (e.g., the cessation of coughing). "Why do you want this?" "How do you value this as significant or important?"

3. *Location 3.* In this location, find the criteria that stop the person from changing. "What stops you?" These values will represent higher level outcomes inasmuch as they stop the outcomes in the second location. Identify the criteria and meta-outcomes at this level (e.g., feeling relaxed, nurtured).

4. *Location 4.* In location 4, find a higher level criterion that can override the limiting criteria of step 3. What do you find *more significant* or *so important* that you would give up smoking even if the smoking triggers feelings of relaxation and nurturing? (e.g., feeling respected by your family). What do you hold as a value even more important than that (e.g., saving your life)?

5. *Anchor 4.* As the person continues to experience the fourth location of the highest values and criteria, amplify and anchor fully.

6. *Transfer the highest values.* Holding the anchor assist the person to step back into location 3, "...noticing what you think-and-feel in this state with this (fire anchor) resource." Do the same as you walk with the person to locations 2 and 1. This pattern accesses the person's highest criterion and applies it to the prior states. It communicates, "Since you value saving your life, bring those thoughts-emotions (values) to bear on this previous state, and this one."

7. *Transfer the submodality codings downward.* Since we now take the criterion of the highest level, along with its submodality codings, into location 3, 2, and 1, as you walk the person through, ask them to identify new ways for them to achieve

their desired outcome. "How else could you feel relaxed and nurtured and *still* stop smoking?" As they notice the submodalities of each state, have them fine tune and adjust them with the submodality codings of the highest experience.

8. *Keep amplifying.* As you use the person's driver submodalities of his or her highest value and apply to each lower level, make each lower state more and more compelling. Also, as you move into each lower location, check to see if the person has the driving Meta-programs of the highest level criterion also.

9. *Future pace and check for ecology.*

#62 *The Thought Virus Inoculation Pattern*

Concept. Sometimes we get hold of ideas that function entirely as dysfunctional beliefs that mentally poison us. We think of such ideas as toxic viruses. Robert Dilts developed this pattern from his work in applying NLP within the health field of applied medicine. He applied the metaphor of *thought viruses* that toxify and sicken mental-emotional life. Via this technology, we can change toxic beliefs and inoculate ourselves, or others, against sick ways of thinking.

The Pattern

1. *Establish literal "spaces" on a floor.* As the person experiences each of these states with their corresponding VAK representations, fully anchor the person at these spaces.

   a) *Neutral meta-position space* where you can review the whole process and access creative, resourceful ideas.

   b) *Old limiting beliefs.* This space represents "Something that you used to believe, but no longer believe," such as a belief in Santa Claus.

   c) *Open to doubting.* Think about a time when you began to doubt that the old belief was true, i.e., when you began to wonder about Santa.

d) *Museum of old beliefs.* This represents those beliefs that you once believed, but which you no longer believe, i.e., a place to leave beliefs you have grown out of. ("B.S." space—a space where you go, "Wrong!" "Doesn't compute.")

e) *A new belief* from which you would like to operate. Check to make sure that the belief operates appropriately. Check also for congruity from the meta-position before actually establishing the space. Ask the person to say the belief a couple of times to polish up the language.

f) *Open to believing.* Think of something you didn't believe in the past that you now feel open to believing.

g) *A sacred space* that represents your mission in life. A space of congruent self-trust that you evaluate as absolutely sacred to you that you will not violate.

2. *Test each space.* Once you have set up anchored spaces for these differing experiences, test each one by having the person step into the space and fully experience it. You may wish to move to the meta-position between each move.

3. *Run a toxic thought through the process.* Elicit a thought, idea, belief that functions toxically for the person and move them through the process until they deposit it in the *museum of old beliefs*. Move to the meta-position and fully identify an empowering thought or belief to put in the void.

4. *Move through all the spaces* using the new belief.

(Note: if at any time the person experiences confusion, move to the meta-position and clarify thoughts and feelings from that position.)

5. *Future pace and check for ecology.*

Conclusion

Meanings completely and thoroughly govern our lives. As a semantic class of life, *meanings* inevitably and inescapably dominate and pervade every aspect of our daily experiences. They especially govern our emotions and therefore our affective-somatic states of consciousness. And yet, simultaneously, we find that *meanings* exist as very plastic and moldable. As creatures of the mind and nervous system, they have a fluidity about them that allows them to shift and change fairly easily.

Meanings do not exist as things and so we can't write them in stone. We *create* meanings in the first place by our *thinking,* evaluating, appraising, connecting, etc., and *so we can also create new and different meanings any time we so desire.* With the patterns in this chapter we have several ways to reframe meanings that may have become unenhancing, dysfunctional, or limiting.

In addition, we can use the Belief Change Pattern and the Decision Destroyer Pattern as further methods for transforming meanings. We can all learn to live by ever increasing and empowering our meanings.

Chapter 10

Strategies

Patterns For Building Empowering Action Plans

Regardless of how we feel, we always have some control over what we do.
>   William Glasser, M.D.

When you know how to do something, it looks so easy—so magical to those who don't!
>   Michael Hall

How do things work? How does a piece of "human subjectivity," e.g., motivation, decision-making, flirting, negotiating, parenting, dieting, fitness, learning, etc, "work?"

- What does a person have to do first in mind-body?
- What next, and next, and next?
- What VAK representations does a person need to make up a given formula?
- What submodalities?
- What Meta-programs?
- What Meta-level responses and states?
- What supporting beliefs and values?

With these questions we have just entered into *the domain of strategies*. In NLP, this refers to "the structure of subjective experience." Building on the Cognitive-Behavioral work of Miller, Galanter, and Pribram (1960) in *Plans And The Structure Of Behavior*, Dilts, Bandler, Grinder, Cameron-Bandler and DeLozier (1980) took their TOTE model and enriched it with the representation systems.

Using the flow chart of human consciousness as it moves through the phases of **T**esting, **O**perating, **T**esting, and **E**xiting (TOTE) [which function as cognitive-behavioral information processing programs], the NLP co-founders greatly enhanced the TOTE model.

Actually, this model began in behaviorism in the S-R model (stimulus-response) of Pavlov and Watson. At this level we have a simple association linkage between *stimulus and response*. Viewing human "mind" and response in this model, the external events (the stimuli) *cause* a response (a feeling, emotion, understanding, behavior, etc.).

Stimulus —> Response

Then, as the early and middle decades of the twentieth century passed, this S-R model became increasingly inadequate for explaining human functioning. Eventually a behaviorist, Tollman (1923), added *a cognitive dimension* to it. He developed S-O-R by bringing in **O**ther Variables (the O). He used this expression rather than the (at that time) dirty word "mind."

Yet the TOTE model had to wait for the cognitive revolution initiated by George Miller (1956) and Neiser (1967) and the refinements that brain researcher Karl Pribram added. This refined the S-O-R model much further. In this model a responding organism *inputs some sensory stimulus* (S) and *tests* it internally against some coded representation of a desired state or criterion (O). As the *testing* proceeds, it either meets the test or fails to meet it. This results in congruity—so that the external and internal representations match (e.g., the volume of the stereo externally matches what the person internally prefers). Or it may result in incongruity, so that the external and internal representations do not match. If they do not match, the person may test again by altering his or her internal representations or by *operating* on the external stimulus (e.g., turning up the volume). Exiting such a "program" of input, processing, and output results in some kind of response or behavior.

Later the NLP co-founders got hold of the TOTE model and dressed it up to make it usable as the structural format for thinking about human strategies—the flow of human consciousness in a formulaic way as it sequences itself until it generates responses.

Many times the problems that we experience in life have to do with the strategy question of *"how to."* We *know* **what** to do. We just don't have the **know how**. We have clarified **what** effective action or response to take. We want to speak assertively, speak before groups with confidence, resolve conflicts with a win/win attitude, forgive, motivate ourselves to complete an unpleasant task, exercise regularly, eat more sensibly, think before we act, etc. But *how* do we pull such things off? What *strategy* (sequence of internal representations) will provide us with the formula for directionalizing and training our brain-body to so respond?

This describes the place for **strategy awareness**, development, accessing, utilizing, etc. So, in this chapter we have included, under the category of strategy, the NLP patterns that provide the formulas (or processes) whereby we can "take effective actions."

#63 *The New Behavior Generator Pattern*

Concept. When we do not know *how to do something*, we need to learn a new pattern, model, or process that will, step-by-step, enable us to discover the formula. Do we know *how* to take criticism well and to use it constructively? Do we know *how* to motivate ourselves? If we don't have a strategy for something, we won't be able to do it. Did you receive a program for resolving conflicts respectfully? For gathering high quality information? For speaking affirmatively and showing affection? Well then, you may simply need to learn or invent such a strategy.

Strategy development occurs whenever and wherever learning occurs. For by learning, we become trained to organize and sequence representations so that they build up various skills.

As we construct these strategies (or parts), we describe them in terms of *what they do*, their **function**, rather than in terms of how they do it, their behavior. In other words, we build parts to *achieve outcomes*. With every strategy we learn, we essentially install a part within ourselves to pull off certain behavioral outcomes. Do you have an assertive part? A forgiving part? A creative part? Of course, the tricky bit lies in creating parts that won't interfere with other parts and outcomes. *Source:* Bandler and Grinder (1979).

The Pattern

1. *Identify a part or function that the person needs.* Determine the specific outcome the person wants. For instance, they might want to build an assertive part, or a part to handle conflict positively, or a part to handle rejection resourcefully, etc.

2. *Access and anchor* the components that make up this part. Identify any past experiences when the person had the ability to do some piece of it. Now relive each situation and experience the desired aspects in all representational systems. Anchor each component piece of this new behavior.

3. *Create scenario within the imagination.* Create a detailed set of images of yourself engaging in this new behavior. Once the person has created a dissociated visual/auditory constructed movie, have them sit back to observe the whole sequence.

4. *Ecological check.* Go inside and ask, "Does any part of me object to this new behavior? Does any part object to making this movie a reality?" Check in all representational systems for objecting parts. (This involves a yes/no question). If you sense an objection, have the signal intensify for "Yes", and decrease for "No", or use finger signals.

5. *Satisfy all objections.* If you discover any objections, use the information to re-edit the movie. Do another ecological check. Continue this process until you find no objections. It becomes important to redefine and satisfy all objections, since in this process we build a new motivational part.

6. *Experience the movie.* Now, have the person step inside the image and go through the sequences in an associated state. "As you then experience yourself successfully engaging in the new behaviors, set up a self-anchor for this state and feeling."

7. *Program it into your unconscious.* Ask your unconscious to analyze the fantasy you have created and to pull from it the essential ingredients of the program you want to have inside you. Your unconscious can then use this information to build a part and give it a dynamic expression. Get what you need to

know from the imagined imagery to build a part of you that can do this exquisitely and easily, and at every moment that it needs to be done.

8. *Test and future pace.* Make sure the part is accessible and responds appropriately. Future pace by seeing yourself use this part effectively in the future.

#63b Adaptation: The Day End Review

Concept. Sometimes, at the end of a day, we find it worthwhile and valuable to *review* our day to make learnings and use the feedback from things that worked or that did not work well, in order to future pace more effective patterns for the future. The following pattern represents an "advanced and user-friendly New Behavior Generator" as designed by Alexander Van Buren (*Anchor Point*, November 1997).

The Pattern

Begin by acknowledging your own personal inner wisdom, strength, and love. This will enable you to center yourself as you presuppose personal resources and capabilities.

1. *Run a movie of the day's activities.* Starting at the beginning of the day, run a movie through your mind of the activities, events, conversations, and people you encountered throughout the day.

2. *Freeze frame the movie at the "rough spots."* Stop the movie whenever you find places where you didn't like the response you got from others or where you didn't like your own behavior. This identifies the problem contexts.

3. *Identify resources to apply.* Ask, "What worked?" What actions, feelings, ideas, responses and ways of being worked well during the day? What other resources could I have used and applied from other contexts?"

201

4 *Identify difficulties to address.* Ask, "What did not work?" Then use the levels of beliefs to ask such things as the following:

a) How would I have liked to have affected others? (Spirit)

b) What kind of a person did I want to be in this situation? (Identity)

c) What did I deem as of the most importance in this situation? (Values)

d) What did I feel certain of or want to feel certain of? (Beliefs)

e) What was I able to do or what would I like to have been able to do? (Capabilities)

f) What feeling or action would I like to have taken? (Behaviors)

5. *Creating the new reality.* Play the movie again seeing yourself doing, feeling, being, acting, etc., with all of the resources you imagined. Do so until you generate a positive emotional response to the new creative movie. To do this, keep recycling back through the resource development step.

6. *Finish backtracking the day's movie.* Future pace, run an ecology check and enjoy.

#64 The Forgiveness Pattern

Concept. When we live with unforgiving feelings toward someone, we experience thoughts-and-emotions of resentment, anger, bitterness, etc. And these neuro-linguistic states will *not* do us any good. We then install the hurt that someone has caused (or that we believe and feel they caused) as a significant memory or reference in our mind. Since we have not released it, resolved it, come to terms with it, etc., we have become *stuck at the point of hurt.* *Subsequently, it keeps* inappropriately signaling our mind-body of hurt, thereby imprisoning the hurt within!

We need to forgive. We need to forgive and release it.

But how? How do we forgive?

Forgiveness, as a neuro-linguistic state, describes a very powerful and useful subjective experience. This forgiveness pattern offers a process that enables us to create the experience of forgiveness.

As a more complex piece of subjectivity, various beliefs can operate that either support or limit our ability to access the strategy of forgiveness. What do you believe about forgiveness? What ideas hold you back from forgiving? How long do you believe it takes to develop forgiveness? What do you believe about the relationship between forgiving and re-entering relationship? With that person?

In shifting from unforgiving to forgiving, we alter our perceptions and meanings from seeing the person/event fused together, as ugly, dark, demonic, etc., to seeing the person and event as two separate phenomena, so that we can sort out our thoughts-feelings about each and not let our rage at the behavior contaminate our compassion for the person.

Figure 10.1
The Forgiveness Continuum

Hurt	Anger	Upset/Stress	Distinguish	Developing New	Good	Serenity	Appreciation	Apology
Dissociation	Numb	Rejection	Person/Behavior	Understanding	Memories	Prayer	of Person	Friendship
Distracted		Occupied	Confusion/Fear	Positive	Distinctions	Return	Reconciliation	
Denial/Avoidance		Revenge	Behind the Hurt	Intentions	Feelings			

Vindictive Bitter/Hateful
Sense of Violation

Behavior / / / Person

Figure 10.2
States And Meta-states In Forgiveness

Integration State
Firm—Compassion—Positive
@ ←

Self-
Esteeming
Centered in
Values/Visions
@ ←

Person/
Behavior
Distinction
Dignity
of Persons
@ ←

Anger
Rage at
@ ←

Releasing
Letting go
Shared Response-
Abilities
@ ←

Esteem
Appreciation
Dignity of
People
@ ←

Compassion
Mercy
Kindness/
Sweet Spirit
@ ←

Hurt...
@ ←

Conscious of Hurting Behaving
that violated values/relationship
in some way

from   a Person

The Pattern

1. *Access a state of self-esteeming.* Center yourself in your values, standards, beliefs, and dignity.

2. *Access state of human dignity of all people:* Get full description (VAK) of people as sacred, special, important, valuable, and fallible.

3. *Distinguish person from behavior.* Imagine making a clear-cut distinction in self and others between expressions of a person and their inner Being. What supportive beliefs would strengthen this?

4. *Give yourself permission to rage against hurtful behaviors.* Once you have permission, then rage against hurtful behaviors. Access the anger in order to draw boundaries against unacceptable behaviors without violating the person.

5. *Give yourself permission to love/validate the person in spite of their hurtful behavior.* Recognize their positive intent, access compassion for their limitations and fallibilities.

6. *Release behaviors by refusing to over-value them.* Access a state of "releasing," or "letting go." De-invest meaning and energy from the behavior. Access supporting beliefs. Become aware of your response-abilities in the matter of the hurt—a tempering awareness.

7. *Integrate boundaries, compassion and releasing.* Imagine the *You* who can establish and communicate effective boundaries, express firmness of character, and compassionately release hurts and bitternesses.

#65 The Allergy Cure Pattern

Concept. An allergic response involves the nervous system's adaptation as sneezing, coughing, skin reactions, etc., to a non-toxic element (the hair of a cat or dog, springtime pollens, etc.) or even to emotional subjects (criticism, certain person, etc.). Conceptually, we understand an allergy as a immune function that has made a mistake. The immune system has associated ("learned") to treat something non-dangerous as a threat. So our immune system attacks some harmless antigens *as if* they threaten us. Yet the body's immune system has simply made a mistake in its coding and cuing of its response. Many times allergies result from a psychological trauma.

This technology involves re-educating the immune system so that it stops attacking a non-toxic element and benign substances. *Source:* Andreas and Andreas (1989).

The Pattern

1. *Calibrate.* "What does it feel like (or sound like, look like, etc.) when you experience the presence of the allergen?" As you ask this question, watch the person's physiology, eye accessing cues, breathing, etc., in order to calibrate to their state and responses.

2. *Frame the allergy as a mistake.* Explain the concept that immune systems can make mistakes and get activated when nothing in the environment necessitates its response.

> "Your immune system has simply made a mistake; somehow it thinks of something as dangerous when actually no danger exists. It has made a mistake about what it needs to attack and what it does not need to attack. We want to re-teach or re-train your immune system so that it can learn, quickly, how to function more effectively."

3. *Check for ecology/secondary gain.*

"How would you experience your everyday life if you didn't have this response? What does having this allergy do for you that may have some secondary benefit? Can you think of anything positive that comes from having this allergy?"

4. *Identify and anchor an appropriate counter-example resource.*

"What can you think of that would serve as a good counter-example to this allergy trigger that seems as similar to the allergen as possible and yet one to which your immune system reacts appropriately. Imagine yourself now in the presence of this similar agent."

Anchor the allergy response and hold the anchor thought the whole process.

5. *Dissociate.* "Now imagine that right in front of you an impenetrable plexiglass shield exists that goes from wall to wall, from floor to ceiling..." While holding the resourceful anchor, ask the person to,

"See yourself over there on the other side of the plexiglass having your immune system functioning appropriately. As you watch, you can remember that this represents *the you with the effective immune system* which allows you to enter into the presence of allergens without reacting..."

6. **Gradually,** *introduce the allergen.*

"As you watch yourself over there behind the plexiglass shield, slowly introduce the allergen that used to cause a problem for you. Let the allergen gradually move behind the glass giving your immune system a chance to get used to it."

Wait at this point until you see a physiological shift indicating that the person's immune system has begun to adjust. Next, ask the immune system for a signal that it has absorbed the new information. The response will essentially signal you that "Yes, all right, I've got it. I'll change the notches on my flag so it doesn't match up with any of the T cells I have."

7. *Re-associate.* Continuing to hold the anchor, "Now allow yourself to step into the you, behind the plexiglass, and fully experience the allergen that used to create an allergic response for you."

8. *Calibrate.* See if the physiology, eye accessing cues, breathing, etc. have changed.

9. *Future Pace.*

"Imagine a time in the future when you will come into the presence of this allergen that caused a problem and you find has no effect now. Step into several of these times and notice how comfortable you feel."

10. *Test.* If you can actually test carefully, do so. If not, imagine the allergen and re-calibrate to see that physiology remains changed.

#66 *The Grief Resolution Pattern*

Concept. Sometimes when we lose someone or something very special to us, we get caught up in excessive and unnecessary grieving. Then we continue to grieve the loss of a loved one, a job, a childhood, etc., and feel sad, depressed, or hopeless, and become unable to get on with life. Perhaps we simply lack a good strategy for bringing closure to the loss, using it for growth, and moving on.

The fact that people in other cultures can experience grief or loss in very different ways from our cultural style suggests that human subjectivity has a wide range of choices. In some cultures, loss triggers people to give up, rage, seek revenge, commit suicide, etc., whilst in others it enables people to celebrate and even rejoice— giving loss the meaning of "a transition to another life."

This illustrates the plasticity of meaning. It underscores that loss does **not** necessitate a prescribed form of grieving. Our subjective experience is always derived from how we represent the loss and the meanings we attribute to it. Again, the map in our heads *about* the territory of loss suggests that there exist multiple maps (hence reactions) that we can experience. What strategy map do we want to choose as we navigate life?

Grief also involves not only an external loss, but also internal losses—a loss of meaning, values, expectations, etc. Experiences of grief arise not only from our loss, but much more from how we perceive the loss. Our meaning determines the experience—and our representational sequence of VAK responses controls the meaning. Resolving grief involves re-establishing connections and values in order to recover. *Source:* Andreas and Andreas

The Pattern

1. *Identify the grief representation.* Think about someone or something you have lost, or a potential loss. Notice how you represent that person or thing. You may experience having the loved one "there, but not really there." Or you may "see them, but only vaguely," in some insubstantial way. Identify the submodalities associated with the sense of loss. Common submodalities include seeing the person as flat, transparent, distant, floating off the ground, unclear, etc. Grief usually involves an unfinished or unreal representation.

2. *Identify your stuck grief representation.* If you have experienced a grief in which you feel "stuck," notice your representations of this. How do you think about it? One man said, "I see her in a small, still picture. It looks very dark and depressing. I don't want to look at it." When someone inquired about this, the man said it represented "the last time I saw her—the day we broke up." Here the *content* controls the representations. If we recall bad times with a loved one, rather than good times, we will increase our sense of pain.

3. *Identify your "special memory" representation.* Think back to a time when you had some special memories associated with this person, when you experienced something of importance. Change any negative associations to positive associations. Identify the meanings and values you wish to keep. What did you especially appreciate and value?

4. *Identify "finished grief" as a resource experience.*

"Now think back to someone who no longer plays a part in your life and yet, when you recall this person, you feel good and enriched. Your thoughts provide you with a sense of their presence perhaps or of their value to you. Now notice how you think of that person."

Identify the modalities and submodalities that you use. Notice also the meanings that you give to them.

5. *Re-code your representations.*

"Would you have any objection to developing a more resourceful way to think about the person you have lost so that you could feel good about him or her? Does any part of you object to keeping the good feelings that you received from this other person and letting them enrich your life?"

6. *Access a valued experience with the person.*

"Think of one of the most special times you had with this person. See him or her as life-size, moving, and over to your left (or whatever driving submodalities the person has). Think of him (her) in the same way as you thought about your old buddy or friend. And even though you have lost him/her, you can still have those good feelings..."

7. *Identify the values.* To preserve the benefits of that relationship and to use them to move into the future, we add this step.

"As you allow yourself to review all of the good experiences you had with this person, notice the things you valued about her (him): warmth, intimacy, spontaneity, variety, stability, fun, adventure, etc.

"As you identify the values that you do not want to lose from this person, make a symbolic image of all these values and then bring that symbol into you...to keep near to your heart."

8. *Check ecology and future pace.* "Now imagine going into your future with these values that you received from that person... let these values enrich you and be an ongoing legacy of that person."

9. *Test.* Now think of that person and notice what you think-and-feel about her/him. See if you can feel as bad and desperate as you did earlier.

#67 The Pre-Grieving Pattern

Concept. The strategy that enables us to effectively grieve, release, and move on with life also empowers us to access the value(s) of what we might have anticipated having lost in the "future" via our imagination, so that we don't have to torture ourselves!

1. *What will you probably lose in the future?* We humans live a fragile and fallible life: we get sick, move through life stages, die, etc. Good ego strength enables us to "look reality in the face" without quivering, whining, throwing a tantrum, etc. It enables us to welcome reality as it exists. Identify the things that we will or could lose.

2. *Determine outcome representations of value.* How do you need to think and represent such events to remind you of their temporal nature so that you can remember them as time-limited? What other things do you value and appreciate even though you know "it too will pass away?" What supporting beliefs and values can empower you in this respect?

3. *Transfer the coding to the future losses.* Use your representations of that valued experience or person to identify your VAK representations of "acceptable loss." Then transfer to the persons, things, events that you may or will lose in the future.

4. *Access resources for coping with such losses.* How might you experience those valued qualities in new and different ways, with new and different people, in your future? Create a representation of doing this. See the resourceful you moving on with life creatively, joyfully, etc.

5. *Ecology check.* Do you have any parts that object to making this resourceful picture a part of your future? If so, take the objections and use them to modify your representations.

6. *Install on your Time-line.* Access your Time-line and then install your representation in the future.

#68 The Healthy Eating Pattern

Concept. Sometimes we don't eat as healthily as we should in order to have the health and fitness that corresponds with a vigorous and energetic life. Do we have a good strategy for healthy eating? We may not. Eating in a healthy way involves listening to the "wisdom of the body" so that we can recognize when we feel "full" and "empty." In so doing, we learn to eat for nutrition, not for some psychological value: comfort, nurture, relaxation, etc.

Eating in a healthy way also involves our decision-making strategy. We need to make good choices that take into account long-term pleasures and criteria, well-being, health, etc., rather than short-term pleasures. Healthy eating also involves the shifting of beliefs—transforming limiting beliefs into empowering beliefs, getting over the old eating "programming" of childhood, and building supportive beliefs about self, body imagery, etc. *Source:* Andreas and Andreas (1989), "The Naturally Slender Eating Strategy."

The Pattern

1. *Obtain your eating time representations.* How do you know the time has come to "eat?" Do you see, hear, or feel something? Imagine that you have worked all day: how do you know the time has come for lunch or supper?

2. *Check your stomach feelings.* What do you feel? What kinesthetic qualities do you experience? Check whether your stomach feels full, empty, or some degree in between. Also check for the overall feelings: tension, relaxation, etc.

3. *Explore.* "What would feel good in my stomach right now?" Ask this of your body wisdom and notice what response you get. Think of an available and healthy food item (e.g., turkey sandwich, vegetable soup, salad, etc.) and imagine eating it. Try as many items as necessary to find the most appropriate one. Recall the sensations that this item creates.

4. *Compare.* Compare the feeling from the favored food item with the feeling you had in your stomach before you imaged eating anything. Which feels better? Imagine what your body will feel like over the next few hours. If you get a "No" that it won't feel better, decline that food. If you get a "Yes," then accept it. Notice that you decide now *based on* which will give you the best feeling over time.

5. *Explore and compare using a non-healthy item.* Visualize an unhealthy food item (e.g., a candy bar). Imagine eating it, and feel it in your stomach. Experience what it feels like now, in a few hours, tomorrow. Imagine what you think and feel about it over time. Compare these feelings with the feelings you got from steps 3 and 4. Notice which feeling you find more pleasurable. Which choices make you feel better?

6. *Future pace.* When you have considered enough possibilities, notice the food items that make you feel the best and imagine yourself taking these choices into your future.

#69 The Resolving Co-dependence Pattern

Concept. What we call "co-dependent relationships" result from becoming overly involved with others so that we assume responsibility *for* things that obviously lie outside our area of response. We think-and-feel responsible for how someone else thinks, feels, and/or behaves. People who fall into the co-dependent pattern usually end up intruding into the responsibility circle of others, and fail to assume proper responsibility for themselves. They typically lack a good sense of connectedness to their own self. This pattern provides a way to reconnect with one's self, to stop co-dependent ways of relating, and to encourage healthy *inter*-dependent relationships.

The Pattern

1. *Think of someone you have become **over-involved with**.* Who do you feel responsible **for** (not **to**, but **for**)?

2. *Identify connection representations.* Scan your body and notice where you sense connections from you to the other person. Such representations usually take the form of various metaphors: ropes, ties, apron strings, etc. Allow yourself to become aware of some metaphorical way that seems to describe how you represent your connectedness.

3. *Sever the ties.* Now imagine, for a moment, that you have become completely free from these ties. Does any part of you object to this? If some voice or part objects, explore its positive intention in creating or keeping the tie. Identify what secondary gain you obtain from the relationship.

4. *Identify your outcomes and meta-outcomes.* Identify your objective in maintaining the connection to this other person. What do you get from this relationship? What do you give to this relationship?

5. *Construct an ideal self.* Use the information you obtained to build an ideal you with all the resources, qualities and abilities necessary to have healthy relationships with yourself and with others. Visually locate this ideal self in just the right location.

6. *Swish to the resourceful you.* As you disconnect each tie from the other person, see yourself reconnecting it to your ideal self. Experience getting your desired outcome now from this ideal self rather than from the other person. Soak in these good feelings and sit with them for a few moments.

7. *Connect other to Resourceful Self.* Send this other person to his/her ideal self that has the ability to maintain good boundaries, keep good distance, and respond appropriately. Imagine helping the other reconnect each tie to his/her resourceful self. Now see you interacting appropriately with this other person in the future.

#70 *The Assertive Speaking Pattern*

Concept. Do you have a good strategy for speaking up and asserting your own thoughts, values, beliefs, feelings, etc.? Assertiveness involves a basic human right—that of owning and claiming responsibility for our own thoughts, values, feelings, etc. Some people simply lack the strategy and training regarding *how* to do it. Others have suffered having permission taken away from them so that they don't allow themselves to voice their feelings. This shows up in *fears about the meaning* of assertive behavior (a Meta-state). "If I speak up, people will not like me; I will be rejected; people will think I'm bossy," etc. Such lack of assertiveness results from dysfunctional beliefs or inadequate programming.

Conceptually, asserting differs from fleeing and fighting—the two responses that arise when we feel afraid, threatened, insecure, violated, etc. In the fleeing aspect of the fight/flight syndrome of general arousal, we become primarily conscious of our fear as a symptom of insecurity and stress. In the fighting aspect of fight/flight, we become primarily conscious of anger as a symptom of our insecurity and stress. Accordingly, aggression lacks the quality and resource of assertiveness as much as does passivity. This pattern adds assertiveness (speaking up kindly and respectfully) as a resource in our communicating and relating. *Source:* Andreas and Andreas (1989).

The Pattern

1. *Discover how the person stops him/herself from speaking up assertively.*

   "Think of a time when you wanted to express yourself in an assertive way, but didn't feel that you could. As you think of that time, notice what pictures you make, where you see them, and how many you have. What else do you notice about those pictures? What do you say to yourself? Whose voice do you use and where do you locate that voice? What feelings do you experience as you notice this, and where do you locate those feelings?"

2. *Locate the belief associated with assertiveness.*

"As you think about speaking up and expressing your own thoughts and emotions, what ideas or beliefs do you have about this? Do you hold any negative thoughts about it? What could serve as a useful purpose in **not** speaking up assertively?"

3. *Invest assertiveness with more value and meaning.* Search for the opposite of discounting and devaluing assertiveness. Identify the benefits supporting becoming more assertive.

"Think for a moment of all the advantages that will accrue for you in learning to speak and relate more assertively. What do you think of other people who express themselves in a respectful and firm way? What can adopting this resource do for you?"

4. *Fully represent assertiveness in a compelling way.*

"What pictures, sounds, feelings and words support the resource of assertiveness for you? What internal pictures would you create if you felt as assertive as you would like to feel? Notice their qualities and location. How would you talk to yourself? Notice your voice tone, rate, location, etc. What feelings would you have if you felt as assertive as you would like to feel?"

Elicit and fully represent times in the person's past when they responded in an assertive way. Integrate these with your pictures of assertively responding now and in the future.

5. *Switch pictures.* Have the person move their pictures and representations of non-assertiveness behind their pictures and representations of communicating with assertiveness. Let the non-assertive pictures take on the qualities of the assertive pictures.

"Now move those non-assertive pictures (indicate their location) over here behind these pictures of you speaking assertively. Change them to reflect you as assertive with the same color, images, and movement as the assertive pictures. Move any non-assertive voices to the place where your internal dialogue supports assertiveness. Change the message so that all voices support assertiveness in the same way. If you find any negative feelings about assertiveness, move them to the location where you hold good feelings about assertiveness. Have them take on the same qualities as the good feelings. Work with these parts until you feel congruent and comfortable with communicating assertively."

6. *Future pace.*

"See yourself clearly in your future as responding assertively in situations where assertiveness would function as a true resource. Step in and fully experience all the good feelings that result from asserting yourself respectfully."

#71 The Responding To Criticism Pattern

Concept. We generally recognize the ability to receive criticism without feeling hurt or judged as an important skill and one well worth developing. This pattern turns "criticism" into *"feedback"* and allows us to feel safe while another offers us a message. We may evaluate that message as unpleasant and undesired whether we find it true or untrue, accurate or inaccurate. This technology enables us to treat the products (words, tones, volumes, etc.) that come out of another's mind and mouth as *theirs*. This frees us from immediately personalizing and feeling bad!

This skill depends upon the concept that "words are not real." They only exist as symbols or maps *of* reality, never reality itself ("The map is not the territory"). Realizing this at *the feeling level* empowers us to develop a good relationship to information, communication, and messages. Accepting that words only exist as symbols in the mind of the sender, we can breathe more easily in the knowledge that "criticism" (a nominalization) also exists only in our mind, not in the world.

The term "criticism" itself, as a nominalization, highlights a hidden verb, "criticize" (also "critique"). It refers to an evaluation and to someone evaluating. Ask yourself, "Have I adjusted myself to the fact that human minds inevitably do what human minds do best—they weigh, compare, evaluate, criticize, etc.? How well adjusted have I made myself with this fact?"

This pattern enables us to have a strategy for responding resourcefully to any critical communication while maintaining presence of mind as well as our own value and dignity.

The Pattern

1. *Access a safety state.* To "hear," receive, and respond effectively to criticism we need to operate from a state wherein we feel unthreatened. Physically distance yourself until you feel safe. If you find this challenging, then imagine putting up a plexiglass screen around you that will shield you from incoming information. Anchor this.

To strengthen and amplify your sense of safety and strength, take a minute to get into a physiologically powerful position. Stand or sit tall, center yourself, distribute weight evenly, breathe deeply.

2. *Acknowledge and validate the other person.* "Bob (use his or her name), I appreciate the time you have taken in talking with me about this issue."

3. *Elicit fuller information.* Ask for specific and quantifiable information that you can picture clearly. "What exactly do you mean. Help me to understand your concerns." Take charge of the conversation by only asking questions. Ask for details.

4. *Fully picture the details offered.* As you hear the person speak, make a mental picture of the criticism on your mind's screen to your right (for constructed images) of the criticism. Maintain a conceptual sense of a comfortable distance from that internal film. To get a complete picture, continue to ask, "Do you have any other details to add?"

5. *Reflect back your understanding.* Reiterate in detail the criticism offered. "So what you specifically object to involves this and this. Do I have that right?" This aims to pace and match the other's understanding, so that he or she, at least, feels understood.

6. *Agreement frame.* When you feel you have a complete picture, ask the other person if he or she has anything else to add. Once you have agreement about the criticism, do not go back and add issues or details.

7. *Check out your own understandings.* On a screen, in your mind, up and to your left, make a picture (with sounds, words, feelings, etc.) of how you view the topic. What do you think, believe, value, feel, etc. about the subject?

8. *Do a comparative analysis.* Compare both pictures and, as you do, look for areas of agreement and disagreement. How close or far away do you stand with your critic?

9. *Graciously communicate your understandings.* Begin with those areas of agreement to establish rapport, " I agree that..." Let him or her know where you agree. And appreciatively thank them, "I'm glad you brought this to my attention." Then let the person know precisely where you see things differently. "I do not agree that..."

10. *Move from "understandings" to decisions.* If the person merely intends to give you information with the criticism, as you thank him or her, say, "I will take your thoughts into consideration," and leave it at that. If you need to negotiate or respond in terms of some action, you might inquire as to what specifically the other wants and/or inform them of what you intend to do in the light of the criticism.

11. *Negotiate the relationship.* If you want to further the relationship, you might want to ask, "What would you like me to do that would make a positive difference for you in regard to this matter?" You can use this format even if you choose not to do anything about the criticism. "Since I plan to do this or that in

order to maintain my own self-integrity with my values, I don't want you to feel rejected. What else could I possibly do that would enable us to feel connected?"

12. *Disagree agreeably.* If you disagree completely with the criticism and plan to take no action regarding it, then aim to offer your disagreement in as agreeable a manner as possible.

"Thanks for sharing your viewpoint about this. Since our views differ so much about this, it seems that we have come to an impasse at this point. Do you have anything else you might want to offer?"

In closing, let the person know that even more than the specific criticism, you really appreciate their openness and willingness to offer you a different perspective.

#72 The Establishing Boundaries Pattern

Concept. We experience "co-dependent" relating when we become overly involved with others and assume responsibility *for* things that we should leave to them. Because co-dependency involves poor ego-boundaries and the failure to assume proper responsibility, people who get into this style of thinking-and-feeling typically lack a good boundary development. This pattern enables us to set personal boundaries, which, in turn, leads to a greater sense of personal power, security, and centeredness.

The Pattern

1. *Identify a boundary problem* that arises from the lack of good, solid, and firm boundaries. For example, you might feel responsible *for* how another feels; you *rescue* them from the problems they create for themselves, or worry more about something in another's life than they do, etc. "Boundaries" refer to ego-boundaries that give us a sense of "me" in contradistinction to "other." Within the "boundary" we experience our values, beliefs, thoughts, feelings, and sense of identity.

2. *Create a sense-of-self space and its boundaries.* Begin with a physical sense of your territorial "space" and imagine it moving out to eighteen inches or two feet as a literal space all around you. Begin filling up this space with qualities, thoughts, feelings, resources, values, etc., that belong uniquely to you (e.g., assertiveness, confidence, dignity, love, trustworthiness, etc.). Anchor it with a color, word, or object.

3. *Solidify the boundary.* At the rim of your personal space imagine an invisible boundary. You might imagine it as a force field as in *Star Trek*, or as plexiglass, or as a boundary form that provides a separate sense of "me" apart from and different from everybody out there. Fully experience this individuation from first person and anchor it.

4. *Take second position.* Step out of yourself momentarily as you take second position with someone who values you and respects your boundaries. From their eyes, see the you with good boundaries. Hear them validating and appreciating these boundaries. Notice anything that you might need to make the resource even better.

5. *Reassume first position.* Identify, amplify, and validate every personal value, belief, and understanding that makes you distinct from other selves. Future pace this way of orienting yourself in the world.

6. *Trouble-shoot.* Imagine meeting someone who does not respect your boundaries and who talks and acts in ways that attempt to pierce your boundaries. See them trying to do this, while your resourceful self expresses the thoughts that keep the boundaries up and in good shape.

7. *Check ecology and future pace.* Imagine using these boundaries as you move into your future. "And you can now imagine how it would feel to move out into the world with this..."

#73 The Magical Parents Pattern

Concept. Some of us find ourselves entering adult life having suffered from inadequate parenting. Somehow we got stuck with parents who skipped Parenting 101 (i.e., parents who did not study how to become good parents!). Today, we need to re-parent ourselves in order to become more mature, loving, assertive, etc. Often the inadequate parenting we received inhibits our developmental growth so that we get stuck at various stages of development. This pattern addresses the deficits we might have experienced as children and gives us the technology to engage in creative and productive self-nurturing. *Source:* Sally Chamberlaine and Jan Prince, *From the Inside Out.*

The Pattern

1. *Identify needs and resources.* Imagine a blackboard or use a piece of paper. On one side, list the emotional needs that you did not receive as a child. On the other side, list the qualities necessary to fulfill these needs (e.g., understanding, empathy).

2. *Identify parental models.* Begin to construct in your mind model parents who possess the qualities necessary to fulfill the needs of the child. See, hear, and feel them completely. Use models that you have seen, read about, or observed. Especially see parents who respond with unconditional love and concern. Anchor this resource.

3. *Enrich the parental model.* Visualize and discuss how these parents relate to each other and to the child. Do this until you have a fully functioning model of effective parenting.

4. *Time-line back to birth.* Float up above your Time-line and go back to the day of your birth. Drop into that experience and, from your adult self, with all your resources, thank the old parents and explain that now your new *magical parents* will take over. Then have the magical parents welcome the child into the world and give the child loving messages. Make sure the child feels protected and cared for as you tell the child of the difference he or she will make in the world.

5. *Time-line up through childhood.* Begin to let the magical parents fulfill all the required emotional needs as you move with that child up through time.

6. *Time-line resourcefully through old negative experiences.* As you move through time, let the magical parents become especially available to the child during the negative incidents in your memory. As you do so, let these situations replay from the new and resourceful perspective of the capable and resourceful child who now has caring and wise parents. Notice the different outcome as you ask your subconscious mind to move to additional times when the child needed supportive parents. Replay these situations with the added resources from the child and parents.

7. *Zoom up the Time-line to the present.* As you Time-line resourcefully through these experiences, fire the anchor for feeling unconditional love from your parents and let your unconscious mind know that "this can generalize as you move more and more rapidly and quicker up through time to the present moment."

8. *Stop, integrate, future pace.* Holding the anchor, allow your unconscious to fully integrate these learnings and feelings and keep these learnings and feeling as you move into a bright future.

#74 The Transforming Mistakes Into Learnings Pattern
(Second "Mistake" Pattern—see #40 for the first)

Concept. When we make mistakes, we frequently respond to them in such a way that we put ourselves into a negative emotional state. The shame and guilt associated with our experience often obscure the lessons that we could learn. With this pattern, we have a strategy for looking past the negative emotions to embrace the learnings available. We can then develop the ability to use mistakes as learning tools. (We presented one format for this in the chapter on neuro-linguistic states; here we offer a second one. Enjoy.)

The Pattern

1. *Identify a mistake.* Identify a mistake which you do not want to make again or a mistake which you have associated with a negative emotion such as guilt or shame.

2. *Clarify your understanding about the "mistake."* Decide how you know it as a "mistake." What criteria do you use? Whose standards? What beliefs and values do you apply?

3. *Amplify the negative feelings.* Begin to increase the intensity of your "negative responses" to the mistake until you become unwilling to experience it again.

4. *Retrieve learnings from the mistake.* Look thoroughly at the cause-effect structure(s) that underlies the mistake. What led to it? What factors contributed? Etc. Identify any and all positive intentions. What did the part of you that generated the mistake seek to do that was of positive value? Identify the benefits or learnings coming from the experience. What secondary benefits resulted from the mistake (someone rescued you, paid you attention, etc.)?

5. *Separate emotions from lessons.* Imagine a box with a very heavy lid. As you separate the negative emotions from the lessons that you have learned from the mistake, allow all of those emotions which no longer serve you to go into that box. Float above your Time-line, back to the place(s) where the mistakes occurred. Put those lessons there in such a way that you can easily recall them.

6. *Test.* Recall the experience. Do any of the negative emotions reoccur or do you find that the emotions have become neutralized? If any of the negative emotions remain, run a movie quickly from the beginning to the end of the situation until only the lessons remain (the V-K Dissociation pattern).

#75 *The Thinking/Evaluating Wisely And Thoroughly Pattern* (SCORE Model)

Concept. What strategy do you have for thinking through a situation, problem, experience, or for gathering complete information? Thinking in a multi-faceted way (a term derived from Systems Theory which means being able to think in multiple ways simultaneously) about causes, contributing factors, systemic processes, etc., describes "wisdom"—the opposite of jumping to conclusions, reacting without thinking, having tunnel-vision, etc.

In NLP, the SCORE model provides a way to consider many of the basic components that make up effective problem-solving and the mental-emotional organizing of data. The letters of this term "SCORE" stand for the words: *Symptoms, Causes, Outcomes, Resources, and Effects.* Dilts, who uses the SCORE model extensively, as well as Tim Hallbom and Suzi Smith, suggest that we ought to consider these elements as comprising the minimum amount of information that we need to make good decisions and create effective changes.

While properly SCORE describes a **model**, and not a technique, a great many techniques come out of this format. In a sense, SCORE describes the overall NLP meta-pattern of thinking about *present state*, *desired state*, and bridging from one to the other with *resources*.

The Pattern

1. *Gather information using the SCORE model.*

Symptoms typically come to our attention and so represent the most noticeable and conscious aspects of a situation or problem. What surface and presenting symptoms do I notice? What other symptoms may I not have attended to? What about long-term symptoms? How do I represent these symptoms? What meanings do I attribute to them?

Causes refer to those effects and factors that bring a situation or problem into existence. What causes this situation? We usually experience these as less obvious and more hidden. What underlying cause could possibly explain this? Sometimes factors that only *contribute* to a situation, but do not actually *cause* it, play an important role. What about other contributing factors that I may not have paid much attention to?

Outcome(s) refers to "the end" or goal we have in mind, and, inasmuch as in the system of human consciousness outcomes feed-forward information, they also play a contributing role. What direction have I put myself in? What orientational focus affects the current situation? If I continue on this path, where will it take me? What other outcomes may arise from those outcomes? What final outcome state do I want to move toward?

Resources refer to those factors and components of thought, emotion, memory, imagination, etc., by which we create our representations, meanings, beliefs, behaviors, etc. Personal resources arise from our RS (VAK) and languaging. What resources do I need to move from this present state to my desired state?

Effects refer to the results or consequences of applying our resources to the situation. What happens when I think this way? Feel this way? Speak or act in this or that fashion? Does the response I get fit with the outcome I want? If not, then we might stop doing what doesn't work and try something else (the resource of flexibility). Frequently we can mistake the desired effect of achieving an outcome for the outcome itself. Thus we get a positive effect from wanting our goal without actually doing anything!

2. *Use your learnings from the SCORE format to guide your decisions and actions.* Do you have clarity about your outcome? Do you have access to sufficient resources? What other information do you need to gather? Where do you stand in the overall picture of the current situation with your resources as they move you to your desired outcome?

The Dancing Score. More recently (1996), Robert Dilts has developed a model of "Systemic NLP" by having a person spatially anchor each of the SCORE components along a line from "past" to "present" to "future." Then he asks the person to establish a *meta-line*—one that runs parallel to the SCORE line—and has the person step into each "meta" position to a person from their history or imagination who has resources, wisdom, or different perspectives. Doing this process exclusively via the kinesthetic modality— meaning *not* talking about it, but *"just knowing it* as you step into each position," enables a person to access his or her "somatic syntax" (as Robert describes it).

Once a person has "walked through" each of the spatial places of the SCORE on both the primary line and then the meta-line, he or she can then move through it more and more quickly—dancing his or her way through the kinesthetic spaces, letting all of the intuitive and non-conscious awarenesses emerge.

#76 A Creativity Strategy (The Walt Disney Pattern)

Concept. What kind of strategy do you have for accessing a creativity state wherein you can invent new responses for yourself and others? Robert Dilts modeled Walt Disney's process and concluded, "...there were actually three different Walts: the dreamer, the realist, and the spoiler (also called the "critic"). You never knew which one was coming to your meeting." *Source:* Robert Dilts.

This strategy moves through these three states as the three processes that enable us to both feel creative and to actually create.

The Pattern

1. Access each of the three states. With yourself, or with someone else, take the time to access, fully describe, and completely experience in an associated way each of the three states. You may want to use some spatial kinesthetic anchoring so that you have a space to which you physically move. Access and anchor each one.

Dreamer. Think of a time when you creatively dreamed up or fantasized about some new ideas without any hesitation or inhibitions. Fully remember it or imagine it and then step into that experience and relive it from first person position.

Realist. Recall a time when you demonstrated a high level thinking realistically and devised some specific plan that then allowed you to put an idea into action. Step into the Realist space and fully experience it. What does this "ready to implement" state feel like?

Evaluator/Critic. When did you engage in good, solid "critical thinking?" Recall a time when you constructively criticized and evaluated a plan so that you sharpened it, honed it, and made it better. Step in and relive it associatedly.

2. Move to a meta-position. Step aside from all of these states (physically or in your imagination) and, as you step back, notice each of them from the meta-level. Now experience your thoughts and feelings *about* each state. As you do, appreciate each as having a valid role and place.

3. Identify a desired outcome and "run it through the pattern." Now move first to your dreamer state and visualize more fully this outcome. See it as a movie playing on the screen of your mind... or as a storyboard—i.e., as a sequence of images about your goal. As you let the dream continue, constantly edit and re-edit your movie.

Now move into the realist position and notice what you need to do, if anything, that would achieve your outcome. What actions do you need to take? How would you implement this vision? What would comprise the first step, the second, the third? Create an action plan for implementing this dream.

Now step into your critic/evaluator space and critically evaluate it—looking for missing pieces, for what might not work, for what you still need, etc. Keep a list of improvements that you can make.

4. Re-dream your dream. Return to your dreamer state and creatively use all of the realistic and critical information you received to make the idea an even better one. Keep re-cycling through this process until every fabric in your being goes, "Yes!"

#77 *The Spinning Icons Pattern* (Integration Pattern)

Concept: This pattern of *the Spinning Icons* creates an iconic metaphor out of any two contrasting experiences for the purpose of generating a higher level generalization [or meta-state].

The process involves eliciting a fairly concrete, sensory representation of two experiences. The next step involves changing the concrete representations into abstract icons. This moves the process of problem-solving, creativity, etc. into a different and higher realm. You then follow this by making a change in the VAK structure at the submodality level of location. By rotating the icons, exchanging locations, and spinning more and more rapidly, a new "metaphor" arises by blending the icons into a single iconic representation. This results in a new connection. The new icon exists as *a symbolic guide* to help a person move from present state to desired state. In the final step, the person *tells a story* about the new icon. In doing this one moves down the ladder of abstraction and frequently gains insights into about how to achieve the goal. The following represents the visual version of the pattern. This operates as an integration pattern useful for virtually any NLP change work. Nelson Zink and Joe Munshaw developed this pattern, originally named "Synthesizing Generalizations."

The Pattern

1. *Identify two states.* Think of a discrepancy between your present state and your desired state or goal. Notice any incongruity between the current state or experience and the state or experience that you want to have, or between your present resources and your desired resources.

2. *Get two visual representations.* As you think of your present state (problem state, stuck state), what visual image or representation do you get? What picture occurs in your mind's eye? Notice particularly where you locate the picture and its distance from you. Describe the picture briefly.

As you think of your desired state (outcome, goal, resources), what visual representation do you get? Notice this picture's location and distance. Describe briefly.

3. *Abstract from the representations to a symbol or icon.* Now, allow your mind to turn the first picture into some kind of abstract symbol or iconic visual representation. Just let the icon appear. Keep the icon in the location of the first picture.

[Note: when you use this with someone, pay special attention to pacing the recipient's vocabulary and experience. Also you may find that the phrases, "stick figure drawing," "cartoon," or "caricature" may work better for some people than the phrase, "iconic visual representation." Some people develop very elaborate and detailed icons while others create pictures with very simple visual representations, sometimes as simple as merely coding a color. The key here lies in guiding the client from a concrete, specific picture to an abstract visual symbolic representation.]

4. *Repeat this same process with the second picture.* Turn it into an iconic image that you find in the same location as the second picture.

5. *Rotate the icons until they spin out wildly.* See the two iconic images at the same time, now, each image in its proper location. [Pause]

Now, s-l-o-w-l-y begin to rotate them, allow them to exchange locations, then move back to their original locations, then exchange locations again, etc. Begin to *rotate or spin* them a bit more rapidly now. Let them go round and round and, as they do, spin more and more rapidly. Now let them move *very rapidly!* Have the person continue to do this for about ten seconds.

[Note: the basic idea here involves getting the icons to move around each other. For some people the word "rotate" will work best; others will respond better to the word "spin." The key lies in the moving relationship between the two icons in relationship to each other.]

6. *Blend the spinning icons.* As you rotate the icons very, very rapidly, now let them blend together into a single image and allow this new image to move right out in front of you, where you can view it easily. What new icon do you see before you? Describe it briefly.

[As you do, get a quick and brief description. Pace the client's emotions and ideas about the new icon. Move as quickly as possible to step seven.]

7. *Language a story.* When you have the new icon in place, immediately begin telling whatever "story" or incident comes to your mind. This could arise from a past memory or incident in your life, a fairy tale or story you have heard, a made-up or constructed story from your life...w-h-a-t-e-v-e-r you have—simply begin telling a story, now.

[Note: At the end of the story begin exploring with the client how the insights gained from it apply to getting the outcome or desired state the client seeks. "How is the story relevant to your difficulty?" The story/metaphor exists as a fairly abstract piece, but less abstract than the icons. The metaphor offers insights into specific elements of how the problem or quest for the goal might now be considered differently.

The story or narrative, discussed in step seven, does not necessarily play an essential role to the change work created in the first six steps. The story simply takes the change which has happened largely at an unconscious level and makes it more conscious and coherent to the client.

For experienced practitioners who work regularly with people, you can add *the Spinning Icons Technique* to your elegant "bag of tricks." Compare and contrast Spinning Icons with what you do, and discover what happens. Zink and Munshaw (1998) have also developed auditory and kinesthetic versions of the Spinning Icon technique. Contact Joe Munshaw at Gateway NLP Institute for a free copy of those instructions: jmunshaw@primary.net

Conclusion

NLP arose from modeling, and continues to model *strategies of excellence*. By identifying the language components of subjectivity, as well as the structural components that make up its syntax, we can accurately describe the "strategy" of subjectivity. We can also discover the strategy of experiences that do not attain their desired outcome, and either redesign it, or simply install a new one.

For other patterns that involve strategies, see the Establishing Value Hierarchy Pattern, the As If Frame Pattern, and the Agreement Frame Pattern.

And The Magic Of Enhancing Patterns Continues ...

We have put into this volume the most extensive list to date of **NLP patterns** for "running your own brain," taking charge of your life, becoming more resourceful, and generatively transforming yourself. And yet this list by no means exhausts the field. Many, many other patterns have already been created as well as a multitude of hybrid patterns that mix and mingle with these to thereby create new mixtures applicable to various fields: health, therapy, sports, business, personal life, hobbies, religion, law, education, etc.

Having recently authored, with Dr. Bobby Bodenhamer, a work on Time-Lines (1997), I (MH) here list a whole set of patterns that we have not included in this book.

1. Entering into the Place of Pure Potentiality
2. Fast Time & Slow Time—Time Distortion Pattern
3. Spiraling Resource Experiences in Time—Collapsing into the Now
4. Accessing the Flow State of the Eternal Now
5. Developing More Time for Patience—Now
6. Chrono-phobia Cure Pattern
7. Transforming "Time" by New Sentence Generator
8. Linguistic Re-Narrating Life
9. Linguistically De-Storying and Re-Storying Life
10. Developing a New Rhythm for "Time"
11. Developing a Neurological Rhythm for "Time" & "Times"
12. "Time" Alignment Pattern
13. Finishing a Past Gestalt
14. Taking Interest to Reframe "Boredom"

Since developing and promoting **the NLP Meta-States Model,** I (MH) also have created and designed numerous patterns that involve taking a meta-level position, as well as reformulating many of the NLP patterns in terms of that model. We have included a few in this text. Others include:

1. The Einstein Pattern of Creativity and Problem-Solving
2. Triangles of Excellence (developed from Nicholas's, 1996, MDI pattern)

3. Synthesizing Generalizations (developed from Zink & Munshaw's pattern, 1996)
4. The Mystery Theater 3000 Pattern (*Anchor Point*, December 1995)
5. Gestalting States Patterns For Resolving Conflicts (Developed from Assagioli's Transpersonal psychology work and book on Psychosynthesis)
6. Interpersonal Meta-Stating (*Anchor Point*, June 1996 and February 1997)
7. Self-Management of Negative Emotions Pattern
8. The Miracle Adjustment Shift (*Anchor Point*, January 1997, developed from Brief Psychotherapy's Miracle Question)
9. The NLP Happiness Pattern (*Anchor Point*, June 1996, and January 1997)
10. The De-Pleasuring Pattern (for deframing addictions)

Of course, these additional patterns only touch the hem of the garment in terms of the scores and scores of other patterns that have arisen and continue to arise in the field of NLP. Monthly in *Anchor Point* (Utah, USA) and quarterly in *NLP World* (Switzerland), and in *Rapport* (London) as well as in other publications, you will see the creativity of this field manifested.

Come, join the revolution of human evolution for excellence!

Part Three

Pattern Applications

Thinking Like A Magician

Chapter 11

Thinking In Patterns

Pattern Thinking As An Art And A Skill

Any sufficiently advanced technology is indistinguishable from magic.

Arthur C. Clarke

When it comes to our choices about *what* to *think* and *how* to *think,* we have a great many options. We referred to this in Chapter 8 with regard to *thinking patterns.*

For instance, we can think **inductively** from many particulars and move up to some general principle. We can think **deductively** down from some global understanding as we move down to specific applications. We can even think, as Gregory Bateson described and recommended, **abductively**, by using metaphors and analogies, and reason across from one thing to another thing. Lakoff and Johnson (1980) and numerous cognitive theorists argue for the metaphorical basis of cognition in making sense of things.

We can also think in sights, sounds, sensations and in words (representational systems). We can think by matching and comparing for similarities or we can think by mismatching and comparing for differences (sorting for sameness versus difference). We can think in terms of what we think and know or what others think and know ("self" and "other" referencing). Indeed, we have many kinds of ways of thinking.

In terms of a **thinking style** that we have assumed throughout this work—we have encouraged a strategic and procedural style rather than an optional or creative style. By identifying *patterned ways* of redirecting consciousness in expanding one's conceptual maps, we have relied on specific *patterns*. In doing so, we have presupposed that you can easily shift to **thinking in** *patterns*. When you do, such *pattern thinking* gives you specific *procedures* for how to use your brain so that you can more effectively manage yourself and your states. This also presupposes that certain processes inherently work better than others and that we can learn specific strategies for effectiveness which govern specific domains. By learning to think in terms of *strategic patterns*, we can more easily adopt the most effective strategies.

This dovetails into the chapter on *Strategies* (chapter 10) wherein we described the importance of *modeling*. After all, these NLP patterns, for the most part, arose from *modeling* as a special kind of *pattern thinking*. Thus the special kind of thinking involved in *modeling* human subjectivity leads us to sort for and think about such things as the following:

- *How* does a person *develop* pattern thinking in order to generate patterns?
- What kind of thinking may interfere with *pattern thinking*?
- Will *pattern thinking* interfere with creative thinking, critical thinking, or intuitive thinking?

Pattern Thinking

The processes that work so efficiently, quickly, and thoroughly in the Cognitive-Behavioral psychologies do so because of the emphasis on **how** rather than **why**. This separates the *"why" models* of human functioning that function on explanation and understanding origins and history (e.g., psychoanalysis, Jungian, Adlerian, Ego, Humanistic Existential, Transpersonal, etc.) from *the "how" models* that focus on process and structure (NLP, Brief, Gestalt, Reality Therapy, REBT, etc.).

How thinking skips over the psycho-theological belief systems about origins and "meanings" and goes right to **structure**. *How* should we code this or that information (as ideas, beliefs, understandings) to create a strategy (or model of the world) that will allow us to function in business, friendship, intimate relationships, recreation, etc., with much more passion and joy? Once we find the *structure* of experience (regardless of *content)* we can change *that* very structure via modalities and submodalities.

This bypasses resistance, psycho-archeology, the need for understanding its source, etc. It enables us to work in a much more solution-focused way. Working at *the structural level* of experience (beliefs, behaviors, emotion, etc.) in our neurology allows us to make changes without knowing a lot of content. Theoreticians designate this approach as *"process psychology."* We look for the process; we ask process questions ("How do you prevent the problem from occurring?"); we identify processes at work ("So when you hear her voice, that loud shrilling voice in your head, that really 'rattles your cage'"); and facilitate trying out new processes ("Now shrink down that picture and allow it to fade out").

Shifting From Content To Process

If *pattern thinking* involves shifting out of the "content" of thoughts to a higher logical level—thinking about the *structure and process* of thoughts—how do we do this? What steps do we need to take to make this shift?

First, we need to recognize the difference between the two. So many people don't. Actually this describes part of the problem— *people get caught up in the content.*

Whenever we develop tunnel vision about a problem or solution, we can only see one thing—and it looms large in our sight. We then filter out "unique outcomes," exceptions, counter-examples, alternatives, etc. Filtering out the positive, we then use our tunnel vision perspective to predict a gloomy future. In becoming more and more caught up in the problem, we personalize, catastrophize, over-generalize, think in all-or-nothing terms, and then end up prophesying, "It's hopeless."

Even therapists frequently don't always operate from a process approach. They can also lose perspective and *get caught up in the content.* At that point, we typically have two people experiencing a stuck state! Therapists who suffer burn-out frequently reach that point because they let the client's languaging of their dilemmas function as an hypnotic induction!

Getting "caught up in the details of the client's content" also occurs when therapists forget that diagnostic labels only operate as symbols and like other words, "they are not real." Labels only exist as linguistic maps and explanatory schemes. Forgetting to treat the labels as just labels, therapists fail to see the person behind the label.

Second, we need the ability to step aside from the content. Once we recognize the difference between content and process, we can step aside from the content. This means that we can put our beliefs on hold, treat them tentatively, not taking our language or stories (or those of others) too seriously.

Using our map-territory understanding of how the nervous system abstracts information from the world to create our under-standings enables us to treat all human constructs as just that— *human constructs.* This helps us to lighten up, reject "seriousness," see things more humorously, and realize that more often than not we (and others) have simply *languaged ourselves for misery.*

General Semantics introduces several *formulations* that can assist us at this point.

1. *The map-territory distinction,* "The map is not the territory".
2. *Consciousness of abstracting* or awareness that our subjective reality arises from and reflects our abstracting and does not necessarily correspond with "reality."
3. *Tentativeness*—a tentative attitude about the "reality" of our maps, our words, our ideas, our feelings. "It seems to me... at this point in time..."
4. *Indexing* the specifics: what, when, where, who, how, in what way, from what source, etc.
5. *Etc.* "I can never say all about anything. Therefore I need to append my statements with 'etc.'" [Ah, now you have an explanation for the apparent over-use of *etc.* in this text!]

Understanding and using these formulations assists us in *not* getting caught up in content. They enable us to maintain a sanity about our human constructions, since *no identity* exists, only *non-identity* exists. In other words, "sameness" does not exist in process reality, only differences. This means that everything continually changes, shifts, alters, transforms. So allness and identity exist as illusions and can lead to unsanity.

Recognizing these things enables us to **step back** or, as Bateson said, to go "meta" to our content and think-feel *about* it at a higher logical level. Taking a higher perspective means using our self-reflexive consciousness and engaging in an advanced form of human thinking—thinking about our thinking.

Third, we need to practice "going meta" and noticing the structural elements in the content. NLP does this in its basic model since we have to step back and identify the different *modes* of awareness. Noticing the visual, auditory and kinesthetic representations (VAK) puts us at a higher logical level than content. Again, we moved to another process level when we began making distinctions in the qualities of the modalities and specified some of the submodalities.

Learning the strategy model facilitates moving from content to process. It operates at the process level to the extent that it causes us to notice how an experience functions. It facilitates our understanding about the syntax of the experience.

The *Meta-States Model* further provides us with a rich awareness of structure, as it moves our awareness even higher through moving up logical levels. This model takes into consideration the structural effect when we bring a state of consciousness (of mind-body) to bear upon another state of consciousness (as in fear of fear, anger at fear, etc.).

Fourth, develop awareness about structures and processes in subjectivity. The more structural facets that we know and understand, the more ability we will have to conceptually step aside and notice process. So far we have offered for your consideration:

- Modalities (Representational Systems)
- Submodalities
- Meta-programs (sorting styles)
- Strategies (TOTEs as sequences of RS)
- Meta-states

Even the transformation patterns gets us thinking more about process and structure than content. This develops our intuitive sense of *how* patterns work, *what makes* them work, *how to generate them* with ourselves and others, how to quality-test them, etc.

Conclusion

NLP, as a model of human excellence and psychosis, began via a process of **modeling**. The founders of this domain initiated their work by asking *process questions*:

- "How does this piece of human subjectivity work?"
- "What patterns of internal processing go into the formula that generates this?"
- "How can we *structurally* describe the patterns and meta-patterns?"

Thus, *modeling a person's strategy* for a piece of genius, or for a piece of psychosis such as schizophrenia, has **structure.** In this chapter we have suggested the importance of thinking in terms of *patterns*—curiosity about structuring patterns, understanding of pattern analysis, skill in replication of enhancing patterns, etc. Accepting and perceiving *patterns* empowers us to recognize, identify, and replicate **patterns of excellence.** We then can "run those patterns" through our own neuro-linguistics.

In the next two chapters we carry this analysis further. First, we will explore *the wisdom* involved in knowing **what** magic to do **when** (the very theme of this work). Then we will identify a few major *domains of application* and how to do pattern thinking in those areas to create ever-increasing levels of excellence.

Chapter 12

Figuring Out What Magic To Do At What Times

Robert Dilts, in the context of thinking about and designing *a "Unified Field Theory of NLP,"* has raised a central question that frequently comes up with regard to using these magical NLP patterns. We have used this question, in fact, as part of our formulation of this work. I (MH) have heard people raise this question repeatedly while conducting NLP training, namely,

---

"How do you know what to do when?"

As we now apply this to *the NLP toolbox* containing scores of patterns, processes, and techniques, *how can we figure out what pattern to use, with what difficulties, at what times, with regard to different individuals?*

In the 1950s, Abraham Maslow noted that, if you only have a hammer, the likelihood increases that you will tend to see every problem as something to hammer. Yet not every tool will work for every problem. The Visual-Kinesthetic Dissociation pattern, as a human technology, will not work for every presenting problem, nor will Six-step Reframing, or Core Transformation. This leads us to postulate several very important questions:

- *When* will a particular pattern work?
- *When* will that same pattern *not* work?
- *What factors* indicate use of a given pattern?
- What factors *counter-indicate* its use?
- What meta-level understandings guide our decisions about *what* pattern to choose?
- What understandings assist us in deciding *when* to use it?
- *What* distinctions about "problems" can help us to sort and separate them?

To date, the NLP model has offered only a few guidelines, and very general ones at that, so we have, *"When what you do doesn't work, try something else."* In spite of the general usefulness of this rule, it actually provides no direction about *what* to do. It only suggests that we do "something" *different*. It offers no distinctions about matching certain problems with certain patterns. Nor does this rule of flexibility prescribe *what* else to try. As such it only offers us a rule for a floundering flexibility rather than *an intelligible flexibility*.

Distinctions Inside "Problems"

Robert Dilts (1995) has suggested that we begin by first looking at *"problems"* themselves and then explore some distinctions that we can make with regard to them. In his 1995 seminar, *Unified Field Theory of NLP,* and in his 1996 article *NLP, Self Organization and Strategies of Change Management,* he suggested two sets of distinctions: *stable/unstable* and *simple/complex.*

- "Is the problem stable or unstable?"
- "Does the problem present itself consistently, regularly, and predictably or does it present itself in an unstable way, inconsistent and random?"

The Stability Factor

Stable problems have a regularity and dependability about them. The person consistently and systemically experiences the problem. They can count on it. You can on it. For example, every time the person steps into an elevator, he freaks out. Or, every time she hears *that* tone of voice, she feels an inner sense of panic.

Problems of this sort have *a stable S-R (stimulus > response) structure.* Thus the strategy that drives it involves a straightforward and habitual pattern. Within this structure, *a synesthesia* drives and organizes it in order to keep it consistently regular. The person never gets into an elevator, rides up, goes into a meeting and then thinks, "Shoot, I forgot to feel panicky!" So we typically find stable problems operating from out-of-conscious awareness (unconscious processes).

Unstable problems operate from, and involve, a very different tone and structure. They come and go. They manifest an ebb and flow that operates, seemingly, without rhyme or reason. Typically we can't figure them out! Nor can we count on them. They occur in random patterns. Now it occurs; now it doesn't. The problem lacks consistency and regularity. You can't count on the problem nor predict it.

Dilts describes this kind of problem as involving *an ever-shifting landscape.* He uses this phrase about "landscapes" as a vivid metaphor for *unstable* problems. For example, a person will suffer from depression on one occasion and from mania on the next. Or, a person can't decide about anything, and then later becomes rigidly dogmatic in his or her decisions. First they experience one set of symptoms, and then they experience another set.

Typically, unstable problems involve more complexity inasmuch as we have more "parts" or facets of personality (mind, emotion, meaning, value, beliefs, contexts, roles, etc.) that play a part in the process. With *unstable* problems we should therefore inquire about the number of component pieces or elements that play a contributing factor to the difficulty.

The Complexity Factor

After the *stable/unstable* distinction, we can look for and take into consideration the complexity of a problem.

- "How simple or complex do we find the problem?"
- "When we examine the structure of the problem, how would we describe the manner of its operation? In a simple or complex manner?"
- "Does it involve just primarily level functions and operations, or does it involve reflexive processes that loop back from output at one time that later becomes input?"

Simple problems involve direct, immediate, and primary level processes. *Phobias* fit this description. So do allergies. When the stimulus occurs, the person then has a direct response to it. Again, *stimulus > response.* Simple problems generally contain just a few elements rather than many components. Dilts, continuing his metaphor, describes this as having a "solid landscape."

Complex problems, on the other hand, involve many elements and may also involve many layers or levels of involvement. Thus Post Traumatic Stress Disorder (PTSD) certainly has the S-R structure to it of a phobia. It also has many other components, i.e. the fear response not only to a sight, sound, sensation, but to many sights, sounds, and sensations. It may also involve many levels. Thus someone suffering from PTSD may have not only a strategy to fear darkness, the sound of footsteps, and other primary level stimuli, but also a strategy to experience a panic attack at the *thought of such a memory,* at the *idea* of abuse, at the *meaning* of being controlled, etc.

With these two factors we can now create a quadrant of four interfaces that allows us to examine problems for simple/complex and stable/unstable.

Figure 12.1

Change Quadrants

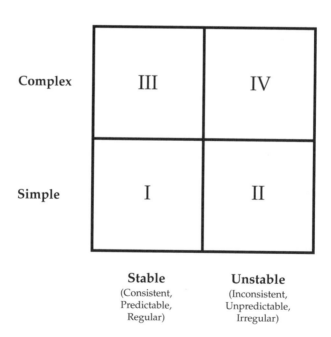

Complex	III	IV
Simple	I	II
	Stable (Consistent, Predictable, Regular)	**Unstable** (Inconsistent, Unpredictable, Irregular)

Problem Analysis

In **Quadrant I** of the chart we have simple and stable problems (e.g., phobias, allergies, stuck in a negative emotional state, decisions, or limitations, unproductive strategies, procrastination, depressions, learned helplessness, etc.) These problems stay put and operate regularly and systematically. So more often than not, *one profound shift at the key leverage point* may create profound, radical, and surprising transformation. *Magic!*

Thus we experience the magical effects of "the phobia cure" in NLP. It works fast, and profoundly. So with other shifts, when we come upon a methodologically regular strategy—and we intervene so that it can't keep functioning as it has. Herein lie most of the highly celebrated interventions of NLP.

In **Quadrant II** we have simple, but unstable, problems. These come and go in a random and unpredictable manner—uncontrollable anger that flares up unpredictably, stress overloads that come "out of the blue," manic-depression, obsessive-compulsive disorders, etc. Sometimes you have these kinds of problems—sometimes you don't. Here a person may *think* he or she has created a solution or resolution to a difficulty, only to find it reappearing at a later date.

Contexts play a crucial role in these kinds of problems. The problem may not occur daily. It probably does not operate as part of one's basic orientation through the world—which also explains why a person doesn't "understand" the problem when it does occur. "I'm not a violent person." "I don't even believe in getting upset with someone." "I don't know why I get into that kind of a mood."

Thus *the context* of the person's ongoing state—that slowly and imperceptibly builds up until they have reached a place where other maps kick in—plays a much more crucial role in these problems. Here, then, we have to explore contexts, contexts over time, identity contexts, meaning contexts, etc.

In **Quadrant III** we have complex and stable problems. Though they involve many components and/or layers, we can predictably count on them. These include such things as PTSD, unenhancing meta-states (self-contempt), eating disorders, identity disorders, etc.

The difficulty with stable-and-complex problems lies in fully specifying all of the complexities that go into generating them.

- What other thoughts-and-feelings do you experience with regard to this problem?
- What other meanings?
- What other component pieces bleed over into this experience?

Here we will typically want to simplify and reduce the "problem" by pulling apart the complexities and treating them as we would problems that occur in Quadrant I.

In **Quadrant IV** we have complex, but unstable problems. These problems also come and go. Here again we can't predict when the complex problems will occur. They don't seem to operate from a systematic strategy. These include such phenomena as: multi-personality disorder, schizoform personality disorder, schizophrenia, etc.

If the stable-and-complex problems of Quadrant III provide a challenge in identifying all of the different component pieces that go into making them up, here we have another complicating problem. The problem won't hold still so that we can take a good clear picture of it. Its lack of stability causes it to continually shift and change, and this can sabotage a clear and precise description of it.

Tracking A Problem's Trajectory

What happens to a simple-and-stable problem (I) when it becomes unstable (II)? When a phobia (I) becomes unstable (II) it ceases to operate as a dependable phobia. As it de-stabilizes, it breaks up the rigid S-R patterning. This destabilization creates a space for change and transformation.

What happens to a simple-and-stable problem (I) when it becomes complex (III)? When a phobia (I) becomes complex (III), it becomes stronger and more rigid, just in new and more complicating ways—as PTSD or agoraphobia. Now the problem takes on new layers and levels so that the person fears his fear, fears time, fears self, fears higher level fears.

What happens when a complex-and-stable problem (III) becomes unstable (IV)? De-stabilizing the rigid synesthesia patterns breaks up the constructions, again making room for change and a new re-construction.

What happens when a simple-and-unstable problem (II) becomes complex (III)? It becomes a quadrant IV problem—complex and unstable.

What happens when a complex-and-unstable problem (IV) becomes simple-and-unstable (II)? It becomes somewhat more manageable and even more so if it becomes simple-and-stable.

Guidelines For Choosing Patterns For Interventions

When we come across a stable, regular, and consistent problem, we may first want to **de-stabilize** it. By de-stabilizing the structure, it frequently becomes de-framed and cannot exist any more. At other times, it simply opens up space for us whereby we can bring about change. Three powerful means for deframing and deconstructing a reality include: Meta-modeling, strategy analysis, and submodality exploration. With these technologies, we can alter the structure of the problem.

When it comes to problems that have much complexity and layeredness, we can focus primarily on **simplifying** and **reducing** their size and shape. This enables us to fragment them. And, in so fragmenting them, we essentially use the strategy of "dividing and conquering." Then it becomes easier to find or create solutions to smaller problems. Reducing the confusion clarifies the processes. Then we can begin to sort out the complexities, discover the time element that operates, etc.

When we encounter an unstable problem, we will want to go to the opposite direction, and **stabilize** it. Stabilizing a problem thereby transforms an unstable and unwielding problem so that it operates with more regularity. And by giving it more stability, we can "hold it still" long enough to identify its underlying strategy and the components that drive it. How do we so stabilize an unstable problem? We can provide more feedback and more reflexiveness from a meta-level about its functioning. These things generally help to stabilize a process. Moving to a higher level of resolution can provide help as it establishes a meta-level of stability, as an "Agreement Frame" does in a conflict.

When instability arises from lack of focus and direction—we can simply begin to identify some goals, values, and outcomes. "On what level do you think or feel this?" "On what level do you want this outcome?"

Levels Of Problems

In an early work on NLP, Robert Dilts (1983) made another set of distinctions about "problems." He sorted out differences, which I (MH, 1995, 1996) have labeled *primary state* experiences and behaviors, from *meta-level constructions*. This refers to the logical levels involved in a problem.

> *The more acute behaviors, such as bad habits, compulsions, and phobias tend to constitute content behaviors and are fairly easily dealt with by employing simple anchoring techniques of deprogramming and program substitution. Behavior such as chronic depression, psychosis, or neurosis will probably require state-altering techniques, such as interruption, exaggeration or the various verbal and non-verbal tracking techniques.*
>
> (Part III, p. 88).

This suggests that when we work with meta-level structures, we can expect more complexity, layeredness, and therefore a longer time element involved in bringing it to resolution. Dilts (1990, page 70) described how he discovered that it took a longer time when he worked with the meta-level nature of beliefs. He noted that this took longer, not because it "should take a long time and be complicated," but because sometimes things have a layered nature to them so that it takes more time to uncover the true structure of things.

If we work on a problem that involves meta-levels *at the same level* of the problem, it will take much longer. But if we move to a higher level and **outframe** the problem from that position—sometimes we can perform *meta-magic* that "in one fell swoop" can change a response in a moment. For more on this see Advanced NLP Modeling—*NLP: Going Meta: Modeling And Engineering Human* (Hall, 1997).

When we have more layeredness within a "problem," we generally have *a structure of reflexivity.* This means that not only do we have some fears or angers about something and that creates suffering, but we have thoughts-and-feelings about those first thoughts-and-feelings. To explore the layeredness of a problem we have to pull apart the reflexivity to find the patterns of psychic energy turning back onto itself. This feedback of previous thoughts-and-feelings and concepts back into the system will indicate how complex a system we have on our hands.

More "Problem" Distinctions

Emotional Intensity. How much *energy* or emotional intensity does a given problem have? How compelling does it feel to the person? How much does it drive them? Do they feel that it operates on the edge of consciousness or at the center? When the "problem" occurs, does it totally consume and drive them or does it just gnaw at them from the edges? How much does the problem enter into *consciousness*? A little, or does it totally consume them?

As we ask these questions about *the emotional intensity* of a "problem," we probe to understand the psychological world of the sufferer. Some "problems" do not even break forth into consciousness. A person may procrastinate, fall into a depression, break forth into a rageaholic episode, and hardly notice it. Another person may experience running the very same behaviors and do so painfully conscious of doing so. One person may run these behaviors, but not *compulsively.* If they notice themselves procrastinating, depressing, raging, etc., they may simply stop doing so.

For them, conscious awareness brings *control.* For the others, conscious awareness only intensifies the pain, as it reminds them that "the problem has them" rather than that they have charge over the "problem."

Nor does the *emotional intensity* element make a "problem" more or less difficult to change. The most raging panic operates according to an internal coding structure and can change almost immediately when a person changes that format (as in the V-K dissociation technique). Prior to this understanding, theorists tended to assume that the emotional intensity of a problem *meant* "more entrenched, deeper, and more difficult to change." But the NLP model suggests that we recognize that the somatic kines-thetics (the emotional intensity) result from the coding. Code a fearful item from an associated perspective—close, loud, etc.—and it will crank up one's responses to it.

Habituation time. Generally, we find it important to inquire about how long a person has had a particular problem. Also, typically, the longer a person has suffered from a "problem," the more entrenched and solid (stable) the problem has become. But not always. By habituating and repeating a certain pattern of thinking, emoting, and responding, it formulates one's neurology. Doing this enables us to *streamline* the strategy and run it without consciousness. This empowers us to "fly into a state of" rage, panic, helplessness, etc. It also enables us to connect more and more things to the state so that we have more anchors for it.

These facets of habituation (more repetitions and associations, becoming more streamlined, with less conscious awareness) deepen the "problem" strategy. Yet the habituation process *alone* does not completely determine a problem's stability or entrenchedness. We do have to maintain it. And we maintain a strategy by giving it importance, significance, and value. It has to keep serving some valued service.

Thus *ongoing continual development of skill and competence*, which typically occurs in human growth and development over the lifespan, can itself temper and even nullify "problems." In this way, we can simply *outgrow* a fear or phobia. Our overall general resourcefulness as a person makes the older fears less significant and realistic.

Accessibility of other resources. Obviously, "problems" do not exist in a vacuum, but within the whole person-as-an-organism in numerous contexts. This means that they exist alongside *personal* and *contextual resources*. Typically, the more resources that a person can access and bring to bear on a difficulty, the less of a "problem" that difficulty presents. And conversely, the fewer resources, the more problematic the difficulty.

Accordingly, in exploring a problem with any person, we will want to probe, detect, amplify, and apply *resources* to the problem. This explains why states of desperation amplify "problems." In such states, we blow things out of proportion, and engage in such cognitive distortions as personalizing, catastrophizing, awfulizing, negative filtering, thinking in dualistic either-or patterns, etc.

Here Brief Therapy, Ericksonian Hypnosis, Narrative Therapy, NLP and other solution-oriented therapies utilize the overall strategy of hunting down, accessing, and creating *resources*. The more *resourcefully* a person thinks and feels depends on the coping and mastering skills that they can access and apply. How existentially safe does a person feel in his or her *person*? How much of a reality orientation does the person have? How skilled at problem-solving? At appropriate risk taking, at living with a sense of purpose and mission, at connecting in loving, affectionate, and supportive ways with others?

Conclusion

All "problems" that challenge and provoke us do not have the same structure. In this chapter we have explored the *pattern of "problems"* by looking at them in terms of stable/unstable and simple/complex. Making these distinctions with regard to stimulating events, information, and experiences allows us to have a better grasp about **what** to do with regard to different kinds of difficulties.

This means that even *a great piece of "magic"* will do you no good if you use it on the wrong problem! Thus—**the right magic for the right problem!**

Chapter 13

Domains Of Use

Hints For Using NLP In Business, Education,
Therapy, Sports, Health, Relationships, Etc.

Business

NLP patterns offer lots of wonderful resources in the realms of business, management, team building, sales, and consulting. Basic communication skills offer resources for making sense of things and communicating with precision and clarity. Numerous authors and trainers have adapted these patterns to the domain of creating and maintaining rapport.

We would direct the business person to chapter 3 on the basic patterns for learning and using "pacing" as well as to the "Precision Model" (Grinder's form of the Meta-model) in chapter 7. Since *"communication"* drives businesses, understanding the basic processes of communicating, and the rules for using the *Meta-model* linguistic muddledness (vagueness) in assisting others to clarify and to offer more precise descriptions, powerfully increases one's effectiveness.

As a professional communicator in the business realm—whether you seek to inform, teach, persuade, sell, market, etc.—you need to have a sense of what your words and non-verbal messages *do* in the minds-and-bodies of those who hear you. To lack this aware-ness limits you to "shooting in the dark," merely hoping that your language use will have its desired effect. But once you know that you always and inevitably *induce* those who listen to you into *states* of mind-and-emotion, you can begin to use your languaging (verbally and non-verbally) more consciously and creatively. Here the patterns in chapter 6 on *state inductions* will provide much assistance.

What state or states do you typically *evoke* in people? What states assist and enhance your work? Which do not? What states would you like to have more power in evoking? How do you recognize such in those around you? This underscores the importance of calibration skills and the ability to work at meta-levels.

Further, in business we inevitably operate out of our own *Meta-programs* that govern how and what we sort for, and so does everybody with whom we interact. We identified the NLP Meta-programs in chapter 8 and suggested that these programs operate as different *channels of awareness,* so to speak. Does the person need details first, or the big picture? Does your boss want you to give him or her a procedure, or several options, for getting a job done? What does your client sort for when he or she decides to make a purchase? What convinces that person?

In business, consulting, managing, selling, marketing, etc., we also sometimes need to have well-developed specific procedures or strategies. We addressed the subject of *NLP strategies* in chapter 10. What does the strategy for effectively managing resistant employees look like? What strategy does a successful person in the stock market use? What supporting beliefs does he or she utilize? How does one effectively manage to "confront" someone making a mistake and do so maintaining and giving dignity to the persons involved? (For full works on strategy analysis and design, see *NLP: Volume I,* and *NLP: Going Meta—Advance Modeling Using Meta-Levels.*)

Education

As a communication model of human learning, NLP obviously has many, many applications in the domain of education and training. Accordingly, we would recommend that an educator begin with the basic patterns (chapter 3) as well as with the NLP model itself (chapter 2) in order to become highly proficient in the representation systems and the kind of learning styles that students use.

This corresponds amazingly well to the work of Dr. Howard Gardner (1983, 1991, 1993) in his books on *Multiple Intelligences*. The eight intelligences that Gardner identified relate closely to NLP.

- Verbal-linguistic intelligence
- Logical-mathematical intelligence
- Visual-spatial intelligence
- Bodily-kinesthetic intelligence
- Musical-rhythmic intelligence
- Interpersonal intelligence
- Intrapersonal intelligence
- Naturalist intelligence

The basic NLP model about "mind" specifies our learning modalities (the VAK representational systems), and then, at a meta-level, the multiple Meta-programs (chapter 8), provide even greater levels of distinctions regarding how we input and process information.

Further, inasmuch as every *learning context* involves a holistic mind-body *state*, educators inevitably have to attend to the mind-body states in which they find their learners. Since *state-dependency* means that a non-enhancing state can actually prevent learning, a professional teacher must work with the neuro-linguistic states that their students bring into class. Without question, in most schools teachers can in fact count on their students probably *not* coming to school in a conducive learning state. This makes the NLP patterns for working with and managing states (chapter 6) very important.

Wisdom, in fact, would suggest, don't you think, that an effective and professional educator would have a well-developed and explicit strategy for eliciting learning states, inducing states of curiosity, wonder, openness, excitement, etc.? And, if we back up one step further, then we would want to explore the best strategy to put ourselves into a state where we even think about modeling excellent examples of teachers (chapter 10).

For fuller works on the application of NLP to education, see Sid Jacobson's three volumes *Meta-Cation*, Joseph Yeager's work *Thinking About Thinking Using NLP,* and Michael Grinder's *ENVoY: Personal Guide to Classroom Management.*

Psychotherapy

Interestingly enough, even though NLP began via a modeling project of three world-renowned therapists from three different psychological models, in the initial work, *The Structure Of Magic, Volume I* (1975), Bandler and Grinder essentially assumed and created a Cognitive-Behavioral model. Subsequently NLP has been located within the Cognitive-Behavioral "school" of psychology ever since (Gilliland, James, and Bowman, 1989, pp. 249). And so it should.

In psychotherapy, the chapters on conflicting parts (chapter 4), identity (chapter 5), meaning (chapter 9), states (chapter 6) and strategies (chapter 10) will offer a wide range of interventions. Yet since these NLP patterns grew out of the way language itself works (chapter 7) and the way human "minds" process it (chapter 8), the interventions at the level of thinking (the Meta-programs) and via Meta-modeling thus become highly generative.

NLP's therapeutic approach to problems, difficulties, and symptoms primarily involves seeking first to understand the *internal structure* and to then "mess" up that structure. In other words, there already exists a *pattern* or *strategy* in every "problem" whether depression, alcoholism, schizophrenia, an eating disorder, etc. So we ask ourselves and sometimes the client, *"How does this problem work?* "Teach me how to have this problem." "What do I have to think or feel or say first, then second, etc.?"

Pattern analysis enables us to follow the course of development of a difficulty from its origin (etimology), contributing factors, risk factors, component parts, symptoms, etc. This enables us to antic-ipate, predict, understand, diagnose, and treat the problem.

Treatment also has a *pattern.* We can trace the development of an intervention designed to ameliorate a problem and lead a person to a more wholesome and well-balanced life. Such *therapeutic "magic"* has structure. So learning its strategy enables us to practice such magic. We can identify and learn the *internal and external structure* of interacting with a client therapeutically so that our conversation, encounters, assignments, feedback, and process leads to solutions.

Inasmuch as NLP presupposes the cognitive-behavioral model, this means that the values, effectiveness, and legitimacy of the Cognitive-Behavioral approach also apply to NLP.

Cognitive-behavioral psychology indeed has now become one of the fastest growing movements in psychology. Since the 1960s it has gradually been replacing psychoanalysis, behaviorism, and Rogerian approaches. Further, it tends to show up in many forms of modern psychotherapy that do not even use that label or identify themselves as "cognitive" (i.e., Reality Therapy, Gestalt, Family Systems, etc.).

1. *Efficacy and Legitimacy.* Since the 1960s the Cognitive-Behavioral approach has demonstrated efficacy with numerous symptoms in multiple studies. It also continues to head the list in terms of efficiency in meta-analysis studies. (See Garfield and Bergin, 1987, *Handbook of Psychotherapy and Behavior Change: An Empirical Analysis*).

2. *Respectful Collaboration.* The Cognitive-Behavioral therapist explains *the actual mechanisms* responsible for change in order to empower the client in owning and using the mechanisms. This reduces the "authority" or "expert" role that the older psychologies relied upon and invites the client to enter into a cooperative and respectful collaboration.

3. *Holistic and Systemic.* The Cognitive-Behavioral approach operates from an holistic understanding. It incorporates models and techniques that affect perception, understanding, and reason as well as neurology, physiology, environmental context, etc. In so doing, it utilizes *a systems approach* which avoids the dualistic and elementalistic problems of the older psychologies.

4. *Efficiency Oriented.* With the growth of managed health care, emphasis has shifted to doing therapy more efficiently so that it works more quickly and with more quality. The Cognitive-Behavioral model assumes that clients not only *can* learn, but *want* to take responsibility for themselves and not depend upon the therapist to inform them as to what their internal processes (dreams, emotions, ideas, passions, etc.) "really" mean. By respecting the dignity and personality of the client, this

approach helps clients actualize potentials. It does so by taking more of an educational and skill development approach. This moves therapy along much more quickly and puts the responsibility for one's own mental-emotional well-being where it belongs—on the client, with the therapist functioning primarily as coach, consultant, helper.

5. *Process Oriented.* The Cognitive-Behavioral approach focuses on processes, mechanisms of change, and models. This supports the idea that we started with in this work on *patterns.* If productively helping another human being to get a better handle on life has *an internal structure,* then, as we discover those *intervention patterns* that we see effective clinicians use, we can model them and their patterns.

The NLP patterns in this work take the best of what works from many schools of psychology. Utilizing the **ABCs model** of Rational Emotive Behavioral Therapy of Ellis and the Cognitive Model of Beck, NLP expands the "Beliefs" in **B** a hundred-fold to a multiple of "intervening variables" (Tollman, 1932). In doing so, it provides a hundred new places for intervention at finer levels of analysis than just "belief change," "disputing irrational beliefs," "disputing with cognitive distortions," etc.

As a form of *Brief* psychotherapy, in NLP therapy, therapist and client *co-create* a therapeutic resolution by working together and establishing desired outcomes as well as methods for gauging and measuring movement toward these outcomes. In this approach, the therapist does not adopt the expert role, but the role of facilitator and coach. *The client fully participates* in the process and *owns* it. This avoids most of the "resistance" issues that plague other approaches.

This *inter-active* style also involves the therapist's playing an *active and directive role,* rather than a passive one. Once the client has identified his or her desired outcome, the therapist assists the client in moving toward the solution state. "Therapy" becomes a matter of structuring, a question about *how* to bridge from present state to solution state. Questions about resources and processes become increasingly important. Brief psychotherapy using NLP takes the following steps:

Step One: Identifying The Problem

Therapy begins with a person's story. The therapist initially only provides the context for the story to be told. By providing this time and space for the problem story, the therapist offers *a touch of grace*—sympathy, empathy, understanding, validation, universalization, etc., of the problem.

Then, as the therapist reflects back an empathetic understanding of "the problem" and it matches or paces the person's felt and perceived sense of "reality," the therapeutic relationship begins. Building this sense of rapport sets the frame in therapy for more disclosure.

(As an aside, this work focuses primarily on the actual *patterns* of transformation which one will use to move a person from a problem state to a solution state. Nevertheless numerous NLP books have detailed the importance of *the therapeutic relationship* itself and the pattern of **pacing** (matching the person's model of the world) as the structure of empathy. See the bibliography.)

Simultaneously, the therapist begins to explore precisely and specifically the client's definitions of "the problem" and how it evidences a problem in life. This generates the **therapeutic focus**. In this exploratory stage, the therapist's empathy leads the client in becoming more and more specific and focused. Using the NLP Meta-model, the therapist gathers *high quality* information. So, as a client talks about "the problem," active Meta-modeling facilitates a new kind of talking or languaging of "the problem." It enables the person to mentally map out the problem with less ill-formedness and more precision and clarity. As this transpires, the person develops a more accurate and useful map for navigating life (chapter 7).

The therapist will use the Meta-model's questions to challenge and enhance the poor mapping. The aim of this? To empower the client to reaccess the experience from which they created their mental map and to then challenge the vagueness, fluff, ill-constructions, etc., of the map. This frees the person to then re-map in much more accurate and empowering ways.

Step Two: Specifying The Well-formed Solution State

Once the client has identified what he or she finds problematic and has explained his/her map of the problem, the therapy quickly shifts to a **solution-focus**.

> "What do you want?"
> "**If** you didn't have this 'problem,' what would you want to have?"
> "Think for a minute about the solution state that you would like to experience, and begin to describe for me what that would look like, sound like, feel like, how you would talk to yourself, etc..."

To develop *a well-formed outcome,* the therapist uses certain criteria to govern the exploration of the client's desired outcome. Doing this *re-directionalizes the client's thinking.* Such questioning also empowers the client to think in terms of specific behavioral actions that they can take, in a step-by-step manner, to allow them to move toward the solution effectively.

Specifying "The Problem"

As therapist and client become more specifically aware of a problem, this hones their therapeutic focus. In this work we have sorted *"problems"* into the seven categories enumerated in chapter 2. Repeated here, we offer a model for thinking about, and working with, *problems.* Using this classification of types or kinds of problems enables us to relate the NLP patterns to them. In other words, we have chosen to sort various "problems" as falling into these kinds of "issues."

- **Parts**—suffering from two or more "integral parts" in conflict
- **Identity**—suffering from having one's sense of self in distress
- **States**—experiencing problematic, unresourceful and/or emotional states of consciousness
- **Language**—experiencing cognitive errors in self-talk and languaging oneself in negative and distressful ways
- **Thinking**—experiencing problems in thinking style, meta-programs, and cognitive distortions

- **Meanings**—Suffering from limiting beliefs and diminished meanings
- **Strategies**—Suffering from not knowing how to engender a part of desired behavior (micro- and macro-behavior)

This purely arbitrary system simply provides a way to organize our thinking about the "issues" that people experience. Obviously a person may suffer from incongruity when one part of the self wants to play during work time and work when it is time to play. The client may also struggle with beliefs about such conflicts and what this implies about their identity, the states they get into, etc. So we do not want to think of these categories as exclusive, but merely as a way to sort out difficulties so we can address them methodically and effectively. If a particular pattern does not shift a "problem," we simply go to another category and address it from that angle.

Figure 13.1 (Figure 2.5 repeated here)

The NLP Algorithm

Present State   **Desired Solution State**

Description: specifically   Specific description in
how a problem   terms of well-formedness

Bridging to—
Kinds of resources needed to move

- Parts—suffering from having two or more "parts" in conflict
- Identity—suffering from having one's sense of self in distress
- States—experiencing problematic unresourceful states of consciousness
- Language—experiencing cognitive errors in self-talk and languaging oneself in negative and distressful ways
- Thinking styles—suffering from cognitive and perceptual distortions or simply inappropriate Meta-programs
- Meanings—suffering from limiting beliefs and unenhancing meanings
- Strategies—suffering from not knowing how to achieve a piece of desired behavior (micro- and macro-behavior)

Now, given these descriptions of NLP therapy, *a good therapist* using NLP patterns will:

1. Build rapport with the client to create a safe place for healing.
2. Use rapport to actively engage the client in the process.
3. Specify "the problem" so that a specific therapeutic focus develops.
4. Think and operate by moving from undesired state to desired state.
5. Access resources in the client for bridging from the now to the solution state.
6. Utilize specific strategies and patterns for change, calibrating throughout the process.

Sports

NLP, in the domain of athletics and sports, plays a key role primarily in terms of *states* and *state-management*. For a number of years, I (MH) worked as a coach for a boys' gymnastics team and as a "mental" coach for a girls' competitive team. As I did so, I focused primarily on assisting the youngsters to learn about how to "run their own brains" so that they could put themselves into the best athletic state. This gave me the opportunity to help them identify resourceful and unresourceful states—and how *mind* inevitably governs *body*.

I found that I used the "state management" patterns a lot in that context (chapter 6), as well as the Desired Outcome Pattern (chapter 3), Anchoring (chapter 3), and Strategies (chapter 10). In the last case, each sport (and even each expert in each sport) will have its own strategy. Thus we can anticipate a different *strategy* for skiing, basketball, swimming, racing, boxing, football, etc.

Here also beliefs about self, capability, possibility, learning, etc., will play a key role in supporting or limiting a person's performance (chapter 5). In this domain also one should consider the role of language. The best gymnasts that I worked with and interviewed had not only shifted to thinking of and defining themselves as a "gymnast," but also had come to effectively language themselves as such (chapter 7).

Health

NLP, in the fields of health, medicine, fitness, etc., has much to say. As a holistic model, the *neuro-linguistic model* begins from the assumption of the mind-body connection. That is, what and how we communicate to ourselves inevitably (and inescapably) has an effect upon our body.

In this domain, therefore, the patterns for working with conflicting "parts" (chapter 4) will play a crucial role. Whenever we have internal conflict within ourselves, we can expect to pay a price for that "conflict." This becomes true with a vengeance when we consider negative Meta-state structures that we create by which we *turn our psychic energies against ourselves.* Such "dragon" states (Hall, 1996) include: contempt of the self, anger against one's anger, fear about fear, rejection of fallibility, hatred of embarrassment, guilt about anger at one's fear, contempt for one's guilt about one's fear, etc.

Specific patterns that relate to health in this volume include the following: the Phobia Cure (#33 the V/K Dissociation pattern), #65 the Allergy Cure pattern, #66 the Grief Resolution pattern, #67 the Pre-Grieving pattern, #68 the Healthy Eating pattern, etc. (chapter 10).

In the domain of health, we will also want to check out identity beliefs (Chapter 5). Many people have defined themselves as sick or diseased, from a family predisposed to heart attacks, cancer, etc. Others have built beliefs and mental maps that put limits on what kinds of experiences and processes can be addressed "psychologically." To carry around such self-definitions inevitably affects treatment.

Similarly, in the area of language and language use, if we *language ourselves* for illness, disease, shortness of life, health problems, we frequently create a self-fulfilling prophecy (chapter 7). Here we need to listen carefully to our language and challenge unenhancing formations, e.g., "She's a pain in the neck," "I always get a cold on holiday," "Committee meetings with him give me indigestion," "Well, no sleep tonight—I've got an important engagement tomorrow."

Relationships

In the area of relationships, much NLP literature has been created. Here everything in NLP about communication: rapport, pacing, representational systems, predicates, anchoring, desired outcome frame, etc. (chapter 3), plays a most important role. Here, too, managing our own states, so that we meet people while in a "good place" (resourceful) rather than when unresourceful, enables us to "be at our best" (chapter 6). Such state management skills and patterns also enable us to bring out the best in others.

And again, the role that language plays in relating to others— disclosing our inner thoughts and feelings, our values and beliefs, our hopes and dreams—enables us to either connect with others, or to feel frustrated (chapter 7). Good relationships involve the ability to connect with each other in terms of understanding and also in terms of good problem-solving and negotiating. Here we need some specific strategies for connecting, parenting, bonding, supporting, etc. (chapter 10).

Conclusion

As a model of *human functioning*, NLP applies to so many domains. And as a model of *excellence* in subjective experience, it provides us with a way of thinking (a model) for us to effectively understand and work with such subjective experiences.

Epilogue

The *revolution in modeling human excellence* has begun, and by now you should have a pretty good idea of *the very structure of how to do magic* with your own personality, with that of others, at work, with loved ones, for fun, etc. Let this empowerment of taking charge of your own dreams and experiences grow and expand until you become the magician you want to become using your own "spells" that you cast in your mind and in your everyday languaging.

By now also you undoubtedly have access and experience to numerous NLP patterns that can work "magic." And, if you have indeed been touched by some aspect of NLP magic, you may also have become curious about how that magic works. Good. That provides you with the basic orientation of modeling. And, if indeed we have just barely scratched the surface of all the magic that lies out there awaiting our discovery, then we need a lot more people with modeling skills. And with that we say...

Let the magic continue...!

Appendices

Appendix A

Eye Accessing Cue Chart

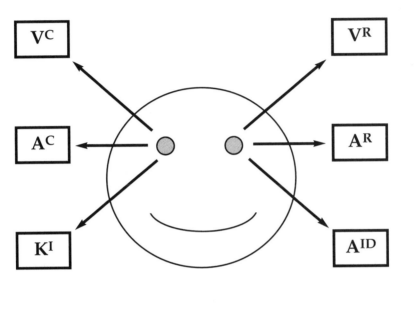

V^C

V^R

A^C

A^R

K^I

A^{ID}

| Their Right Side | | Their Left Side |

(The Person Looking At You)

Appendix B

Calibration Exercise

For Agree/Disagree or Yes/No

Pair up with another person and engage in a pleasant conversational style of asking simple and easy questions. For this exercise, ask light-level questions and then confirm them with "Yes/No" questions while you simultaneously pay attention to the non-verbal responses the other person gives you as he or she verbally says "Yes/No" in agreement or disagreement with what you say.

> "You say your name is Bob?"
> "What do you like to be called?"
> "Bobby? So you prefer that?"
> "Were you born in California?"
> "Do you own your own car?"

Calibrate to what constitutes a yes/no response non-verbally for your partner. Notice differences between the non-verbal responses for "Yes" and from those that accompany "No."

For example, some people will spontaneously and unconsciously tense their jaw muscles for "No," and relax them for "Yes." Some people will have a paler complexion for "No," and a redder or flushed look for "Yes." Some will tilt the head forward when conveying "Yes," and back for "No."

As you calibrate, notice muscle tension, eye movements, gesturing, eye relaxation/tension, mouth, breathing, etc.

When you feel that you can distinguish between the "Yes" and "No" messages that a person gives at the non-verbal level, then ask your partner to not answer the question verbally, but only non-verbally. Then continue to ask questions and observe responses. After each question, let your partner know whether you think he or she gave a "Yes" or "No" answer. When you get four right answers in a row, switch roles.

Doing this will train your intuition for the "Yes, I agree" non-verbal signals and the "No, I disagree" signals for a given person. Practice with several people so that you can become even more aware of the variations in people. Then spend an entire day or two just noticing these kinds of agree/disagree cues that people give you.

Appendix C

There "Is" No "Is"

Did you even notice that we wrote this book using the General Semantic extensional device called **E-Prime** (except for quotations from others)? We did.

E-what? **English**-*primed* of the verb "to be" (is, am, are, was, were, be, being, been). Invented by D. David Bourland, Jr. and popularized by Bourland and Paul Dennithorne Johnston in *To Be Or Not: An E-Prime Anthology*, E-Prime and E-Choice empower people to not fall into the "is" traps of language.

The "is" traps? Yes, Alfred Korzybski (1941/1994) warned that *the "is" of identity* and *the "is" of predication* present two dangerous linguistic and semantic constructions that map false-to-fact conclusions. The first has to do with identity—how we identify a thing or what we identify ourselves with—and the second with attribution—how we frequently project our "stuff" onto others or onto things without realizing it.

Identity, as "sameness in all respects," does not even exist. It can't. At the sub-microscopic level, everything involves a "dance of electrons" always moving, changing, and becoming. So no thing can ever "stay the same" even with itself. So nothing "is" in any static, permanent, unchanging way. Since nothing exists as eternal, but since everything continually changes, then nothing "is." To use "is" mis-speaks, mis-evaluates, and mis-maps reality. To say, "She is lazy...," "That is a stupid statement...," falsely maps reality. And Korzybski argued that unsanity and insanity ultimately lie in *identifications*.

Predication refers to "asserting" something. So to say, "This is good," "That flower is red," "He is really stupid!" creates a language structure which implies that something "out there" contains these qualities of "goodness," "redness," and "stupidity." The "is" suggests that such things exist *independent of the speaker's experience*. Not so. Our descriptions speak primarily about our internal experience indicating our judgments and values. More accurately we could have said, "I evaluate as good this or that," "I see that flower as red," "I think of him as suffering from stupidity!"

"Is" statements falsely distract, confuse logical levels, and subtly lead us to think that such value judgments exist outside our skin in the world "objectively." Wrong again. The evaluations (good, red, stupid) function as definitions and interpretations in the speaker's mind.

The "to be" verb dangerously presupposes that "things" (actually events or processes) stay the same. Not so! This verb invites us to create mental representations of fixedness so that we begin to set the world in concrete and to live in "a frozen universe." This verb codes the dynamic nature of processes statically. "Life is tough," "I am no good at math."

Do these statements not sound definitive? Absolute? "That's just the way it is!" No wonder Bourland calls "is," "am," and "are," etc., *"the deity mode."* "The fact is that this work is no good!" Such words carry a sense of completeness, finality, and time-independence. Yet discerning the difference between the map and the territory tells us these phenomena exist on different logical levels. Using E-Prime (or E-Choice) reduces slipping in groundless authoritarian statements which only closes minds or invites arguments.

If we confuse the language we use in describing reality (our map) with reality (the territory), then we *identify* differing things. And that makes for unsanity. **There "is" no "is."** "Is" non-references. It points to nothing in reality. It operates entirely as an irrational construction of the human mind. Its use leads to semantic mis-evaluations.

Conversely, writing, thinking, and speaking in E-Prime contributes to *"consciousness of abstracting"* (conscious awareness), that we make maps of the world which inherently differ from the world. E-Prime enables us to think and speak with more clarity and precision as it forces us to take first-person. This reduces the passive verb tense ("It was done," "Mistakes were made."). It restores speakers to statements, thereby contextualizing statements. E-Prime, by raising consciousness of abstracting, thereby enables us to index language. Now I realize that the person I met last week, Person$_{last\ week}$, "is" not equal in all respects to the person who stands before me, Person$_{this\ week}$. This assists me in making critical and valuable distinctions.

E-Choice differs from E-Prime in that with it one uses *the "is" of existence* (e.g., "Where is your office?" "It is on 7th. Street at Orchard Avenue."), *the auxiliary "is"* (e.g., "He is coming next week.") and *the "is" of name,* (e.g., "What is your name?" "It is Michael." "My name is Bob."). Though we wrote this in E-Prime, we have decided to begin to use E-Choice so as to avoid some circumlocution that we have used in the past(!).

Appendix D

NLP As Therapy

In A Managed Care World

While NLP originally arose from modeling several therapy processes, *NLP itself is not a therapy*. Rather, NLP operates as a communication model about human mental-and-neurological functioning.

Nevertheless it does translate as a meta-psychological model very easily, as noted in *The Structure Of Magic* (1975). Applying NLP to the therapeutic process of assisting a hurting human being to find resolution of difficulties and empowerment in life, we offer the following as an overview of the process. Here we have sorted it into six sessions (to fit current Managed Care criteria).

Session 1. Build rapport, pace the client's current experiences of thoughts and feelings, begin to develop an empathic understanding of the situation and how the client finds it distressing or problematic, begin to identify the therapeutic focus—what the person will have and experience when they don't have the problem.

Session 2. Building of therapeutic goals that meet the criteria of well-formedness. This means: the desired outcome stated in specific, small chunk behaviors and skills, means for measuring or determining progress, awareness of potential obstacles to success, and beginning to develop resources.

Sessions 3-5. Employ specific *patterns of transformation* as strategies whereby a client can begin to move from problem state to solution state. Give lots of therapeutic support and encouragement, with constant review of performance goals, etc.

Session 6. Terminate the therapy with review, future pacing gains and resources, rehearsal for set-backs, etc.

Elements That Make NLP Therapy A "Brief" Psychotherapy Process

Managed Care focuses on therapy as short-term, time-limited, and strategic. Using NLP in this way necessitates that we make sure that we have certain component elements in place. Namely:

A focus on precision and specificity. Imprecision, vague thinking, fuzzy definitions, etc., work as "problems" in human consciousness. Therefore clarity, precision, focus, and specificity play a very crucial role.

A goal-directed sense of support from the therapist. When a client senses that the therapist has skill and knowledge in facilitating the therapeutic direction, this can instill hope, trust, and motivation.

Specific tools ("technologies") for achieving goals. "Just talking," in the hope of gaining some insight that will change problems, isn't short-term, goal-directed brief psychotherapy. It consists of specific processes, strategies, and patterns for actually moving from one state to another.

A co-created exchange. Start with what the client already *wants* to accomplish, align with their objectives, and prove trustworthy, knowledgeable, and skilled by helping them get what they want. Letting the client have and own responsibility for the outcomes cuts out any need for them to resist. The therapist plays the role of coach and facilitator, not parent.

The ability to think strategically. The expertise of the therapist rests primarily in having knowledge and skills in empowering the person to develop resources, reframe unproductive ways of looking at things, increasing motivation to take effective action, etc.

A view that therapy also occurs beyond the office. The therapist gives assignments between sessions that will access resources, develop insights, practice changed ways of thinking and behaving, so that the "talk" in the office becomes the lifestyle outside the office.

The ability to check up on progress and measure it. Every session after the first should involve "holding the client responsible" by inquiring about how things have begun to change, what they learned, how they functioned, etc. This presupposes their active involvement, their motivation, and their ownership. Rating symptoms on a scale (0 to 10) and checking on progress conveys the belief, hope and expectation of change.

Therapy Checklist

____ Did I establish rapport? Pace the client?

____ Did I establish a desired-outcome state with the client?

____ Did it meet the conditions of well-formedness?

____ Did the client seem engaged?

____ Did I seem engaged with the client?

____ Would I classify the client as: Visitor, Customer, or Observer?

____ Did I use an intervention?

- What?

- For what purpose?

- Did it seem successful?

- Based upon what evidence?

____ Did I prescribe some homework? If so, what?

____ What issues, problems, process will come next?

____ What issues do I need to explore and clarify?

____ How far along has client moved from Problem State to Solution State?

____ Do we yet have a well-defined solution state in mind?

EAP Audit

1. What is the presenting problem?

2. The signs and symptoms of such?: _____

3. Why does this client seek assistance now?

4. Treatment focus: _____

5. Treatment goals: _____

Impact:

1. Amount (1-10) that the client seemed engaged in the process: __

2. Assessment of the problem: _____

    _____

3. Treatment focus: _____

    _____

4. Cooperative goal setting by client with therapist: _____

    _____

5. Interventions and decision points in the process today: _____

    _____

6. Homework prescribed: _____

7. Documentation about the therapy process: _____

8. Client's evaluation of today's therapy (1-10):

    —— Understanding

    —— Ownership of process

    —— Motivation

9. Level of client's current ability to function:

    —— Personally

    —— Vocationally

    —— In Relationships

    —— Other

Appendix E

List Of NLP Centers*

USA

The following is a list of current NLP Centers in the USA. In the following **"P"** stands for NLP **P**ractitioner Training, **"MP"** stands for **M**aster **P**ractitioner Training, **"T"** stands for NLP **T**rainer Training. As the field of NLP grows, more and more specialized trainings have developed and will continue to develop. Centers now offer courses in Photoreading, Core Transformation, Hypnosis, etc.

Originally we had hoped to have devoted a good section to each training center—until we discovered all of the following Centers in the USA. We put out a press release via *Anchor Point* Magazine and via the Internet for information—those who responded have their information included.

New England Institute of NLP
505 Pratt Corner Road
Amherst, MA 01002-9606

Massachusetts Institute of NLP
PO Box 99
198 Jewett St.
Georgetown
Georgetown, MA 01833

Judith A. Swack & Associates
400 Hillside Ave.
Ste. 11
Needham, MA 02194

The Northeast Institute for NLP
Zero Kinsley Street
Nashua, NH 03060

Northeast NLP Institute
351 Simpson Rd.
Saco, ME 04072

NLP America/Blue Dell Systems
61 Steamboat Wharf, Suite #1
P.O. Box 259
Mystic, CT. 06355
(860) 536-2249
joeizh@worldnet.com

Also:
22320 Calibre Court, Suite 905
Boca Raton, FL. 33433
blu_ize@compuserve.com
P & MP trainings, Intro. & Adv. Hypnosis, Generative Imprint Model, Persuasion Technology, the Vision Gate Leadership Model.

NLP Center of Connecticut
Jack H. Bloom
23 Sherman Street
Fairfield, CN. 06430

NLP Seminars Group International
PO Box 424
Hopatocong, NJ 07843

NLP Applied Behavioral Technologies
1 International Blvd., Suite 400
Mahway, NJ 07495-0025

Institute for Education & Cognitive Psychology
c/o FEA,
12 Centre Drive
Jamesburg, NJ 08831
(690) 860-1200
Fax: (609) 860-6677
NJPSA@aol.com
Http://www.njpsa.org
Specializes in training in redirectional thinking and accelerated learning. Most of the Institute's work centers on improving education & the lives of children. Also conference on peak performance, personal & professional development.

Ocean NLP Center
1845 Old Freehold Rd.
Toms River, NJ 08755

New York Training Institute for NLP
155 Prince Street
New York, NY 10012
(212) 674-3194
Http://nlpcenter.com
P & MP trainings, hypnosis, teaching in USA, Europe, and Israel.

The NLP Center of New York
24 East 12th Street, 4th, Ste 402
New York, NY 10003
212 647- 0860
800 422- 8657
Fax 973 509-9599
nlp@earthlink.net
http://www.nlptraining.com
P, MP, & T; Ericksonian Hypnosis, Core Transformation, Workshops for Educators, Corporations, Businesses.

Dynamic Wellness Center
38 West 26th. Street #10B
New York City, NY 10010

Upstate Centre for NLP
333 Hudson Street
Cornwall-On-Hud, NY 12520

Upstate Centre for NLP
PO Box 6018
Syracuse, NY 13217

Success Enterprises/NLP
161 C. Monroe Ave. PO Box 426
Pittsford, NY 14534

Creative Growth Unlimited
510 W. Union St.
Newark, NJ 14513

Olic Production Trainings
1903 Walnut Street, # 400
Philadelphia, PA 19103
(215) 467-5035
Robmarket@aol.com

Neuro Energetics
111 Centerville Rd.
Lancaster, PA 17603

NLP Training Systems
2129 Spring Garden St.
Phildelphia, PA. 19130

Neuro Synergy
1012 Bethleham Pike, PO Box 269
Spring House, PA 19477

Choicework Institute
6118 Park Heights Avenue
Baltimore, MD. 21215

Advanced Behavioral Modeling / INLPTA
1201 Delta Glen Court
Vienna, VA 22182-1320
(703) 757-7945
Fax (703) 757- 7946
Wyattwoodsmall@compuserve.com
http://www.hookup.net/-inlpta
Advanced trainings, esp. In modeling and T trainings.

NLP Institute of D.C.
1600 Crystal Drive, Suite 1612
Arlington VA. 22202
Administrative Off.:
One Brittany Terrace
914 496- 4081
Fax 914 496-6708
Rock Tavern, NY 12575-5105
P, MP, Training, with emphasis in business
applications

NLP of Gastonia / Institute Of
Neuro-Semantics
1516 Cecelia Dr.
Gastonia, NC 28054
704 864-1545
Fax 704 864-1545
Bob@neurosemantics.com
http://www.neurosemantics.com
P, MP trainings with an emphasis on
personal integrity and training both the
conscious and the unconscious mind.

South Carolina NLP
PO Box 1140
Pawleys, SC 29585

Peak Performance Corp.
1640-8 Powers Ferry Rd., #300
Marietta, GA 30067

Avatar Industries
4370 Georgetown Square
Atlanta, GA 30338

The Connecting Link
243 Blazing Ridgeway
Lawrenceville, GA 30245

Rivijon Training Institute
1093 A1A Blvd., #390
St. Augustine, FL 32084
904 471-7161
rivijon@aug.com
P, MP trainings, with a special interest in
health, wellness, personal & professional
development, PhotoReading. Located in
Jacksonville, FL.

Learn Institute Of Neuro-Semantics®
PO Box 3990
Plant City, FL 33564
(888) 532-7697
LION-S@learnusa.com
http://www.learnusa.com

Southern Institute of NLP/
International NLP
PO Box 529
Indian Rocks Beach, FL 33785
(813) 596-4891
Fax (813) 595- 0040
Sunnlp@intl-nlp.com
P, MP & T trainings. Focuses on interna-
tional trainings in Europe.

Mid-South Institute of NLP
2906 Garth Road S.E.
Huntsville, AL 35801

The NCS Institute
422 Gay St.
Knoxville, TN 37902

NLP of Ohio
676 Everwood
Columbus, OH 43214

L.E.A.D. Consultants
PO Box 664
Reynoldsburg, OH 43068

Ohio Valley NLP
PO Box 9854
Cincinnati, OH 45208

IDHEA Seminars
12605 W. North Ave. Suite 291
Brookfield, WI 53005
1-800-414-790-1991
1-800-REX-SIKES
train@idea-seminars.com
www.idea-seminars.com
Focuses on applying NLP for personal
development, offers P & MP trainings, and
tools for living a more enjoyable &
successful life.

Learning Strategies Corp.
900 E. Wayzata Blvd.
Wayzata, MN 55391

Entertrainment
1236 North Astor St.
Chicago, IL. 60610

Boundaries Unlimited
PO Box 904
Evanston, IL 60204

Health Dynamics
4601 N. Claremont
Chicago, IL 60625

NLP Institute of Chicago
PO Box 25184
Chicago, IL 60625

Tranformational Technologies
PO Box 18476
Chicago, IL 60618

NLP Institute of Chicago
1532 W. Victoria St.
Chicago, IL 60660-4223

In-Training The Future
210 W. Jefferson Street
Macomb, IL. 61455-0817

Gateway NLP
1227 Lindenwood Avenue
Edwardsville, IL. 62025-2321
1-800- 252-3100
(618) 692-6868
Fax: (618) 692-2038
www.gatewaynlp.com
jmunsha@siue.edu
Offers P & MP training through Apprenticeship Program working directly with Dr. Munshaw, Professor of Speech Communications at Southern Illinois University.

NLP St. Louis
227 Hillsdale
Ballwin, MO. 63011
(314) 391-0906
Fax (314) 230-8217
NLPStLouis@aol.com

NLP Midwest
8416 Kauai Dr.
Papillion, NE 68046

NLP Midwest
4009 North 104th. Plaza
Omaha, NE. 68138

Gestalt/ NLP Institute of New Orleans
1421 Napoleon Avenue
New Orleans, LA. 70115

The South Central Institute of NLP
PO Box 1213
Mandeville, LA 70470
(800) 347-3615
(504) 626-7424
Fax: (504) 626-7424
sidjacob@pipeline.com
Offering P & MP training, emphasis on NLP in business & education, international training, Singapore: Integrative Learning Corp., 197 Jalan Pelikat, Singapore, 537650. (65) 784-7905.

Mind-Body Harmony Institute
6509 Government St., Suite C
Baton Rouge, LA. 70806
(504) 673-4873
mhhl@eatel.net
Offers P & MP Trainings, Meta-States, Mind-Body Integrations.

NLP Center of New Orleans
4058 Franklin
New Orleans, LA 70122

Success Skills / NLP of Oklahoma
5400 N. Grand Blvd, Suite 100
Oklahoma City, OK 73112
(405) 942-4371
(800) 775-3397
Fax: (405) 947-3046
success@ionnet.net
Offering P & MP courses, specializing in
learning disabilities such as ADD.

Change Point
Box 42227
Oklahoma City, OK 73123

Accelerated Transformation
PO Box 831612
Richardson, TX 75083

NLP Learning Systems, Corp.
4050 W. Park, Suite 102
Plano, TX. 75075

Taylor, Johnson & Associates
PO Box 871224
Dallas, TX 75287

NLP Institute of Houston, Inc.
4900 Woodway, Ste 700
Houston, TX 77056

The NLP Center of Texas
4600 Post Oak Place, Suite 204
Houston TX 77027
(713) 439-0011
(800) 625-1925
Fax: (713) 439- 0030
rodas@blkbox.com
Web: www.nlpcenteroftexas.com
NLP Center since 1981. Emphasis: NLP as
applied in business and corporate settings,
P & MP trainings, Meta-States training.

Access NLP Seminars Group
PO Box 1257
Austin, TX 78704

Institute for Advanced Hypnosis
10508 Lockerbie Dr
Austin, TX 78750

The Institute of NLP
8820 Business Park Dr. #400
Austin, TX 78759-7456

El Paso NLP Help Center &
TimeLine Therapy Institute
1501 Arizona, Suite 7-F
El Paso, TX 79902
(915) 532-8881
Fax: (915) 532-8881
crow@nlpelpaso.com
www.nlpelpaso.com
Offering P & MP trainings, Time Line
Therapy & Hypnosis certification.

NLP Comprehensive
12567 West Cedar Drive
Suite 102
Lakewood, CO 80228

Institute Of Neuro-Semantics
PO Box 9231
Grand Junction, CO 81501
(970) 523-7877
Michael@Neurosemantics.com
http://www.neurosemantics.com

The Center
3900 Amity Rd. #24 Box 5775
Boise, ID 83705

Personal Enrichment Center
P.O. Box 111   (208) 234-1159
Pocatello ID 83204-0111
P & MP trainings, stress reduction, focus
on health, well-being, pain & disease
management, career transition, work place
effectiveness.

Transitioner Management Inc.
1981 E Murray-Holladay Rd #250
Salt Lake City, UT 84117

Western States NLP Training
346 South 500 East Suite 200
Salt Lake City, UT. 84102

NLP Trainings Unlimited, Inc.
PO Box 2800-291
Carefree, AZ 85377

NLP Advantage Group
4067 E. Grant Road, Suite 202
Tucson, AZ 85712

**New Mexico Connection/ Whole
Brain Communication**
Route 19, box 124 D.F.
Santa Fe, NM 87505

NLP Wellness Center
2141 North Alvernon Way
Tuscon, AZ. 87131

NLP Hummingbird Wellness
5055 E. Broadway Blvd. C 214
Tuscon, AZ. 85711

NLP of Southern California
4387 York Blvd
Los Angeles, CA 90041

Southern California Center for NLP
2075 Palos Verdes Dr., Ste 200
Lomita, CA 90717

Adept International
One World Trade Ctr., Ste. 800
Long Beach, CA 90831
Success Design International
11934 Oceannaire Lane
Malibu, CA 90265
800-807-5666
(310) 457-7062
NLPIDEA@worldnet.att.net
*P & MP Trainings, Core Transformation,
Personal Productivity, IDEA, ENVoY.
Emphasis on making a positive difference
for individuals and businesses.*

The Holman Group
21050 Van Owen Street
Canoga Park, CA 91303

Robbins Research International
9191 Towne Center Drive
San Diego, CA. 92122

**NLP Institute & Training Center
Time Line Therapy Institute**
675 Camino De Los Mares, Suite 302
San Clemente, CA 92673
(714) 248-7377
Fax: (714) 248-7379
75152.344@compuserve.com

Neuro-Concepts Institute
25822 Evergreen Rd.
Laguna Hills, CA 92653

Hypnosis & NLP Institute
16842 Von Karman Ave. Suite 475
Irvine, CA 92714

NLP Associates
775 Burnett Ave. #2
San Francisco, CA 94131

The VAK
700 E. El Camino Real, #110
Mountain View, CA 94040

First Institute of NLP
44 Montgomery St. 5th Floor
San Francisco, CA 94104

The Essence Works
5115 Merced Avenue, Ste 125
Oakland, CA 94611

NLP Marin
Carl Bucheit & Robert S. Hoffmeyer
13 Quail Court
San Rafael, CA 94903
(415) 499-0639
*P & MP trainings, free introduction
seminars. Emphasis in trainings on
making them fun, practical, and profound.*

New Life Power Associates
PO Box 508
Walnut Creek, CA 94597-0508

NLP of California, Inc.
230 Mt. Hermon Rd. Ste 214
Scotts Valley, CA 95066

NLP University/ Dynamic Learning Center
PO Box 1112
Ben Lomond, CA 95005
Offering training in P, MP, and Trainers levels along with most of the other trainings associated with NLP.

Quantum Leap
PO Box 67359
Scotts Valley, CA 95067

The NLP Connection
PO Box 7818
Santa Cruz, CA 95061

Sound Resources
230 Mount Hermon Rd., Ste 207
Scotts Valley, CA 95006

Meta-Outcomes
366 Hihn Street
Felton, CA. 95018
(408) 335-3727
Fax (408) 335-5919
Center for Professional Development
245-M Mt. Hermon Rd., #323
Scotts Valley, CA 95066

Syntax Communication Modeling Corp.
PO Box 2296
Los Gatos, CA 95031
(408) 395-0952
Fax (408) 395-9662
syntax@syntx.com
www.syntx.com
Offering advanced professional development for facilitators and consultants, inside & outside of organizations. Reflected in book: Smart Work: The Syntax Guide For Mutual Understanding In The Workplace. *Complimentary newsletter.*

Advanced Neuro Dynamics
615 Piikoi Street, Suite 501
Honalulu, HI 968814

Training Center in Portland
3250 Payne Rd.
Medford, OR 97504

Cascade Center, Inc.
4903 Linden Ave. N., #3
Seattle, WA 98103

NLP NorthWest, INC.
462 Deer Lane
Anacortes, WA 98221

Other-Than-Conscious Communications
PO Box 697
Friday Harbor, WA 98250

Michael Grinder & Associates
16303 NE 259th St.
Battle Ground, WA 98604
(360) 687-3238
Fax (503) 283-1048
Web: //members.aol.com/mggrinder /homepage.html
Emphasis—NLP & education, ENVoY classroom management program, Summer Institute on Learning Style.

The Human Solution
P.O. Box 776
Washougal, WA. 98671-7822

UK NLP Centres

ANLP
P.O. Box 10
Porthmadog
LL48 6ZB
0870 787 1978

The Bowland Partnership
22 Painter Wood
Billington
Clitheroe
Lancs BB7 9JD
01254 822 060

Brian Morton Human Resource Development
1 Roson Court
356 Poole Road
Poole
Dorset BH12 1AW
01202 251 087

Calabor Business And Training
48 St James Road
Carlisle
Cumbria CA2 5PD
01228 599 899

Centre NLP
16 Glenville Avenue
Glenfield
Leicester LE3 8BE
0116 287 3356

Changeworks
Woodside
Shire Lane
Chorleywood
Herts WD3 5NH
01923 291044

Christina Bacchini
15 Fulwood Gardens
Twickenham
Middlessex TW1 1EN
020 8891 3068

The Development Partnership
2 Barnfield
St Michaels
Tenderden
Kent TN24 8EU
01580 765 023

The Developing Company
9 Southwood Lawn Road
London N6 5SD
020 8341 1062

Diana Beaver
The Cottage
Temple Guiting
Near Cheltenham
Glos GL54 5RP
01451 850 863

Excel Communications HRD
45 West Street
Marlow
Bucks SL7 2LS
01628 488 854

Frank Daniels Associates
103 Hands Road
Heanor
Derbs DE75 7BH
01773 532 195

Future Pacing
5 Wellington Square
Cheltenham
Glos GL50 4JU
01242 221 788

Hidden Resources
21 Wood View
Birkby
Huddersfield HD2 2DT
01484 549 515

NLP Academy
35-37 East Street
Bromley
Kent BR1 1QQ
020 8402 1120

Insight Trainings
145 Chapel Lane
Longton
Preston PR4 5NA
01772 617 663

Integration Training Centre
12 Prince Of Wales Mansions
Prince Of Wales Drive
London SW11 4BJ
020 7622 4670

International Training Seminars (ITS)
73 Brooke Road
London N16 7RD
020 8442 4133

John Seymour Associates
17 Boyce Drive
Bristol BS2 9XQ
0117 955 7827

Lambent Trainings
4 Coombe Gardens
New Malden
Surrey KT3 4AA
020 8715 2559

Marlin Management Trainings
Broomfield Cottage
Hatfield Heath
Herts CM22 7DZ
01279 731 649

NLP Northeast
Bongate Mill Farm House
Mill Hill
Appleby
Cumbria CA16 6UR
01768 351 934

Organisational Healing
48 Walton Road
Stockton Heath
Warrington WA4 6NL
01925 861 600

Pegasus NLP Trainings
9 Ridley Road
Bournemouth BH9 1LB
01202 543 250
01202 534 250

Performance Enhancement
1 Manor Court
Barnes Wallis Road
Segensworth East
Fareham
Hants PO15 5TH
01489 889 000

Performance Partnership Ltd
11 Acton Hill Mews
310 Uxbridge Road
Acton
London W3 9QN
020 8992 9523

Personal Growth Training Ltd
41 Ilges Lane
Cholsey
Oxon OX10 9NX
01491 652 265

Pilgrims
Keynes College
University Of Kent
Canterbury
Kent CT2 8BF
01227 762 111

Post Graduate Professional Education
St Luke's Hospital
Blackmoorfoot Road
Huddersfield HD4 5RQ
01484 654 711 (ext. 3276)

PPD Personal Development
Unit 30A
The Loning
Colindale
London NW9 6DR
020 8200 4944

Realisation at Stenhouse
36 Plasturton Gardens
Pontcanna
Cardiff CF1 9HF
02920 377 732

Reeve & Atteridge
18 Holmes Close
Sunninghill
Ascot
Berks SL5 9DJ
01344 872 026

Resourcing Solutions Ltd
Royal Station Court
Station Road
St Twyford
Berks RG10 9NF
0118 901 6610

Sensory Systems
162 Queen's Drive
Glasgow G42 8QN
0141 424 4177

The Society Of NLP
McKenna Breen Ltd
Aberdeen Studios
22/24 Highbury Grove
London N5 2EA
020 7704 6604

Sue Knight Associates
Great Oaks
Green Lane
Burnham
Bucks SL1 8 QA
01628 667 868

Training Changes
7 Spenser Avenue
Cheltenham
Glos GL51 7DX
01242 580 640

* These details are all correct at time of going to press.

Bibliography

General NLP References

Andreas, Connirae; Andreas, Steve (1987). *Change Your Mind—And Keep The Change: Advanced NLP Submodalities Interventions.* Moab, UT: Real People Press.

Andreas, Connirae; Andreas, Steve (1989). *Heart Of The Mind.* Moab, UT: Real People Press.

Bandler, Richard; Grinder, John. (1975). *The Structure Of Magic.* Palo Alto, CA: Science & Behavior Books.

Bandler, Richard; Grinder, John. (1979). *Frogs Into Princes: Neuro-Linguistic Programming.* Moab, UT: Real People Press.

Bandler, Richard; Grinder, John. (1982). *Reframing: Neuro-Linguistic Programming And The Transformation Of Meaning.* Ut: Real People Press.

Bandler, Richard; MacDonald, Will (1988). *An Insider's Guide To Sub-modalities.* Cupertino, CA: Meta Publications.

Bandler, Richard. (1985). *Using Your Brain For A Change: Neuro-Linguistic Programming.* UT: Real People Press.

Bodenhamer, Bobby G.; Hall, Michael. (1998). *The User's Manual For The Brain: The Complete Manual For Neuro-Linguistic Programming Practitioner Certification.* Bancyfelin, Carmarthen, Wales, UK: Crown House Publishing; Grand Jct. CO: ET Publications.

Cooper, John F. (1995). *A Primer Of Brief Psychotherapy.* NY: W.W. Norton & Co.

Dilts, Robert; Grinder, John; Bandler, Richard; DeLozier, Judith. (1980). *Neuro-Linguistic Programming, Volume I: The Study Of The Structure Of Subjective Experience.* Cupertino. CA.: Meta Publications.

Dilts, Robert. (1983). *Applications Of Neuro-Linguistic Programming.* Cupertino CA: Meta Publications.

Dilts, Robert B. (1983). *Roots Of Neuro-Linguistic Programming.* Cupertino, CA: Meta Publications.

Dilts, Robert (1990). *Changing Belief Systems With NLP.* Cupertino, CA: Meta Publications.

Grinder, John; Bandler, Richard (1976). *The Structure Of Magic Volume II.* Palo Alto, CA: Science & Behavior Books.

Grinder, John; LeLozier, Judith. (1987). *Turtles All The Way Down: Prerequisites To Personal Genius*. Scotts Valley, CA: Grinder & Associates.

Hall, L. Michael. (1996). *Accessing Your Ferocious Self As A Presenter*. Grand Jct. CO: ET Publications.

Hall, L. Michael (1995). *Meta-States: A New Domain Of Logical Levels, Self-Reflexiveness In Human States Of Consciousness*. Grand Junction, CO: ET Publications.

Hall, L. Michael (1998). *Advanced NLP Modeling: NLP Going Meta: Modeling And Engineering Human Excellence*. Grand Junction, CO: ET Publications.

Hall, L. Michael. (1998). *The Secrets Of Magic: Communicational Excellence For The 21st Century*. Bancyfelin, Carmarthen, Wales, UK: Crown House Publishing.

Hall, L. Michael. (1996). *The Spirit Of NLP: The Process, Meaning And Criteria For Mastering NLP*. Bancyfelin, Carmarthen, Wales, UK: The Anglo American Book Company Ltd.

Lewis, Byron A.; Pucelik, R. Frank. (1982). *Magic Demystified: A Pragmatic Guide To Communication And Change*. Portland, OR: Metamorphous Press, Inc.

McClendon, Terrence L. (1989). *The Wild Days: NLP 1972 — 1981*. Cupertino, CA: Meta Publications.

O'Connor, Joseph; Seymour, John (1990). *Introducing Neuro-Linguistic Programming: The New Psychology Of Personal Excellence*. Great Britain: Mandala.

Rooney, Gene; Savage, John S. (1989). *Neurological Sorts And Belief Systems*. Reynoldsburg, OH: L.E.A.D. Consultants, Inc.

Spitzer, Robert S. (1992). "Virginia Satir And Origins Of NLP," *Anchor Point Journal*, July, 1992.

Wright, Clifford (1989). *Basic Techniques, Books I & II*. Portland, OR: Metamorphous Press, Inc.

Yeager, Joseph. (1985). *Thinking About Thinking With NLP*. Cupertino, CA: Meta Publications

NLP For Therapy

Andreas, Connirae; Andreas, Tamara. (1994). *Core Transformation: Reaching The Wellspring Within*. Moab, UT: Real People Press.

Bandler, Richard. (1985). *Magic In Action*. Moab, UT: Real People Press.

Bandler, Richard and Grinder, John. (1982). *Reframing:* Neuro-Linguistic *Programming And The Transformation Of Meaning*. Ut: Real People Press.

Bandler, Richard ; Grinder, John. (1975, 1976). *Patterns Of The Hypnotic Techniques Of Milton H. Erickson, M.D., Volumes I and II*. Cupertino, CA: Meta Publications.

Bodenhamer, Bobby G.; Hall, L. Michael. (1997). *Figuring Out People:* Design *Engineering With Meta-Programs*. Bancyfelin, Carmarthen, Wales, UK: The Anglo American Book Company Ltd.

Bodenhamer, Bobby G.; Hall, L. Michael. (1997). *Time-Lining:* Patterns For *Adventuring In 'Time.'* Bancyfelin, Carmarthen, Wales, UK: The Anglo American Book Company Ltd.

Gordon, David. (1978). *Therapeutic Metaphors:* Helping Others Through The *Looking Glass*. Cupertino, CA: Meta Publications.

Flaro, Floyd Meanding. (1989). *Cognitive Ability Patterning For Success For Learning*. Edmonton, Alberto, Canada: Learning Strategies Groups, Inc.

Hall, L. Michael. (1996a). *Dragon Slaying:* Dragons To Princes. Grand Jct. CO: ET Publ.

James, Tad; Woodsmall, Wyatt. (1988). *Time Line Therapy And The Basis Of Personality*. Cupertino, CA: Meta Publications.

Woodsmall, Wyatt (1988). *Lifeline Therapy*. Arlington VA: Advance Behavioral Modeling.

NLP For Business

Bandler, Richard; La Valle, John (1996). *Persuasion Engineering:* Sales And *Business, Language And Behavior*. Capitola, CA: Meta Publications.

Charvet, Shelle Rose. (1996). *Words That Change Minds:* Mastering The Language *Of Influence*. Dubuque, IO: Kendall/Hunt Publ. Co.

Cleveland, Bernard F. (1987). *Master Teaching Techniques:* NLP. Stone Mountain, GA: Connecting Link Press.

Dilts, Robert B.; Epstein, Todd; Dilts, Robert W. (1991). *Tools For Dreamers:* Strategies For Creativity And The Structure Of Innovation. Capitola, CA: Meta Publications.

Dilts, Robert B. (1994/ 1995). *Strategies Of Genius, Volumes I, II & III*. Capitola, CA: Meta Publications.

Dilts, Robert B. (1993). *Skills For The Future: Managing Creativity And Innovation.* Capitola, CA: Meta Publications.

Dilts, Robert B. (1995). "NLP, Self Organization And Strategies Of Change Management," Salt Lake City, UT: *Anchor Point*, Vol. 10, pp. 3-10.

Dilts, Robert B. (1996). *Visionary Leadership Skills.* Capitola, CA: Meta Publications.

Grinder, John; McMaster, Michael. (1983). *Precision: A New Approach To Communication.* Scotts Valley, CA: Grinder, Delozier & Associates.

Hall, L. Michael; Bodenhamer, Bobby. (1997). *Mind-Lines: Lines For Changing Minds; The Magic Of Conversational Reframing.* Grand Jct. CO: E.T. Publications.

Jacobson, Sid. (1997). *Solution States: A Course In Solving Problems In Business With The Power Of NLP.* Bancyfelin, Carmarthen, Wales, UK: The Anglo American Book Company.

Knight, Sue. (1995). *NLP At Work: The Difference That Makes A Difference In Business.* Nicholas Brealey Publishing.

Laborde, Genie Z. (1984). *Influencing With Integrity: Management Skills For Communication And Negotiation.* Palo Alto, CA: Syntony Publishing Co.

Lisnek, Paul M. (1996). *Winning The Mind Game: Negotiating In Business And Life.* Capitola, CA: Meta Publications.

McMaster, Michael. (1994). *Performance Management: Business Techniques That Guarantee Successful Business Systems.* Portland, OR: Metamorphous.

Reese, Edward; Bagley, Dan, III. (1988). *Beyond Selling: How To Maximize Your Personal Influence.*

Robbins, Anthony. (1986). *Unlimited Power: The New Science Of Personal Achievement.* NY: Simon & Schuster.

Robbins, Anthony. (1991). *Awaken The Giant Within.* New York: Simon & Schuster.

Woodsmall, Wyatt. (1988). *Business Applications Of NLP.* Vienna, VA: Advance Behavioral Modeling.

Zarro, Richard; Blum, Peter. (1989). *The Phone Book: Breakthrough Neurolinguistic Phone Skills For Profit And Enlightment.* Portland, OR: Metamorphous Press, Inc.

NLP For Education

Jacobson, Sid. (1983, 1986). *Meta-cation: Prescriptions For Some Ailing Educational Processes, Volumes I, II, & III.* Cupertino, CA: Meta Publications.
Grinder, Michael. (1989). *Righting The Educational Conveyor Belt.* Portland, OR: Metamorphous Press. Inc.

Lloyd, Linda. (1990). *Classroom Magic: Amazing Technology For Teachers And Home Schoolers.* Portland, OR: Metamorphous Press, Inc.

Nagel, C. Van; Reese, Maryann; Reese, Edward; Siudzinski, Robert. (1985). *Mega-Teaching And Learning.* Portland, OR: Metamorphous Press, Inc.

O'Connor, Joseph. (1997). *Not Pulling Strings.* Surrey, England, UK: Lambent Books

Other References

Assagioli, Roberto (1965). *Psychosynthesis: A Manual Of Principles And Techniques.* NY: Penguin Books.

Assagioli, Roberto (1973). *The Act Of Will.* NY: Penguin Books.

Bateson, Gregory. (1979). *Mind And Nature: A Necessary Unity.* New York: Bantam Books.

Bateson, Gregory. (1972). *Steps To An Ecology Of Mind.* New York: Ballatine Books.

Beck, A.T. (1963). "Thinking And Depression: I. Idiosyncratic Content And Cognitive Distortions", *Archives Of General Psychiatry, 9,* 342-333.

Beck, A.T. (1976). *Cognitive Therapy And The Emotional Disorders.* New York: International University Press.

Bourland, David D. Jr.; Johnston, Paul Dennithorne. (1991). *To Be Or Not: An E-Prime Anthology.* San Francisco, CA: International Society for General Semantics.

Bourland, David. D. Jr.; Johnston, Paul Dennithorne; Klein, Jeremy. (1994). *More E-Prime: To Be Or Not II.* Concord, CA: International Society for General Semantics.

Cade, Brian; O'Hanlon, William Hudson. (1993). *A Brief Guide To Brief Therapy.* NY: W.W. Norton & Co.

de Shazer, Steve. (1988). *Clues: Investigating Solutions In Brief Therapy.* New York: W.W. Norton & Co.

de Shazer, Steve. (1991). *Putting Difference To Work*. New York: W.W. Norton & Co.

de Shazer, Steve. (1994). *Words Were Originally Magic*. New York: W.W. Norton & Co.

Ellis, Albert. (1957). *How To Live With A Neurotic*. New York: Crown.

Ellis, Albert. (1962). *Reason And Emotion In Psychotherapy*. New York: Lyle Stuart.

Ellis, A. (1971). *Growth Through Reason:* Verbatim Cases In Rational-Emotive Psychotherapy. Palo Alto: Science & Behavior Books.

Ellis, Albert. (1973). *Humanistic Psychotherapy:* The Rational-Emotive Approach. New York: Julian Press.

Ellis, Albert; Harper, Robert A. (1976). *A New Guide To Rational Living*. Englewood Cliffs, NJ: Prentice-Hall, Inc.

Furman, Ben; Ahola, Tapani. (1992). *Solution Talk:* Hosting Therapeutic Conversations. New York: W.W. Norton & Co.

Gardner, Howard (1985). *Frames Of Mind:* The Theory Of Multiple Intelligences. New York: Basic Books.

Gardner, Howard (1993). *Multiple Intelligences:* The Theory In Practice. New York: Basic Books.

Gardner, Howard (1991). *The Unschooled Mind:* How Children Think And How School Should Teach. New York: HarperCollins.

Garfield, Sol L.; Bergin, Allen E. (1987). *Handbook Of Psychotherapy And Behavior Change:* An Empirical Analysis. New York: John Wiley & Sons.

Hall, Michael L. (1996). *Languaging:* The Linguistics Of Psychotherapy. Grand Junction. CO: E.T. Publications.

Johnson, Lynn D. (1995). *Psychotherapy In The Age Of Accountability*. NY: W.W. Norton & Co.

Korzybski, Alfred. (1941/1994). *Science And Sanity:* An Introduction To Non-Aristotelian Systems And General Semantics, (5th. ed.). Lakeville, CN: International Non-Aristotelian Library Publishing Co.

Lakoff, George; Johnson, Mark. (1980). *Metaphors By Which We Live*. Chicago: University of Chicago Press.

Macnab, Francis (1993). *Brief Psychotherapy:* CMT: An Integrative Approach To Clinical Practice. NY: John Wiley & Sons.

Miller, George. (1956). "The Magical Number Seven, Plus Or Minus Two: Some Limits On Our Capacity To Process Information." *Psychological Review*, 63, 81-97.

Selekman, Matthew D. (1993). *Pathways To Change: Brief Therapy For Troubled Teens*. NY: The Builford Press.

Vailhinger, A. (1924). *The Philosophy Of 'As If': A System Of The Theoretical, Practical And Religious Fictions Of Mankind*. Translated by C.K. Ogden. NY: Harcourt, Brace and Co.

Walter, John L.; Peller, Jane E. (1992). *Becoming Solution-Focused In Brief Therapy*. NY: Brunner/Mazel Publishers.

Glossary of NLP Terms

Accessing Cues: The ways we tune our bodies by breathing, posture, gesture and eye movements to think in certain ways.

As-If Frame: Pretending that some event has happened, so thinking "as if" it had occurred, encourages creative problem-solving by mentally going beyond apparent obstacles to desired solutions.

Analogue: Continuously variable between limits, like a dimmer switch for a light. An analogue submodality varies like light to dark, while a digital submodality operates as either off or on, i.e., we see a picture in either an associated or dissociated way.

Analogue Marking: Using one of the senses (visual, auditory, kinesthetic, olfactory or gustatory) exclusive of words to **mark out,** or bring special attention. It works best when one does not make it known consciously to the other person. Their unconscious will pick up the marking. The speaker may use a gesture like a hand, arm or eyebrow movement, or change the tone or pitch of his/her voice to make note of an idea and to mark it out.

Anchoring: The process by which any stimulus or representation (external or internal) gets connected to, and so triggers, a response. Anchors occur naturally and intentionally (as in analogue marking). The NLP concept of anchoring derives from the Pavlovian stimulus-response reaction, classical conditioning. In Pavlov's study the tuning fork became the stimulus (anchor) that cued the dog to salivate.

Association: This refers to mentally seeing, hearing, and feeling from inside an experience. Associated contrasts with dissociated. In dissociation, you see a young you in the visual image. Generally, dissociation removes emotion from the experience, while, with association, we experience the information emotionally.

Auditory: The sense of hearing, one of the basic Representation Systems.

Backtrack: To review or summarize, to feed back to the other person their key words, posture, tonality, etc. The Backtrack Frame refers to a simple but eloquent way to deepen rapport.

Behavior: Any activity we engage in, "micro" like thinking, or "macro" like external actions.

Beliefs: Thoughts, conscious or unconscious, which have grown into a generalization about causality, meaning, self, others, behaviors, identity, etc. Beliefs address the world and how we operate in it. Beliefs guide us in perceiving and interpreting reality. Beliefs relate closely to values. NLP has several belief change patterns.

Blow-out: A submodality shift process wherein you take a problem situation, use one submodality, make it quickly get worse by degrees or levels until it becomes ridiculously distorted—in either a terrifying or humorous way. It then blows out the boundaries of representation and/or neurology. The person can then *not* get back the original experience.

Calibration: Becoming tuned-in to another's state via reading non-verbal signals previously observed and calibrated.

Capability: An ability, a successful strategy for carrying out a task.

Chunking or Stepping: Changing perception by going up or down levels and/or logical levels. Chunking up refers to going up a level (inducing up, induction). It leads to higher abstractions. Chunking down refers to going down a level (deducing, deduction). It leads to more specific examples or cases.

Complex Equivalence: A linguistic distinction wherein someone makes two statements to mean the same thing, e.g., "He is late; he doesn't love me."

Congruence: A state wherein one's internal representation works in an aligned way. What a person says corresponds with what he/she does. Both their non-verbal signals and their verbal statements match. A state of unity, fitness, internal harmony, not conflict.

Conscious: Present moment awareness. Awareness of seven +/- two chunks of information.

Content: The specifics and details of an event, answers *what?* and *why?* Contrasts with process or structure.

Content Reframing: Giving a statement another meaning. Created by asking, "What else could this mean?"

Context: The setting, frame or process in which events occur and provides meaning for content.

Context Reframing:	Changing the context of a statement which gives it another meaning, created by asking, "Where would this represent an appropriate response?" All meaning operates as context-dependent. So meaning changes whenever we change context.
Conversational Postulate:	An hypnotic linguistic distinction, a question people naturally interpret as a command. "Will you now learn NLP?"
Criterion:	A value, what one finds important in a particular context.
Cross Over Mirroring:	Matching one's body movements with a different type of movement, e.g., tapping your finger in time to someone's breathing.
Cues:	Information that provides clues to another's subjective structures, e.g., eye accessing cues, predicates, breathing, body posture, gestures, voice tone and tonality, etc.
Deep Structure:	The complete linguistic form of a statement from which the surface structure derives.
Deletion:	The missing portion of an experience either linguistically or representationally.
Digital:	Varying between two states, e.g., a light switch—either on or off. A digital submodality: color or black-and-white; an analogue submodality: varying between dark and bright.
Dissociation:	Not "in" an experience, but seeing or hearing it from outside as from a spectator's point of view, in contrast to association.
Distortion:	The modeling process by which we inaccurately represent something in our neurology or linguistics. Can occur to create limitations or resources.
Downtime:	Not in sensory awareness, but "down" inside one's own mind seeing, hearing, and feeling thoughts, memories, awarenesses; a light trance state with attention focused inward.
Ecology:	The question about the overall relationship between idea, skill, response and larger environment or system. Internal ecology: the overall relationship between person and thoughts, strategies, behaviors, capabilities, values and beliefs. The dynamic balance of elements in a system.

Elicitation:	Evoking a state by word, behavior, gesture or any stimuli. Gathering information by direct observation of non-verbal signals or by asking Meta-model questions.
Empowerment:	Process of adding vitality, energy, and new powerful resources to a person; vitality at the neurological level, change of habits.
Epistemology:	The study of how we know what we know. NLP operates as an epistemology.
Eye Accessing Cues:	Movements of the eyes in certain directions indicating visual, auditory or kinesthetic thinking (processing).
First Position:	Perceiving the world from your own point of view, associated; one of the three perceptual positions.
Frame:	Context, environment, meta-level, a way of perceiving something (as in Outcome Frame, "As-If" Frame, Backtrack Frame, etc.).
Future Pace:	Process of mentally practicing (rehearsing) an event before it happens. One of the key processes for ensuring the permanency of an outcome, a frequent and key ingredient in most NLP interventions.
Generalization:	Process by which one specific experience comes to represent a whole class of experiences, one of the three modeling processes in NLP.
Gestalt:	A collection of memories connected neurologically, based on similar emotions.
Gustatory:	The sense of taste, one of the representation systems.
Hard Wired:	Neurologically-based factor, the neural connectors primarily formed during gestation, similar to the hard wiring of a computer.
Hypnosis:	A state altered from usual states, an inward focus of attention, trance, a state measurable on an EEG.
Identity:	Self-image or self-concept; the person you define yourself.
Incongruence:	State wherein parts conflict and war with each other; having reservations; not totally committed to an outcome, expressed in incongruent messages, signals; lack of alignment or matching of word and behavior.

Installation: Process for putting a new mental strategy (way of doing things) inside mind-body so it operates automatically, often achieved through anchoring, leverage, metaphors, parables, reframing, future pacing, etc.

Internal Representations: (IR) Patterns of information we create and store in our minds, combinations of sights, sounds, sensations, smells and tastes.

Kinesthetic: Sensations, feelings, tactile sensations on surface of skin, proprioceptive sensations inside the body; includes vestibular system or sense of balance.

Leading: Changing your own behaviors after obtaining rapport so another follows. An acid test for high level of rapport.

Lead System: The representation system that inputs information into consciousness, often a different system from the primary RS.

Leverage: Information or stimulus that motivates a person; change point in a system.

Logical Level: A higher level, a level *about* a lower level, a meta-level that drives and modulates the lower level.

Loop: A circle, cycle, story, metaphor or representation that goes back to its own beginning, so that it loops back (feeds back) onto itself. An open loop: a story left unfinished. A closed loop: a finished story. In strategies: loop refers to getting hung up in a set of procedures for which there is no way out, the strategy fails to exit.

Map of Reality: Model of the world, a unique representation of the world built in each person's brain by abstracting from experiences, comprised of a neurological and a linguistic map, one's internal representations (IR).

Matching: Adopting facets of another's outputs (behavior, words, etc.) to enhance rapport.

Meta: Above, beyond, about, at a higher level, a logical level higher.

Meta-Model: A model with 11 (or 12) linguistic distinctions that identifies language patterns that obscure meaning in a communication via distortion, deletion and generalization; 11 (or 12) specific challenges or questions by which to clarify imprecise language (ill-formedness) to reconnect it to sensory experience and the deep structure. Meta-modeling brings a person out of trance. Developed, 1975, by Richard Bandler and John Grinder. Basis of all other discoveries in NLP.

Meta-Programs: The mental/perceptual programs for sorting and paying attention to stimuli, perceptual filters that govern attention, sometimes "neuro-sorts," or meta-processes.

Meta-State: A state about a state, bringing a state of mind-body (fear, anger, joy, learning) to bear upon another state from a higher logical level, generates a gestalt state—a meta-state, developed by Michael Hall.

Metaphor: Indirect communication by a story, figure of speech, parable, simile, allegory, etc., implying a comparison, a "carrying over" of meaning by presenting something on the side. Use: to bypass conscious resistance and communicate to unconscious mind directly.

Milton Model: Inverse of the Meta-model, using artfully vague language patterns to pace another person's experience and access unconscious resources. The Milton Model induces trance.

Mirroring: Precisely matching portions of another person's behavior for the purpose of building rapport, becoming a mirror image of another's physiology, tonality and predicates.

Mismatching: Offering different patterns of behavior to another; breaking rapport for the purpose of redirecting, interrupting, or terminating a meeting or conversation; mismatching as a meta-program.

Modal Operators: Linguistic distinctions in the Meta-model that indicate the "mode" by which a person "operates"—the mode of necessity, impossibility, desire, possibility, etc.; the predicates (can, can't, possible, impossible, have to, must, etc.) that we utilize for motivation.

Model: A description of how something works, a generalized, deleted or distorted copy of the original.

Modeling: The process of observing and replicating the successful actions and behaviors of others; the process of discerning the sequence of IR and behaviors that enable someone to accomplish a task; the basis of Accelerated Learning.

Model of the World: A map of reality, a unique representation of the world via abstraction from our experiences; the total of one's personal operating principles.

Multiple Description: The process of describing the same thing from different viewpoints.

Neuro-Linguistic Programming: The study of excellence, a model of how people structure their experience; the structure of subjective experience; how humans become *programmed* in their thinking-emoting and behaving in their very *neurology* by the various *languages* they use to process, code and retrieve information.

Neurological Levels: Known as the different levels of experience: environment, behavior, capability, belief, identity and spirituality constructed by Dilts, not true "logical" levels (MH).

Nominalization: A linguistic distinction in the Meta-model; an hypnotic pattern of trance language; a process or verb turned into an (abstract) noun; a process frozen in time.

Olfactory: The sense of smell.

Outcome: A specific, sensory-based desired result. Should meet the well-formedness criteria.

Overlap: Using one RS to gain access to another, to overlap from one highly developed RS to a less developed system.

Pacing: Gaining and maintaining rapport with another by joining their model of the world by saying what fits with and matches their language, beliefs, values, current experience, etc. Crucial to rapport building.

Parts: Unconscious parts, sub-personalities created through some Significant Emotional Experience (SEE); disowned and separated functions that begin to take on a life of their own, a source of intra-personal conflict when incongruent.

Perceptual Filters: Unique ideas, experiences, beliefs, values, meta-programs, decisions, memories and language that shape and color our model of the world.

Perceptual Position:	Our point of view, one of three positions: first position: associated, second position: from another person's perspective, third position: from another other position.
Phonological Ambiguity:	Two words that sound alike, but we can see there/their difference in a plain/plane way if we look to see/sea it.
Physiological:	The physical part of the person.
Predicates:	What we assert or predicate about a subject; sensory based words indicating a particular RS (visual predicates, auditory, kinesthetic, unspecified).
Preferred System:	The RS that an individual typically uses most in thinking and organizing experience.
Presuppositions:	Ideas that we have to take for granted for a communication to make sense; assumptions; that which "holds" (position) "up" (sup) a statement "ahead of time" (pre).
Punctuation Ambiguity:	Ambiguity created by merging two separate sentences into one can always try to make sense of them. In that sentence notice that "one" both ends the first sentence and begins the second: a punctuation ambiguity.
Quotes:	Bandler once said that Grinder said that Erickson said that, "It is a linguistic pattern wherein someone else expresses our message." Quotes displace resistance from the speaker, an hypnotic pattern.
Rapport:	A sense of connection with another, a feeling of mutuality, a sense of trust, created by pacing, mirroring and matching, a state of empathy or second position.
Reframing:	Taking a frame of reference so that it looks new or different; presenting an event or idea from a different point of view so it has a different meaning; content or context reframing, a change pattern.
Representation:	An idea, thought, presentation of sensory-based or evaluative based information.
Representation System (RS):	How we mentally code information using the sensory systems: Visual, Auditory, Kinesthetic, Olfactory, and Gustatory.
Requisite Variety:	Flexibility in thinking, emoting, speaking, behaving; the person with the most flexibility of behavior controls the action; the Law of Requisite Variety.

Resources: Any means we can bring to bear to achieve an outcome: physiology, states, thoughts, strategies, experiences, people, events or possessions.

Resourceful State: The total neurological and physical experience when a person feels resourceful.

Satir Categories: The five body postures and language styles indicating specific ways of communicating: leveler, blamer, placator, computer and distracter, developed by Virginia Satir.

Second Position: Perceiving the world from another's point of view, in tune with another's sense of reality.

Sensory Acuity: Awareness of the outside world, of the senses, making finer distinctions about the sensory information we get from the world.

Sensory-Based Description: Information directly observable and verifiable by the senses; see-hear-feel language that we can test empirically, in contrast to evaluative descriptions.

Significant Emotional Experience (SEE): A high level emotional event during which we tend to make intense learnings that become imprinted, the generation of unconscious parts.

State: Holistic phenomenon of mind-body emotions, mood, emotional condition; sum total of all neurological and physical processes within individual at any moment in time.

Strategy: A sequencing of thinking-behaving to obtain an outcome or create an experience, the structure of subjectivity ordered in a linear model of the TOTE.

Submodalities: Distinctions within each RS, qualities of internal representations; the smallest building blocks of thoughts, characteristics in each system.

Surface Structure: A linguistic term for the spoken or written communication derived from the deep structure by deletion, distortion and generalization.

Synesthesia: Automatic link from one RS to another, a V-K synesthesia involves seeing —> feeling without a moment of consciousness to think about it; automatic program.

Syntactic Ambiguity: Ambiguous sentence where a verb plus "ing" serves as either an adjective or a verb, e.g., "Influencing people can make a difference."

Third Position: Perceiving the world from viewpoint of an observer's position, one of the three perceptual positions, position where you see both yourself and another.

Time-line: A metaphor describing how we store our sights, sounds and sensations of memories and imaginations, a way of coding and processing the construct "time."

Timeline Therapy™ Technique: An NLP therapeutic technique developed by Tad James; a process for dealing with problems in one's constructs of past or future events.

Trance: An altered state with an inward focus of attention; hypnosis.

Triple Description: The process of perceiving experience through first, second and third positions to gain wisdom of all three viewpoints.

Unconscious: Everything not in conscious awareness, minor RS.

Unified Field: The unifying framework for NLP, a three-dimensional matrix of Neurological Levels, Perceptual Positions and "Time" codings.

Universal Quantifier: A linguistic term in the Meta-model for words that code things with "allness" (every, all, never, none, etc.); a distinction that admits no exceptions.

Unspecified Nouns: Nouns that do not specify to whom or to what they refer.

Unspecified Verbs: Verbs that have the adverb deleted, delete specifics of the action.

Uptime: State where attention and senses directed outward to immediate environment; all sensory channels open and alert.

Value: What is important to you in a particular context? Your values (criteria) are what motivate you in life. Every motivational strategy ends with a kinesthetic representation. You feel the value of your representations.

Visual: Seeing, imagining; the RS of sight.

Visualization: The process of seeing images in your mind.

Well-Formedness Condition: The criterion that enable us to specify an outcome in ways that make it achievable and verifiable; powerful tool for negotiating win/win solutions.

Index

The User's Manual For The Brain
The Complete Manual For Neuro-Linguistic Programming Practitioner Certification
Bob G. Bodenhamer, D.Min. & L. Michael Hall, Ph.D.

Available for the very first time in bound-book format, this is the most comprehensive manual to date covering the NLP Practitioner course. A fully revised and updated edition, it contains the very latest developments in Neuro-Linguistic Programming, particularly with regard to the Meta-states model and the Meta-model of language. For all those embarking on Practitioner training or wishing to study to Practitioner level at home, this book is your essential companion. Written and designed by two of the most important theorists in NLP today, *The User's Manual For The Brain* covers every aspect of the Practitioner programme, including the very latest insights. *The User's Manual For The Brain:*

- **fully explains the NLP model and techniques**
- **systematically examines the NLP Language Model and the NLP Neurology Model**
- **provides an introduction to Advanced NLP.**

Thoroughly structured and expertly organized, *The User's Manual For The Brain* is written in an inviting manner, punctuated by key points, and packed with useful illustrations and diagrams that make NLP highly accessible. Providing a wealth of exercises and techniques, this guide simply presents the reader with an excellent opportunity to *get the most out of NLP.*

CLOTH   424 PAGES   ISBN: 1899836322

Also available:

The User's Manual For The Brain PowerPoint Overheads
An outstanding set of PowerPoint overheads to accompany the most comprehensive guide to date covering the NLP Practitioner course, *The User's Manual For The Brain.* The whole course is summarized by over 200 pages of slides making this an essential resource for NLP Practitioner trainers who wish to use *The User's Manual For The Brain* as the basis for their trainings. The overheads are designed by two of the most important theorists working in the field of NLP today.

ISBN: 1899836519

USA *orders to:*
Crown House Publishing
P.O. Box 2223, Williston, VT 05495-2223, USA
Tel: 877-925-1213, Fax: 802-864-7626
www.CHPUS.com

Canada *orders to:*
Login Brothers Canada, 324 Saulteaux Crescent
Winnipeg, MB, R3J 3T2
or 291 Traders Blvd. E., Mississauga, ON, L4Z 2E5
Phone: 800-665-1148, Fax: 800-665-0103
E-mail: info@www.lb.ca
www.lb.ca

UK & Rest of World *orders to:*
The Anglo American Book Company Ltd.
Crown Buildings, Bancyfelin, Carmarthen, Wales SA33 5ND
Tel: +44 (0)1267 211880/211886, Fax: +44 (0)1267 211882
E-mail: books@anglo-american.co.uk
www.anglo-american.co.uk

Australasia *orders to:*
Footprint Books Pty Ltd.
Unit 4/92A Mona Vale Road, Mona Vale NSW 2103, Australia
Tel: +61 (0) 2 9997 3973, Fax: +61 (0) 2 9997 3185
E-mail: info@footprint.com.au
www.footprint.com.au

Singapore *orders to:*
Publishers Marketing Services Pte Ltd.
10-C Jalan Ampas #07-01
Ho Seng Lee Flatted Warehouse, Singapore 329513
Tel: +65 6256 5166, Fax: +65 6253 0008
E-mail: info@pms.com.sg
www.pms.com.sg

Malaysia *orders to:*
Publishers Marketing Services Pte Ltd
509 Block E, Phileo Damansara, Jalan 16/11,
46350 Petaling Jaya, Selangor, Malaysia
Tel: 03 7553588, Fax: 03 7553017
E-mail: pmsmal@po.jaring.my

South Africa *orders to:*
Everybody's Books
Box 201321 Durban North 401, 1 Highdale Road,
25 Glen Park, Glen Anil 4051, KwaZulu NATAL, South Africa
Tel: +27 (0) 31 569 2229, Fax: +27 (0) 31 569 2234
E-mail: ebbooks@iafrica.com